Writing the
Horror Movie

Writing the Horror Movie

Marc Blake and Sara Bailey

BLOOMSBURY ACADEMIC
NEW YORK · LONDON · OXFORD · NEW DELHI · SYDNEY

BLOOMSBURY ACADEMIC
Bloomsbury Publishing Inc
1385 Broadway, New York, NY 10018, USA
50 Bedford Square, London, WC1B 3DP, UK

BLOOMSBURY, BLOOMSBURY ACADEMIC and the Diana logo are trademarks
of Bloomsbury Publishing Plc

First published 2013
Reprinted 2014, 2017, 2018, 2019, 2020 (twice)

Bloomsbury Publishing Inc does not have any control over, or responsibility for, any
third-party websites referred to or in this book. All internet addresses given in this
book were correct at the time of going to press. The author and publisher regret any
inconvenience caused if addresses have changed or sites have ceased to exist, but
can accept no responsibility for any such changes.

Library of Congress Cataloging-in-Publication Data
Blake, Marc.
Writing the horror movie/by Marc Blake and Sara Bailey.
pages cm
Includes bibliographical references and index.
ISBN 978-1-4411-9618-7 (pbk.: alk. paper) 1. Horror fi lms–Authorship.
2. Motion picture plays–Technique. I. Bailey, Sara. II. Title.
PN1995.9.H6B59 2013
808.2'3–dc23
201300600

ISBN: PB: 978-1-4411-9618-7
ePDF: 978-1-4411-9506-7
eBook: 978-1-4411-9347-6

Typeset by Fakenham Prepress Solutions, Fakenham, Norfolk NR21 8NN
Printed and bound in the United States of America

To find out more about our authors and books visit www.bloomsbury.com
and sign up for our newsletters.

The truth is that the screenplay is a bastard form of literature. It is not a play nor book nor movie, and not just simply a blueprint for a film. All movies, regardless of genre, depend on the screenplay. However it is the director who makes the movie by realizing the printed words of the script on film. I have seen mediocre screenplays made into very good films. And I have seen excellent screenplays made into bad movies by incompetent directors.

Again, it's important for people to understand that the screenplay's essential role in film making is the same regardless of the genre of the film.

Jon Landis, 2012[1]

The authors of the book would like to thank the following for their help and input. Lee Cook, for his tireless research and pestering of the famous and busy. Michelle Kisbee for her work on the filmography. Stephen Cleary, whose lectures on genre were inspirational. Kim Newman, Axelle Carolyn and Alan Jones for their analysis, perception and excellent writing on the subject of horror in all its forms. Martha Bailey and Tom Bellhouse. Christopher Smith, Steven Goldmann, Victor Miller, Jane Goldman, Stephen Woolley, Jason Ford, Terry Bird and all our other interviewees. Marc would like to thank the attendees of his horror classes at City University, London, including Paul Bland, Eric McNulty, Russell Garwood, Josh Upstart, Dorinda Montgomery, Simon Timblick and the evil twins Samantha and Vicky. Marc and Sara would like to thank all their students past and present at Southampton Solent University for their continued support and enthusiasm.

---

[1] Personal communication.

Contents

Introduction: Welcome to the Nightmare

The horror movie is currently experiencing a third golden age, following the Universal Studios Monster era of the 1930s and the movie brat auteurs of the 1970s. Today's technological advances are allowing scary movies to be produced as a cottage industry and to be distributed worldwide. This genre has traditionally been seen as a 'way in' to the movie business and it is a truism that it is a great medium for budding directors and writer-director hyphenates. Horror has a track record of appealing to producers; however, the writer is most likely to get his work seen if it follows genre conventions. It is to this end that this book is dedicated.

In order for the writer to sell his script, he must know his craft and understand the demands of the genre. Our intention is to give a thorough grounding in the history, tropes, subgenres, and in particular the pace and rhythm of horror, as well as its underlying meanings and subtexts, so that the writer will be armed and ready to face those legions of undead producers who are after his succulent brainzzz.

Chapter 1

Why Do We Like To Be Scared?

The first thing any writer needs to understand is 'know your audience'. What is the attraction of horror? Why do we like to be scared? These questions have been addressed by myriad writers, philosophers and academics. The writer of horror movies requires an understanding of the theories behind the nature of horror.

For the academic, the definition of horror is: 'fear of some uncertain threat to existential nature and disgust over its potential aftermath'.[2] The writer, in the case of author Stephen King, sees horror as something that serves as a 'barometer of those things which trouble the thoughts of a whole society'.[3] For Aristotle, horror (in drama) gave an audience the opportunity to purge itself of negative emotions through catharsis.

Horror, in essence, is the fear of the *unknown*.

Taking each concept in turn, let us examine them in more detail.

Fear and disgust

I recognize terror as the finest emotion, and so I will try to terrorize the (reader) audience. But if I find I cannot terrify him/her, I will try to horrify; and if I find I cannot horrify, I'll go for the gross-out. I'm not proud.

(STEPHEN KING 1981, p. 37)

---

[2] R. Tamborini and J. B. Weaver. 'Frightening entertainment: A historical perspective of fictional horror'. In J. B. Weaver and R. Tamborini (eds), *Horror films: Current research on audience preferences and reactions*. Mahwah, NJ: Lawrence Erlbaum, 1996; p. 2.

[3] King 1981, p. 31.

It is easy to bring to mind half a dozen movies that raise issues of fear and disgust: the 'Saw' franchise (Wan 2004–10), *Texas Chainsaw Massacre* (Hooper 1974), *Hostel* (Roth 2005), *The Human Centipede* (Six 2009), *Martyrs* (Laugier 2008) to name but a few. These films contain graphic scenes of violence, physical suffering and elements of Grand Guignol – a term for gore-laden horror derived from the Elizabethan/Jacobean theatre genre.

In 1894, 'Le Théâtre du Grand-Guignol' was established by Oscar Metenier as a venue for naturalist performances. The building was originally a church with gothic structures placed about the walls of the building, exuding a feeling of eeriness from the moment audiences arrived. They endured the terror of the shows because they wanted to be filled with strong 'feelings'. Many attended these shows to obtain feelings of arousal: beneath the balcony were boxes, originally built for nuns to watch church services, which were available for theatregoers to rent during performances, as they would often become aroused by the action happening on stage. It has been said that audience members were so boisterous that actors would break character and yell out, 'Keep it down in there!' There were also audience members who could not handle the brutality of the action on stage. Frequently the 'special effects' were too realistic, and audience members would faint and/or vomit during performances.

Such is the appeal of disgust to an audience. The first popular example of this type of entertainment in cinema was Herschel Gordon Lewis's *Blood Feast* (1963), where, in a pale echo of *Frankenstein* (Whale 1931), a scientist is engaged in collecting body parts. Rather than re-creating human life, this one needs body parts from women to conjure up a deceased Egyptian goddess. The film contains scenes of torture, dismemberment, decapitation and cannibalization, and is considered to be the first real 'gross-out' material of its time. Two decades later a spate of 'video nasties' was denied theatrical release and (in the UK) went out only on VHS. Censorship slipped away towards the end of the twentieth century, heralding a broader attitude to the cultural climate. Having said that, *Hostel* (Roth 2005) was considered to be 'torture porn' by critic David Edelstein, and the term has been applied retrospectively to the 'Saw' series (beginning in 2004), *The House of 1000 Corpses* (Zombie 2003), *Wolf Creek* (Mclean 2005), *Ichi the Killer* (Miike 2001) and *Baise moi* (Virginie Despentes, Coralie 2000) as well as many more. These movies show extreme torture sequences, headless torsos, sledgehammer blows etc., and yet many are mainstream Hollywood product with a wide release. Indeed, the torture porn (or 'Gorno') subgenre has been hugely profitable. The 'Saw' franchise has grossed over $100 million worldwide to date. *Hostel*, which cost less than $5 million to make, has grossed $80 million. Much of the attraction of these films is aided by the development of filming techniques, advances in CGI, prosthetics, special effects and high production values, all of which add to the 'gross-out' effect felt by the viewer.

Theoretician Julia Kristeva wrote on the phenomenon of disgust and horror in her essay on the *abject* – a concept that exists between the concept of an object and the concept of the subject. The abject is seen as 'other', as something that as members of society we reject. Kristeva likens this rejection to the repulsion we feel when confronted by body fluids such as blood or semen and waste products like urine and faeces – things that were once a part of us but are no longer. We are at once repelled by and attracted to these internal–external elements. It is a fascination with the corporeal, which we will explore in greater detail in Chapter 3 (Werewolves and body horror). At its simplest, the *abject* is the scab on your knee which, as a child, you were repulsed by, but could not resist picking.

In mainstream entertainment, there has been a growing fascination with the interior spaces of the body, as seen in TV franchises such as *CSI*. The body has become in part a transgressive intertext as well as a multimedia space. We have had exhibitions by artists such as Marc Quinn, who exhibited 4.5 litres of his frozen blood in the Saatchi Gallery (1992) placed in a mould to represent his own head, and Gunther Von Hagens' notorious 'Body Worlds', a sensational exhibition of

authentic human bodies, willed by donors through the Institute for Plastination's Body Donor Program, and preserved using a process called plastination … [they] show the inner workings of the body and the striking whole-body specimens show the human body in real-life poses, as never seen before.[4]

How far can horror go? Censorship and taboo

It is worth considering the influence of censorship on the writer and his work. Creating a screenplay and/or movie which is so extreme that it attracts opprobrium may be good publicity, but if this is merely down to gratuitous sex, violence or bad taste, then instead of horror it is pure sensationalism, and that is a different thing.

In order to understand censorship, we should first look at its history and how tolerances have shifted over time. The Hays Code,[5] named after Hollywood's

---

[4]http://www.bodyworlds.com/en/prelude.html/ The German horror film *Anatomy* (Ruzowitzky 2000) has people being killed and plastinated by a secret sect, the Anti Hypocratic Order.
[5]While the Hays Code was voluntary and self-regulating, it was put in place to avoid government intervention and rationalize a system that was becoming too unwieldy. Prior to this, individual states had their own censorship policies. By 1921, legislators in 37 states had introduced almost 100 movie censorship bills.

chief censor of the time, Will H. Hays, was formed in the belief that audiences needed moral protection. Father Daniel A. Lord and Martin Quigley, a lay Catholic, created a code of standards in 1929, which they then presented to Hays, their particular concern being the effect of films on children. Several studios met with Lord and Quigley and, after some revisions, they agreed to the stipulations of the Code. One of the main factors in adopting the Code was to avoid government intervention: police yourself before others do it for you.

The Code was divided into two parts, the first a general set of principles, which mostly concerned morality. The second was a set of particular applications involving a list of elements that could not be shown on screen, such as the mixing of race. Nowadays, in most countries, to stipulate this would not only be unacceptable to audiences, it would be against the law. Further dictates of the Code were that sexual relations outside of marriage could not be portrayed as attractive – a reason why the opening scene of *Psycho* (Hitchcock 1960) was taboo-busting (Crane and Loomis were unmarried). Criminal action had to be seen to engender punishment, and neither crime nor criminals could be portrayed to elicit sympathy from the audience. It is hard to imagine something like *Silence of the Lambs* (Demme 1990) being passed under this regime.

In 1966 Jack Valenti became president of the Motion Picture Association of America (MPAA) and decided that the Hays Code was out of date. A new system had to be introduced.

On November 1, 1968, the voluntary MPAA film rating system took effect, with three organizations serving as its monitoring and guiding groups: the MPAA, the National Association of Theater Owners (NATO) and the International Film Importers & Distributors of America (IFIDA).

The original movie ratings were:

G: General Audiences – Suggested for general audiences (all ages)
M: Mature Audiences – Suggested for Mature Audiences; Parental discretion advised
R: Restricted – People under 16 not admitted unless accompanied by parent or adult guardian
X: Adults Only – People under 18 not admitted (changed to under 17 later that year).

The content classification system was originally to have three ratings, with the intention of allowing parents to take their children to any film they choose. However, the National Association of Theater Owners urged the creation of an Adults Only category, fearful of possible legal problems in local jurisdictions. The 'X' rating was not an MPAA trademark: any producer not submitting a movie for MPAA rating could self-apply the 'X' rating (or any other symbol or description that was not an MPAA trademark).

With the introduction of a rating system, the US was a latecomer as far as film classification was concerned. In the United Kingdom, the BBFC (British Board of Film Classification) had relaxed its views in the early 1960s and it was as early as 1932 that an H for Horror certificate was placed to alert parents to horror-themed material. Though this was removed in favour of the universal 'X' rating in 1951, it was again altered, to '18', in 1982. Today the highest ratings are '18' and 'R18' (restricted to those aged 18 and older) and only available at licensed cinemas and sex shops, the latter not requiring a licence to sell 'R18' films.

There are many myths about how the BBFC rates movies (one of which apparently involves using a protractor, although this has been repudiated). 'Broadly speaking you will not see real male erections below an 18 [certificate]. But at 18 it's OK', says David Cooke, Director of the Board. 'Probably the nearest we get these days to getting out the protractor is on language.'[6]

The Board has reluctantly concluded there is no substitute for counting the swear words in a film. 'It doesn't mean that's the only thing we look at – particularly with the f-word and the c-word – we'll look at whether they're comically mitigated, or aggressively aggravated, for instance. But if you don't count, you discover there's no stable boundary. So the rule of thumb is four fucks maximum at 12A.' (ibid.)

The board is aware of the changes in what an audience will and will not tolerate: 'When you look at some of the films from the Video Nasty era, like "House on the Edge of the Park" [Ruggero Deodato 1980], which has lingering shots of women being mutilated, that just wouldn't be made today. It's always been rated, but with cuts. There's a really unpleasant sequence where a teenage girl is forced to strip and her breasts are cut with a razor blade. It's really highly sexualized. ... People think you should be free to make up your own mind about what you watch, provided it's not illegal or harmful. That means we do pass some very strong material at 18. But we're not just doing it because we're inventing it – that's in line with that particular public finding.' (ibid.)

The Exorcist (Friedkin 1974) was considered so shocking to moviegoers that many were subject to nausea, convulsions, fainting and shocking displays of anger: one viewer in San Francisco attacked the movie screen, attempting to kill the demon. Paramedics were called to screenings, and it wasn't long before picket lines appeared at theatres. The film was banned on video for 14 years in the UK.

The Texas Chain Saw Massacre (Hooper 1974) is known for its extreme acts of violence, but actually shows little blood and no close-up of fatal blows, making it much tamer than its successors in the genre. Despite this, it was banned in Australia, Brazil, Finland, France, West Germany, Chile, Iceland, Ireland, Norway, Singapore, Sweden and the UK. France banned the film twice, claiming it would incite violence. It was not issued uncut in the UK for 25 years.

---

[6]http://www.guardian.co.uk/film/2012/jul/26/sex-violence-swearing-film-100-years-bbfc

The Last House on the Left (Craven 1972) was Craven's feature debut. His portrayal of two teenage girls kidnapped by escaped convicts, who then rape and torture them, proved too real for moviegoers. Craven defended the film by saying it was 'a reaction on my part to the violence around us, specifically the Vietnam War', and yet the movie was censored in many countries including the UK, where it was banned for 17 years and subject to censorship until 2008.

More recently, the BBFC has 'only allowed a certificate to *The Human Centipede 2* after 32 cuts had been made, including the "graphic sight of a man masturbating with sandpaper around his penis".'

In 2010 *A Serbian Film* (Spasojević 2010) was pulled from International Horror film festival FrightFest, not because it was deemed too horrific but because its organizers had planned to show the picture in its original uncut version and were overruled by the local council in Westminster, London. 'FrightFest has decided not to show *A Serbian Film* in a heavily cut version because, as a festival with a global integrity, we think a film of this nature should be shown in its entirety as per the director's intention,' said event co-director Alan Jones. Subsequently, Raindance Film Festival picked up the film at Cannes in May and then held the UK premiere, finding a way around the ban by billing the screening as a 'private event'. The *Sun*, a UK tabloid newspaper, described the film as 'sick' and 'vile' following the festival's 2010 press launch. In March 2011, *A Serbian Film* won the Special Jury Prize in the 31st edition of Fantasporto, Portugal's biggest film festival, in Porto.

The answer to the question 'How far can I go?' depends on you. What it is that you want for your movie? If you are putting in elements of horror that are nothing to do with plot, narrative and story arc, then you are no longer in control of the story.

The social barometer

Stephen King suggests that horror acts as a barometer for issues that bother us as a society. For the writer of horror it is useful to consider the concept and to study past movies for evidence of this.

Carrie (De Palma 1976) is a prime example. In the early 1970s, the fear of the feminine was a real issue as second-wave feminism rolled across the USA. The film begins with an almost pornographic view of pubescent high school girls in a communal shower. It is accompanied by cheesy music, which becomes dark and intense as the story unfolds to show teenage bullying and Carrie's first period. The horror for Carrie really begins as she steps over the threshold into womanhood and her powers increase to demonic levels. This could be read as a societal concern about the growing power of women, particularly young women as they learn to express themselves and their own powers of intellect and expression.

More recently, *The Mist* (Darabont 2007) picks up on fear of 'alien' invasion – a theme that has often fascinated moviemakers – and also scientific investigation into new methods of warfare. It is a throwback to the old monster movies of the 1950s wherein the scientists were up to no good 'up at the plant'. The story then twists to its darker heart, the rise of Fundamentalism – in this case, Christian. It is all wrapped up in the fear of the outsider, the invisible entity bearing down upon us.

This is not new. It was explored in Shakespeare's *The Tempest*, and in the 1956 movie *Forbidden Planet* (Wilcox 1956) in which Doctor Morbius (Pigeon) and his beautiful daughter Altaira are the only survivors on planet Altair (formerly inhabited only by scientists). A rescue mission finds them in thrall to a mysterious invisible beast, the Krell, which roams the planet.

In *The Mist*, rather than concentrate on what might or might not have been going on at the military base (the vague 'Project Arrowhead'), we are invited to concentrate our attention on events in the supermarket. Mrs Carmody is a religious zealot who feeds off the fear of the others. She begins as a figure of pity and contempt (in effect, the local bag lady) but, as events worsen, Mrs Carmody lures in those who dismissed her, and soon the crowd are caught up in her hysteria. Her monstrous ideology is a direct reflection of the monster outside – manifesting itself as awful abjections: tentacles, moth-like primordial creatures, stinging flying things that burst open to reveal hundreds more replications. King is addressing contemporary fears head-on – fundamentalism in both religion and science.

Catharsis

Catharsis is the opportunity for the audience to purge itself of negative emotions in a safe environment. Within the confines of the viewing area – a cinema or a living room – the audience feels a sense of relief once the film is over. There have been suggestions that catharsis can result in audiences finding what they see on the screen exciting, and that exposure to these images will increase subsequent acts of aggression – an alarming idea for the screenwriter. However, there is strong evidence[7] that suggests it has the opposite effect, that horror acts as

---

[7] B. J. Bushman and R. G. Geen. 'Role of cognitive-emotional mediators and individual differences in the effects of media violence on aggression'. *Journal of Personality and Social Psychology*, 58. 1990.

a safety valve rather than an incitement to justified aggression. This theory is known as Excitation Transfer[8] by which the audience experiences an intensification of positive effect in response to plot and resolution – i.e. where the evil is overcome by the hero/heroine. It would also appear that it is not reliant on a happy ending, but simply on a satisfactory resolution – in effect, that it follows the plot points expected of the genre. We will see how this works in greater detail in Chapter 4. Of all genres, Horror is perhaps one of the most strict when it comes to obeying the rules.

A film such as *The Orphanage* (Bayona 2007) takes us through each stage towards catharsis. There is a sense of unease as Laura arrives at the orphanage. The house looms above her and we wonder if she has seen something. There is a growing sense of dread as we see the child with the sack over his head, as doors slam and children are heard in the empty house. Then there is the disappearance of Simón – the horror of losing your child, and the growing fear that he might be gone forever, brings us to the most horrific element of all – his death, not only that but at Laura's unwitting hand. At the end, Laura commits suicide and so is reunited with Simón. Though not a happy ending, it brings a sense of resolution. This is catharsis.

The Orphanage deals with the loss of a child and a sense of guilt, and is similar in tone to *The Awakening* (Murphy 2011), which has a more ambiguous ending. Here a nanny, Maud, has poisoned herself and ghost hunter Florence so as that they might be together with Tom, a dead child. Florence, however, tells Tom she doesn't want to die now but that she will always be with him (he is her deceased sibling). The child helps Florence by obtaining the medicine that will make her regurgitate and thus purge herself of the poison. The final scene shows us Florence leaving the school, ignored and unseen by senior staff members. This is perhaps either because she is a 'mere' woman (it was set in 1921) or because she has indeed become a ghost, a fact suggested by her white coat. It is left to the audience to draw its conclusions, but emotional catharsis has been achieved in Florence's new and full awareness. Previously, she had been in denial of the truth, a trope we see recurring in characters such as Eleanor Lance in *The Haunting* (Wise 1963) and Dr Malcolm Crowe in *The Sixth Sense* (Shyamalan 1999).

There is a huge risk in leaving your resolution undecided, and you need to be confident in your skills as a writer to attempt it. In some ways, loose ends make for better movies in this genre, but if you go for this, you must still aim for closure in your catharsis.

---

[8]Glenn D. Walters. 'Understanding the Popular Appeal of Horror Cinema: An Integrated-interactive Model'. *Journal of Media Psychology*. 9(2). 2004.

The psychological

Both Freud and Jung have presented theories on the catharsis of drama. For Freud, horror was the manifestation of recurring thoughts and feelings that had been repressed by the ego but that seem vaguely familiar to the individual.[9] For Jung, however, horror gained popularity from its connections and relationships with important archetypes, particularly with shadow archetypes such as shadow mother or father – or both, as in *Mum & Dad* (Shell 2008). Here, 'Mum' and 'Dad' live under the flight path of London's Heathrow Airport. Their 'adopted' (kidnapped) children, Birdie and Elbie, work at the airport in menial jobs. When Lena, a young Polish cleaner, is befriended by Birdie, she is drawn into the family's world of torture, murder and perversity. Treated 'like one of the family', Lena is designated as 'Mummy's Girl', which is when the horror begins. Her only options are to join in the madness or die. Here, the traditional role of loving parents has been subverted into darker shadow archetypes. Dad is 'given' Lena by Mum for Christmas – whether for sexual or cannibalistic gratification, we are unsure. The family, as with the cannibal Hillbilly's in Tobe Hooper's *The Texas Chain Saw Massacre* (Hooper 1976), play on the accepted language of familial relationships but as an inverse nightmare parody.

This shadow archetype is also seen in Kubrick's *The Shining* (Stanley Kubrick 1980) with great effect. Not only does Kubrick use the father figure as shadow father, but also as shadow king – the Overlook Hotel symbolizing his castle. Kubrick uses mirrors and doubling, further distorting the image of the 'father' figure. Jack is often talking to himself in the mirror, and the huge, wall-sized mirrors of the ballroom reflect the stages of his growing dementia. His son Danny, too, demonstrates an understanding of the world as being inverted, with his constant referrals to 'redrum'.

For these kinds of movie to work, the audience needs to suspend its disbelief. For the horror fan, this suspension has to be rooted in an understanding of what is real and the perception of a supernatural force or gross abnormality. Whether it is the supernatural idea of a house being haunted, the King of Darkness rising from the dead or that a child could be possessed by the Devil, we have to believe for 90 minutes that these things are *just* possible in order to enjoy the experience. Even films that are not supernatural still require the same suspension. *Jaws* (Spielberg 1975) asks us to believe that a shark with a brain the size of a walnut can outwit a Chief of Police, a highly educated marine biologist, and a seasoned shark hunter. It is this dependence on suspension of disbelief that has driven the medium from the beginning. It is the screenwriter's

---

[9]Walters 2004.

art to create a meaningful and consistent reality for a producer and director to buy into. In order to do this, a study of the form, with expectations running high and quality a necessity, is today mandatory.

Chapter 2

Horror Movie History

Horror stories have been with us for centuries, fireside tales developed into stories and novels, plays, and now movies and games. The horror movie began with monsters, most especially the 'undead'. The fear of what happens *after* death feeds into this. What if you're not really dead? What if you come back as something 'other'? What if you become neither fully dead nor fully alive? These fears are born out of both man's desire to be immortal and the complexities of the psyche and its inability to make sense of death.

Mary Shelley's *Frankenstein*, written in Switzerland in 1816 (published in 1818), is a gothic romance: entertainment for friends while Shelley was trapped indoors by inclement weather during a holiday with her lover.[10] It was Lord Byron, a friend and neighbour in Switzerland, who set the competition to see who could write the best ghost story.

The Frankenstein story follows the bringing to life of a body constructed from the parts of other bodies. Shelley takes elements of the Abject and combines them with that most horrific of ideas, that man can be created by man and not by God: thus a monster is born. It is commonly believed that it is the creation that is *Frankenstein*, whereas it is in fact the creator – who therefore ought to be viewed as the real monster. The novel appeals because of the taboos it deals with. At a time when good Christian folk believed absolutely in man as the divine creation of God, to have a mortal attempt to create life was both shocking and horrific. Mary Shelley subtitled her story 'The Modern Prometheus', referring to the god who angered Zeus by bringing fire to mankind. The story appeals on many different levels and this is at the root of its popularity and longevity. Horror deals with taboos but must simultaneously appeal to the masses. It reaches us

---

[10] Although Mary was actually Mary Godwin at the time, the two travelled as Mr and Mrs Shelley. Shelley was still married to Harriet, who died later that same year on 3 December. Mary Godwin and Percy Shelley were married on 30 December.

at a deep psychological level and allows us to explore areas of the psyche within the confines and safety of a story.

Vampires are the most common enduring monsters in horror. Bram Stoker's *Dracula* was written in 1897 and, though it is a work of fiction, part of its appeal lies in its historical roots. How much Stoker was aware of this can only be a matter of conjecture, but connections between Stoker's Count Dracula and the Transylvanian Vlad III Dracula of Wallachia have often been stated. During his reign (1456–62), 'Vlad the Impaler' is said to have killed up to a hundred thousand people (including political rivals, criminals, and anyone else he considered to be useless) by impaling them on sharp poles. For this he was revered as a folk hero. The name Dracul is derived from a Chivalric order called 'The Order of the Dragon', founded in 1431; due to his bravery in fighting the Turks, Vlad II was awarded the order, which was passed on to his son Vlad III (Dracula meaning son of Dracul). It is believed that Stoker came across the name in his reading on Romanian history and renamed his villain, who was originally called 'Wampyr'. Other influences on Stoker's work are the Irish writer Sheridan Le Fanu's vampire novel *Carmilla* (1872), the *sidhe* (from Gaelic mythology including stories of women who drank blood), Jules Verne's novel *Castle of the Carpathians* and Anne Radcliffe's *The Mysteries of Udolpho*. That Stoker frequently visited the Yorkshire coastal town of Whitby is well recorded, and he used many real locations both from there and in London, distorting the geography from time to time for the sake of the story.

Dracula was adapted into a play by Hamilton Deane in 1924, though Stoker himself wrote the first theatrical adaptation, presenting it at London's Lyceum Theatre under the title *Dracula, or 'The Undead'* in May 1897 shortly before the novel's publication. It was the first adaptation to be authorized by Stoker's widow, and was performed only once, perhaps because it lasted for more than four hours! The play opens with Renfield, the servant of Count Dracula, offering a prologue. He explains that most people go through life not knowing their creator. He (Renfield) however, does. He explains that Dracula, his master, created him and he is the man who gave him immortality – 'For which I will never forgive him.' Renfield then bites into a rat, and the play begins.

Tod Browning's 1931 movie *Dracula*, starring Hungarian actor Bela Lugosi, popularized the screen image of the vampire, but it was by no means the first. There is a lost Russian horror film called *Drakula* from 1920 as well as the more widely known *Nosferatu: A Symphony of Horror*. This classic German Expressionist film[11] directed by F. W. Murnau (1921) starred Max Schreck. It was

---

[11]There is debate about whether or not *Nosferatu* can be called a horror movie. The 'Horror Movie' was not recognized as a genre until the release of *Dracula* (Browning 1931). *Frankenstein* (Whale 1931) was the first film to be commissioned as a 'horror' by a studio.

an unauthorized adaptation of the tale, and names and other details had to be changed, as the studio was unable to obtain the rights to the novel. The film works well, because Schreck held off as much as possible in the reveal of the monster, as happened later with James Whale's *Frankenstein* (1931). *Nosferatu* was the only production of Prana Film studio (founded in 1921 by Enrico Dieckmann and Albin Grau). Grau maintained that the idea came from his war experience, when, in the winter of 1916, a Serbian farmer told him his father was a vampire and one of the undead. Grau and Dieckmann asked Henrik Galeen to write a screenplay based on Stoker's novel. Galeen had already had experience in working in this area with his film *Der Golem, wie er in die Welt kam* (*The Golem: How He Came into the World*). *Der Golem* was a silent horror[12] made by Paul Wegener in 1920 as part of a series begun in 1915 about the mythological Jewish Golem, an anthropomorphic being made from inanimate clay brought to life by the Hebrew word 'emet' (truth) written on its forehead. Removing one letter changed this to 'met' (death) and the Golem was thus deactivated.

Filming for *Nosferatu* began in July 1921, mostly in Wismar, a small port in Northern Germany, although exterior shots of Transylvania were actually shot in northern Slovakia. Cameraman Fritz Arno Wagner only had one camera and therefore only one original negative. Murnau followed Galeen's screenplay carefully, using handwritten instructions on camera positioning and lighting, though this didn't stop him rewriting 12 pages of the script as some of Galeen's text was missing from the director's working copy. This concerned the last scene of the film, where Ellen sacrifices herself and the vampire dies in the first rays of the sun. That vampires are vulnerable to sunlight was not entirely Murnau's concept. In Stoker's novel, Dracula is weakened by it, but in *Nosferatu*, sunlight is fatal.

Nosferatu keeps the main characters of Jonathan and Mina Harker, as well as the Count, but Arthur and Quincey don't appear and the names of the characters have changed. Nor too does Orlock create other vampires by sucking their blood: he kills his victims outright. Bram Stoker's estate sued Prana Film for copyright infringement and won, resulting in the company declaring bankruptcy. The court ordered all existing prints of *Nosferatu* burned, but one copy had been distributed around the world and, from this, duplicates were made. The film has a strong cult following and is considered a seminal work for film students and fans of horror.

The film was marketed with a warning for the unwary, stating that '*Nosferatu* is not just fun, not something to be taken lightly', and posters declaring 'Its Only

---

[12] As with *Nosferatu*, *Der Golem, wie er in die Welt kam* can be regarded as a horror movie only retrospectively.

A Movie ... Only a Movie ...'[13] The makers of *Frankenstein* picked up this idea of warning the audience and heightening the suspense by using the actor, Edward Van Sloan (who played Dr Waldam), to step out from behind a curtain and deliver this friendly warning to the audience.

> We are about to unfold the story of Frankenstein, a man of science who sought to create a man after his own image without reckoning upon God. It is one of the strangest tales ever told. It deals with the two great mysteries of creation – life and death. I think it will thrill you. It may shock you. It might even horrify you. So if any of you feel that you do not care to subject your nerves to such a strain, now's your chance to – uh well, we warned you.
>
> *Frankenstein*; James Whale 1931

Tod Browning's *Dracula* was released in 1931, based on the play by Deane. After Bram Stoker's wife sued Prana, Carl Laemmle Jr saw the box office appeal and legally obtained the novel's film rights. Originally, it was thought that Lon Chaney would play the lead, having already played a fake vampire in *London After Midnight* (aka *The Hypnotist*: Browning 1927). However, Chaney was diagnosed with throat cancer in 1928 and was too ill to take up the role. Lugosi had played the role on Broadway and happened to be in Los Angeles when the film was being cast. There were several other actors up for the part, but Lugosi eventually won the studio over. It might have been his persistence in lobbying the executives, but it might also have been his willingness to accept the role for $500 a week, a lower figure than any other actor would accept.

Universal decided to film a simultaneous Spanish-language version of the movie, using the same sets and costumes. This was common practice in the early days of sound and, although few versions still exist, *Dracula* is the exception. George Melford directed the Spanish version. The star, Carols Vilarias, was permitted to see the rushes of the English version so that he might imitate Lugosi's performance. The Spanish crew watched the dailies and were able to work out better camera angles and lighting. Melford encouraged this in an attempt to 'top' the English version. For many, the Spanish *Dracula* is the superior movie. As well as these two versions, a silent copy of the film was also released. This enabled the film to be shown in as many movie theatres as possible and helped its popularity.

There are over 200 film versions of the Dracula story. Whale's *Frankenstein* was so successful it spawned the first sequel, *Bride of Frankenstein* (1935), in which Elsa Lanchester played both the Bride and Mary Shelley. As the Bride she

---

[13] A gimmick that was later used to publicize Wes Craven's *Last House on the Left* (1972).

only appears at the end of the movie and steals the picture. Despite this, she remains the only female horror icon of that time (and there have been precious few since then).

Universal then monopolized the horror genre for over a decade, but other studios caught on to the financial benefits of developing horror stories. In 1942, Val Lewton at RKO produced *Cat People*, directed by Jacques Tourneur and based on Val Lewton's short story *The Bagheeta*, published in 1930. The film tells the story of Irena (a young Serbian woman) who believes she is descended from a race of people who turn into cats when sexually aroused. The film is most famous for the invention of the horror technique known as the *Lewton Bus*. The term derives from a scene in which Irena is following her love rival, Alice. At the height of the scene, just as the audience is expecting Irena to turn into a panther at any second, the camera focuses on Alice's terrified face, and a hissing sound breaks the silence. It is a regular bus pulling up front of screen. It is a false shock, which completely dissipates the tension and has become a widely imitated technique that is used to this day.

A year later, Val Lewton followed up his success with *I Walked with a Zombie* (Tourneur 1943), based on an article of the same title written by Inez Wallace for *American Weekly* magazine. RKO loved the melodrama of the title and asked Lewton to come up with a movie to fit. The first version of the film was written by Curt Siodmak, who had written screenplays for *The Wolf Man* (Waggner 1941), *Frankenstein Meets The Wolfman* (Neill 1943), *Ghost of Frankenstein* (Kenton 1942) and *The Invisible Woman* (A. Edward Sutherland 1940). Ardel Wray, a young woman hired by Lewton from RKO's Young Writer's Project, reworked the script – the only woman credited with writing a Lewton film. Wray was brought in to flesh out the theme based on Haitian voodoo. Lewton is purported to have announced that the film would be a West Indies version of Charlotte Bronte's *Jane Eyre*. Lewton later reworked the script a third time, by which time Siodmak had left the production.

In 1932, Victor Halperin directed *White Zombie*, starring Bela Lugosi, for Universal. This film capitalized on the voodoo zombie themes of Seabrook's book of 1928, *The Magic Island*, and introduced the term 'Zombie' into movie parlance. Jacques Tourneur was to direct the better known *I Walked with a Zombie* in 1943.

It could be argued that *The Cabinet of Dr. Caligari* (Wiene 1920) was the first 'Zombie' movie, but there is a sea change here. Caligari's creature, Cesare, is a somnambulist who sleeps in a coffin under the power of Dr. Caligari. This is closer to the stories of Haitian voodoo zombies that were controlled by one person – the *bokor*. Tourneur's *I Walked With a Zombie* tries to keep to the Haitian template, but after this, the undead creature in thrall to its master mutates into an uncontrolled rampaging monster. The undead of old could not be fed, otherwise they would return to the grave. The new zombie attacks at will and is not under the control of any outside person. Later versions owe more to Norse mythology, which tells of a *draugr* – an animated corpse that roams beyond its grave to attack, eat and infect the living. A human killed by a *draugr* is destined to become one too.

Romero's *Night of the Living Dead* (Romero 1968) breeds the zombie with the vampire and creates the modern monster of the apocalypse. These 'zombies' can come back to life for almost any reason, but their bite will infect. Romero's undead have a limited memory of their previous life, but can walk and use their hands. They understand doors and windows and have enough instinct to eat. They are not intelligent, having the single drive to seek out and consume living flesh. Romero showed the undead eating animals as well as humans. There is no reason for their need to eat flesh, just a driving will. Their gait is shambling and slow, and they can barely walk, let alone run. Nowadays we see zombies who sprint, climb walls and appear to have a higher level of intelligence than their earlier versions. This development came with *28 Days Later* (Boyle 2002) and Zack Synder's remake of *Dawn of the Dead* (Synder 2004), and is seen in force in *La Horde* (Dahan and Rocher 2009).

In order to kill a zombie you must destroy its brain or cremate it. Body parts severed will become animated. In a recent development in *[REC]3 Genesis* (Plaza 2012) zombies are rendered ineffective by being read to from the bible. Go figure.

It has been said that Hollywood invented the werewolf, but lycanthropic myths exist in ancient Greece, where references to it are to be found in the 'Histories' of Herodotus (450–20 BC). The Neuri, a Scythian tribe, were transformed into wolves once every year for several days and then changed back into human shape. Ovid (43–17 BC) also spoke of men being transformed into wolves in his 'Metamorphosis' (completed in AD 8).

Werewolves in European folklore are said to show lupine traits in their human physical form, such as eyebrows meeting in the middle, long, curved fingernails, low-set ears and a loping gait. One way of checking to see if a man was a werewolf was to cut his flesh and see if there was fur in the wound. Russians believed that a man who was a werewolf would have bristles under his tongue. In animal form, he is seen as indistinguishable from other wolves, except for having no tail, human eyes and a voice. Swedish folklore believed the werewolf would run on three legs, stretching out the fourth so that it looked like a tail. It was also believed that werewolves were in the habit of digging up and eating recently buried corpses. By the nineteenth century, werewolves were no longer just male. In Scandinavia, they were believed to be old women who had poison-coated claws and were able to paralyse with a look. It was thought that werewolves were born that way – but also that sleeping under a full moon, wearing a pelt of wolf skin or having epilepsy might transform a human into a werewolf.

Transformation by bite or scratch by another werewolf is a modern device, perpetuated by horror fiction and movies, but this kind of transmission was rare in the myths and legends and bears more than a passing resemblance to the contagion of biting by vampire. In medieval Europe, the corpses of people executed as werewolves were cremated rather than buried to stop them coming back as vampires.

The first werewolf movie was made by Universal and entitled *Werewolf of London* (Walker 1935). It starred Henry Hull who plays Wilford Glendon, a wealthy English botanist, attacked and bitten by a mysterious creature while on a field trip in Tibet. When he turns into a werewolf he has an instinctive desire to hunt and kill, but is later filled with remorse. He is ultimately shot and killed as a werewolf and reverts to human form as he dies.

The film was not a success at the time, being regarded as too similar to *Dr Jekyll and Mr. Hyde* (Mamoulian 1931). Since then it has come to be regarded by film historians as a classic.[14] One of the similarities between the two films is that, each time a man transforms, he becomes more animalistic than before, suggesting a progression in the development of the monstrous. *The Wolf Man* (Waggner 1941) starring Lon Chaney Jr is much the better known film and was Universal's biggest hit of the year. Although *Cry of the Werewolf* (Levin 1944) depicts a female werewolf, it was not until *Ginger Snaps* (Fawcett 2000) that the female werewolf made any impact on the genre. The werewolf tended to be a very masculine monster, but *Ginger Snaps* has bred two equally good sequels and there are signs that we may be seeing more of the female werewolf or werevixen.

With the outbreak of the Second World War, the horror movie made way for war movies, propaganda and documentaries, but a decade later it was again picking up on the zeitgeist and making our fears manifest.

Mass invasion, the atomic bomb and bad science all had moviegoers seeking out new horizons, and there followed an exponential growth in a blend of Horror and Science Fiction, which too was heralding a new golden age. Movies such as *The Thing from Another World* (Nyby 1951), *War of the Worlds* (Haskin 1953), and *The Day the Earth Stood Still* (Wise 1951) are excellent examples of this crossover.

This period also saw the reprise of the ghost story, perhaps the oldest form of horror closely linked to short stories and novels, as well as the beginnings of

---

[14] It achieved an Oscar for Best Actor in a Leading Role (for Fredric March) and was nominated for Best Cinematography (Karl Struss) and Best Adaptation Writing (Percy Heath and Samuel Hoffenstein).

portmanteau horror,[15] with Ealing Studios' *Dead of Night* (Cavalcanti 1945) – a must-see movie, even now.

The House on Haunted Hill (Castle 1959) stands out from the crowd partly for its camp creepiness and partly for its proximity to *Psycho* (Hitchcock 1960) in introducing the idea of the psychotic killer. Eccentric millionaire Frederick Loren (Vincent Price) invites five people to a party in a rented house, promising each of them $10,000 if they stay the night. As they arrive, each is given a pistol for protection. Loren's wife tries to warn the guests that her husband is deranged. The tale is a mix of ghost story and whodunnit, with guests hunting for a killer who may or may not be a ghost. It makes its claim for horror with the emergence of a skeleton from a vat of acid, supposedly the dead Vincent Price – a trick replicated in cinemas with a real skeleton suddenly sweeping over the audiences, although this was later a cue for a volley of popcorn boxes. Castle was something of a showman and huckster, and created many gimmicks for his B movies, such as *Percepto* (*The Tingler* 1959), which shocked audiences in their seats, *Illusion-O* (*13 Ghosts* 1960), red and blue cellophane glasses, and a 'fright break' 45 minutes into *Homicidal* (1961).

The question of places being haunted as opposed to people is not a new one. In Rene Clair's *The Ghost goes West* (1935) an American businessman buys a Scottish castle and ships it brick by brick to America, to his chagrin finding that a centuries-old ghost has come along with it. That it is *people* who are haunted was explored in *The Haunting* (Wise 1963) which examined the psychoses of its lead character, Eleanor Lance, and which since then has become the dominant trope.

If horror reflected the concerns of a society (fears of science, atomic bombs, men from Mars/Communists), the other overriding concern of this time was the psyche. America had discovered Freud's talking cure, and 'seeing a shrink' was no longer the domain of the psychotic, more that of the neurotic. In *The Haunting*, Dr Markway is doing research to prove the existence of ghosts and visits Hill House to explore its tales of violent death and insanity.[16]

The Haunting was shot in black and white, a decision Wise had to fight for. He also had to sign an agreement accepting full responsibility for the effect of an experimental lens he had been sent and wanted to use, which distorted many of the images. The film was a success. Wise puts this down to the source of terror being 'the unknown', rather than a threat of physical pain or death. By refusing

---

[15] This is a subgenre that was popularized in the 1960s by the UK's Amicus productions, but with roots in cinema's earliest anthology *Unheimliche Geschichten* or *Five Sinister Tales* (Oswald 1919), which featured Edgar Allen Poe's 'The Black Cat' and R. L. Stevenson's 'The Suicide Club'.
[16] Note the similarity in title to the *House on Haunted Hill*. The film was adapted from the novel by Shirley Jackson called *The Haunting of Hill House*, published in 1959.

to resolve the film's many questions, or to show the audience any direct ghostly manifestation, it became in effect a ghost story with no ghosts. The audience's imagination created their own ghostly fears, making the experience of watching the film deeply personal. It was all done by suggestion, an important lesson to remember – and one forgotten, it seems, for the 1999 remake.

The story of modern horror begins with *Night of The Living Dead* (Romero 1968), and it is from here on in that we see the clear divisions and subdivisions of the genre.

Chapter 3
Subgenres

Horror divides into several clear subgenres, and it is important that the writer approaching a horror project has an understanding of the tropes and the underlying aspects of each subgenre. At the time of writing, the mash-up has become commonplace. Bleeding out of the ubiquitous zombie pictures of the late 2000s, it has led to literary attempts (*Pride and Prejudice and Zombies*), historical (*Abraham Lincoln, Vampire Hunter*), monsters (*Megashark vs. Giant Octopus*) and even an SF/Western crossover (*Cowboys vs. Aliens*). None of these were much good, and nor were the monster clashes of the 1940s, Hammer's cheesier later sequels, *Godzilla vs. Mothra*, *Freddie vs. Jason* or *Van Helsing*, but their proliferation implies a regular rebirth for an easily sated audience. The mash-up is essentially collage, the early twentieth-century artistic experiment coined by Picasso and Braque. Unless you have a stupendous idea that will sell to a studio executive on its title alone, as did *Snakes on a Plane*, it is probably best avoided.

In essence the horror genre can be divided into the following:

- The undead (see Chapter 2 for the history), including vampires and zombies
- Monsters (see Chapters 2 and 5)
- Psychological horror
- Demons, possession, and child possession
- The supernatural: Ghosts, Hauntings and Poltergeists
- Witchcraft and curses
- Werewolves and body horror
- Bad science
- Slasher.

The undead

Mankind has always been fascinated by what comes after life, and indeed most religions have been founded on it, but what attracts the horror fan about the afterlife is that it's going to come out of the grave and bite you in the neck.

The Undead are the abject *in extremis*, at once both alive and dead, yet still mobile despite their extreme state of decomposition. In *The Cabinet of Dr. Caligari* (Wiene 1920) the dead are hypnotized, but in George Romero's *Night of the Living Dead* (Romero 1968) they are a shambling mass that needs to feed. These ghouls can only be killed by severing the brain stem – a rule that still holds true to this day.

There have been several explanations for the catatonic horde in this progenitor of the modern horror film, including their being a comment on the Civil Rights struggle, the Cuban Missile crisis or the Vietnam War. The sequel to *Night of the Living Dead*, *Dawn of the Dead* (Romero 1978), is thought to be about our wasteful consumerist society and/or our cold war/nuclear anxiety. In recent years zombies have illustrated post-9/11 fears, American foreign policy, the SARS epidemic and the inevitable collapse of capitalism. They are a multi-purpose analogy. One zombie fits all.

They can also be broadly satirical. Joe Dante's chapter in the *Masters of Horror* TV series (Season 1, 2005–6, Episode 6: 'Homecoming') used the living dead as social satire, having undead soldiers come back to fight a re-election in the US. George Romero made his trilogy of 'Dead' movies but shifted towards the satirical position in *Land of the Dead* (Romero 2005). Here, the Dead walk the land but the rich are safe in fortified cities, an obvious metaphor for the class struggle or perhaps a post-9/11 immigrant situation (though Romero wrote the first draft before 9/11). His *Diary of the Dead* (Romero 2007) uses the found footage, documentary style beloved of recent years and tells the tale of students making a horror film at the time of the first outbreak. It has much to say about the culpability of the media and our obsession with documenting events rather than getting involved. There is also his misanthropic ending in which we begin to wonder if the human race is really worth saving.

Danny Boyle's *28 Days Later* (Boyle 2002) is technically not a zombie film, as the Rage virus which infects the population keeps its victims very much alive, though partial to flesh eating (as in Romero's *The Crazies*, 1973). There are, however, enough parallels and homages to the Romero canon to take them 'as read'. The big difference was that these mothers could run! Zack Snyder's *Dawn of the Dead* remake (Snyder 2004) was also tarred with this brush, although Romero has pointed out that, if they ran, their tendons would snap. This simple shift offered writers a choice. Do they continue to shamble on, as in the excellent 2004 rom-zom-com *Shaun of the Dead* (Wright, 2004), or sprint for brains as in Boyle's *28 Days Later* or *Resident Evil* (Anderson 2002)? There is no question that the undead are with us and here to stay. They can equally represent Osama Bin Laden's terrorists: *Ozombie* (Lyde 2012); or urban isolation: *Colin* (Price 2008). They can be metaphors for Mad Cow disease: *Dead Meat* (McMahon 2004); or retrodden as comedy in such dubious pleasures as *Night of the Living Dorks* (Dinter 2004), *Dead and Breakfast* (Luetwyler 2004), *ZombieLand* (Fleischer 2009) or the sublime, silly and sexy *Zombie Strippers* (Lee 2008). The subgenre has reached its baroque stage and there seems little more to say, but genres are cyclical and, in a few years' time, who can tell what will leak out of the head of an undead writer.

The other kind of Undead, in the form of vampires and their iconic chief, Count Dracula, is also continually subject to reinvention. We have had *Buffy the Vampire Slayer* on TV, then *Interview with the Vampire* (Jordan 1994) and, of late, the *Twilight* saga of five movies to date (Hardwicke 2008–), although these are more properly described as romantic fantasy, merely appropriating some of the traits of the vampire and werewolf. However, each has taken a new slant on an old story and there is always more to come.

Monsters

With advanced technology, green screen, CGI and the like, it has become possible to create almost any kind of multi-fanged and tentacle-endowed monster for a reasonable budget. Having said that, this is a *studio* budget, and excellent creature features such as *Monster Man* (Davis 2003), the *Feast*[17] trilogy (Gulager 2005, 2008; Adam 2009) and *Cloverfield* (Matt Reeves 2008) require studio input and deep pockets. Gareth Edwards's lone effort, *Monsters* (Edwards 2010) was made over some considerable time and its 250 CGI effects represented months of hard work. Once you are properly studio funded you get to make *King Kong* (Jackson 2005) or *Prometheus* (Scott 2012) but until then it's best to conceive of something we can only glimpse for most of the movie. Better yet, there is the inner monster, which is cheaper to film.

---

[17] See Appendix 2: Interviews (p. 202).

Psychological horror

Psychological horror is the creaking door, the eerie doll, the boarded-up house, the scraping behind the wall, the fleeting image. It is the sudden ring of the phone – a good scare. It is internalized, and so there is no room for gore; instead, there is tone and mood and mist and shadow. It is the horror we create with our own imagination.

Psychological horror deals with the unknown in the shape of humanity itself and our struggle to come to terms with our own nature. The idea is to access our psyche, the bits of ourselves that we see in dreams, in nightmares, madness, visions or fits. Nearly all psychological thrillers deal in madness or consciousness gone awry. This requires a complexity of character, such as with killer Robert Rusk in *Frenzy* (Hitchcock 1972) or Carol LeDoux in *Repulsion* (Polanski 1965). This creates a real difficulty for film-makers. How do you show that which is the unknown? From the German expressionist cinema of the 1920s to the Asian horror of the 2000s, the aim has been to find a way to map the innermost workings of the (twisted) mind on screen.

The reasoning of psychological horror is to question what a person really is in their mind, to establish order and to solve the puzzle. Often the story is framed in such a way that the protagonist/victim is paranoid and no one will believe her, throwing her into a position where she must defend her sanity and prove she is not seeing things – or, if she is, that she is right and there is something evil out to get her. The ultimate threat here is not death but madness. It is perpetual insanity, which is why many stories end with the protagonist bound in a straitjacket, pulling back to her mad cell and the insane cacophony of the other inmates. *Carrie* (De Palma 1976) was an excellent example of a shock 'mad' ending,[18] and *The Shining* (Kubrick 1980) was a graphic illustration of the disintegration of sanity. Jack Torrance's death is only a result of the inability to cope with the new conditions he finds himself in. He is still trying to impose order right up until the end, but his natural state is that of a murderer.

The main conflict is between the conscious and the unconscious, between control and disorder. The danger is in our basic human drives, our repressed fears, phobias, urges and compulsions, shown best in films like *Peeping Tom* (Michael Powell 1960). This kind of movie debates the nature of humanity itself. What are we when stripped of community and forced to rely on our wit and instinct? Self-knowledge is the key to survival in these movies, in discovering your true nature – for better or worse. They can often be Freudian in essence,

---

[18]Although not for the protagonist, Carrie, but for the popular Sue Snell.

and you will see parents or parental figures everywhere: the love of, the memory of, the fear of and the abuse by.

In a number of tales, the worst fear has already happened. The protagonist is unaware of this and the mystery that unfolds is for them to reach a point of catharsis, resolution and self-knowledge – but alas, too late. Some examples of movies that do this quite expertly (spoiler alert) are *Carnival of Souls* (Harvey 1962), *The Sixth Sense* (Shyamalan 1999), *Dead of Night* (Cavalcanti 1945) *Dr. Terror's House of Horrors* (Francis 1965) and lately John Carpenter's *The Ward* (Carpenter 2010). These tales all demand careful seeding and preparation so that the audience is not ahead of you. This was most effectively done in *Haute tension* (Aja 2003), though some found its extremes illogical (the blow job and severed head scene for one).

The hero in a psychological horror movie has to have a strong logical objective. This means a strong plot, often with the most interesting ideas and characters. An obscure British picture starring Roger Moore, *The Man Who Haunted Himself* (Dearden 1970) is a marvellous example of a man drawn into a situation he cannot fathom, and is perhaps the former Bond actor's finest role. Following a car accident, businessman Harold Pelham is operated on and briefly dies on the operating table. As he is brought back, two heartbeats appear on the monitor and, as he returns to daily life, he discovers that he has a doppelganger. This is Jekyll and Hyde once more, man and Monster, the duality of nature.

Psychological horror explores this field, often splitting in two quite literally those things we call good and evil, the coexisting sides of our nature. Showing two as one, as in R. L. Stevenson's tale, is such an enduring story that it has been remade many times: as two men in *Fight Club* (Fincher 1999); as woman and her alter ego in *Haute tension* (Aja 2003); and as a multiplicity in *Identity* (Cooney 2003).

The vocabulary we use about these aspects of our humanity is in itself psychoanalytic. Terms like repression, bi-polar, OCD, ADD, obsession and multiple personality disorder are terms with which we have become familiar, but are themselves terms from clinical psychology. We have slowly adopted them since the days of *Psycho* (Hitchcock 1960).[19]

The term 'serial killer' has been attributed to FBI profiler Robert Ressler, who coined it during a lecture in 1974, but it has since been claimed that he was referring to 'serial homicide'. Regardless of the actions of John Wayne Gacy, Ted Bundy and Aileen Wuornos it was the huge success of *Silence of the Lambs*

---

[19] It is worth rewatching *Psycho*, stopping at the reveal of Mother's corpse, and asking 'Are the subsequent 10 minutes of psychological deconstruction really *necessary*?'

(Demme 1991) that popularized the term, despite the stark *Henry: Portrait of a Serial Killer* (McNaughton 1986), a mordant and more realistic examination of the mind of a mundane multiple killer.

Psycho begins as a robbery thriller with the over-arching question, 'Will Marion succeed?', but the central question later evolves to 'Can Norman keep her murder a secret?'. We have in effect changed genres and protagonists. Hitchcock repeated the trick in *Frenzy* (Hitchcock 1972), where Rusk, the murderer, has to break the fingers of a dead woman's body in a potato truck in order to retrieve a tie pin which she managed to grab from him in the heat of his attack. Hitchcock had to work hard to make this long scene effective, introducing black comedy in order to help us sympathize with the devil because we are wedded to genre and find it hard to change horses midstream. Nowadays, the concept of the antihero has become commonplace, and in drama we are ready to accept the convention of the redemptive journey of a Keitel, Travolta or Eastwood character.

Before *Psycho* introduced us to the psychological aspect, movies were solely thrillers, policiers or detective stories. Killings were motivated by lust, revenge or greed, and the concept of the killer who kills as part of what he *is* was simply unknown. One possible exception, although considered a 'noir', is Fritz Lang's *M* (Lang 1931) where the child killer played by Peter Lorre presents the case for his compulsion to a kangaroo court of locals. It is interesting to note that its central conceit of setting a thief to catch a thief later shows up in *Silence of the Lambs* (Demme 1991), which too is a horror/thriller blend.

Demons, possession and child possession

If God exists, then so too must the devil. If there is the concept of infinite wisdom and goodness beyond man's understanding then, 'as above, so below', there must be original sin and Hades, fire and brimstone, and endless suffering. If not, then the horror film with a religious (Judaeo-Christian) ethic will not affect you at all. *The Exorcist* (Friedkin 1973) was one of the all-time horror blockbusters and remains for most the *ne plus ultra* of horror movies. This and *The Omen* (Donner 1976) produced several sequels of variable quality and gave rise to *The Exorcism of Emily Rose* (Derrickson 2005) and *The Last Exorcism* (Stamm 2010), plus such underrated movies as *Stigmata* (Wainwright 1999).

Whilst most Americans consider themselves to be Christian, Europe is more pantheistic, yet the origins of Catholicism go back a long way and the concepts of demons, rites and possessions are still rooted in deep belief. The Catholic Church in Rome has recently reinstated exorcisms after a relatively short period of denying the practice. The idea of the Black Mass (*The Devil Rides Out*: Fisher 1968) is an inversion of the Christian 'White' one, in that it has ritual, ceremony, incantation, a cross (inverted) and transubstantiation, substituting real blood as sacrifice instead of the symbolic wine, plus a summons for the (Dark) Lord to hear the prayer. It is transgression, pure and simple.

In encountering demons, devils or possessions, there are usually three distinct stages, a kind of 'close encounters' of the evil kind. First there is *contact*, which may be in the form of a séance or the use of a Ouija board. In this, the idea is to contact the spirits for information or as proof of their existence. This does not preclude the idea of evil, but it is a relatively small physical manifestation. Next there is the *summoning up* of a demon, which is more serious. Here, we introduce the pentacle and the charmed circle out of which you must not step: also, a necronomicon or black bible of sorts – a spell, a tome or a lost scroll (usually in Aramaic) to contain the spell that will conjure up the dark forces. Now we are moving towards the gaining of power and the invocation of a demon to do our bidding: a golem, an evil spirit, an acolyte. Finally there is *blood sacrifice*, aiming to summon Satan, Baphomet, Mephistopheles, the Prince of Darkness, Old Nick, Belial, Shaitan, Leviathan, the Horned One, Beelzebub or the Antichrist. This, as in *Hellraiser* (Barker 1987), is when things have really gone a bit too far.[20]

Only someone mentally disturbed would believe that they could have any power over, or make any kind of contract with, the Great Beast – and movies in which the Devil is raised never end well for the pilgrim of evil. They do, however, attract big stars, and in the past the whiff of sulphur has been liberally spread about by Robert De Niro (*Angel Heart*: Alan Parker 1987), Al Pacino (*Devil's Advocate*: Taylor Hackford 1997) and Jack Nicholson (*The Witches of Eastwick*: Miller 1987) as they madly chewed the scenery.

It is better to focus on possession, ideally that of a young child by an evil spirit. The fear here is a transgression of the idea of innocence combined with that of childhood disease. That your child is not really your child but a destructive foreign agent is a dread all parents will know, and the idea your offspring is simply evil is one that will occur on more than one sleepless night. It takes four years to socialize a child and to inculcate in them an understanding of right and wrong, and most of childhood is a battle to tame their feral natures. The concept

---

[20] A New-Age version of this, *Tears of Kali* (Marschall 2004) is well worth a look.

of any kind of pristine 'childhood' is a recent invention and the horror of the 'evil' child is one that recurs often.

Possessed children in the movies began in earnest with *Village of the Damned* (Rilla 1960) an adaptation of John Wyndham's 1957 novel *The Midwich Cuckoos*, in which all the inhabitants of the English village of Midwich, and anyone in a five-mile radius, suddenly fall unconscious. This is not explained (aliens are hinted at), but two months later all the women are pregnant, later giving birth on the same day to blonde haired, pale skinned children. It transpires that a similar thing has happened in other countries (Russia, Canada and Australia) but that the children died or were murdered by their parents. The kids grow at an alarming rate, and by the age of seven they are impeccably polite but show no sign of conscience or love. They develop a group mind and psychic powers that can halt those who try to stop them. The movie was followed by the equally superb *Children of the Damned* (Leader 1963) and a lesser remake by Wes Craven in 1995 (*Village of the Damned*: Craven, 1995). Stephen King's 1977 short story, *Children of the Corn* (published in *Night Shift* magazine in 1977), also became a movie (Kiersh 1984) – an homage to the same idea.

Another superb early example of the evil child is *The Bad Seed* (LeRoy 1956), based on a 1954 novel by William March and a play written by Maxwell Anderson and performed in 1955 – in which prim and proper little girl Rhoda Penmark is suspected of drowning her classmate Claude over a penmanship medal. She later admits this to her mother Christine, and also to the killing of a neighbour. It is revealed that Christine is the daughter of serial killer Bessie Denker and was adopted at the age of two. Rhoda's killing spree continues, and her mother attempts to cover up her daughter's activities, before finally trying to kill her and then commit suicide. After the credits roll, the cast is introduced in theatrical style, and Christine administers an old fashioned spanking to the child (the Hays Code would not permit crime to pay). Naughty possessed child! Bad girl.

The greatest story of child possession is *The Exorcist* (Friedkin 1973). The film was adapted from the 1971 novel by William Peter Blatty, a mythic story of a man trying to regain his faith with terrible consequences, wrapped around the demonic possession of Regan McNeil. It was based on a true event. The 1949 Mt Rainer exorcism case was that of a 14-year-of boy who experimented with a Ouija Board and apparently become possessed by the devil, later being 'successfully' exorcized by Catholic priests after several failed attempts. Blatty approached one of the exorcists, Father John Bowdern, who agreed to help him research a novel based on the events with the condition that he change the possessed child to a girl to protect the family. He later showed a draft to his neighbour Shirley Maclaine, who had appeared in another possession film, *The Possession of Joel Delaney* (Hussein 1972). Maclaine passed it to movie mogul

Lew Grade, but his offer was not accepted. Warner Bros eventually picked it up and many directors were considered before they settled on William Friedkin, whom Blatty favoured.

The script of *The Exorcist* was heavily re-written, with Blatty as producer, and the year-long shoot was plagued with problems and rumours of priests being on set to bless the participants – a sort of holy Health and Safety. Warner Bros did not preview the film, afraid of causing offence, opening it at 30 cinemas where it played for six months. It became a huge blockbuster, with hysterical reactions from audience members having heart attacks and miscarriages, and ushers using cat litter to clear up the (presumably pea-green) vomit. The Catholic Church was besieged with requests for exorcisms and, rather than declare the film blasphemous, the *Catholic Times* saw it as profoundly spiritual. *The Exorcist* played in some cinemas for two years after its release. *The Exorcist* was re-released on its 25th anniversary in Britain, having been finally granted a certificate by the BBFC, containing excised footage including the famous 'spider walk'.

There has been much talk about subliminal imagery in *The Exorcist*. Friedkin himself has stated that it is 'not subliminal because you can see it'. The Demon's face is visible in two single frames, one during Regan's medical examination and one where his mother is in the kitchen. The image was apparently part of the testing for the dummy to be used for the revolving head sequence. Linda Blair's body double, Eileen Dietz, was being tested for make-up and this image was superimposed on the dummy. It is an incredibly effective scare, and that's saying something in a film stuffed full of relentlessly shocking imagery. It entirely unsettles you after flashing momentarily in your peripheral vision. Using stark single frames like this has, to our knowledge, only been done twice since: once, visible in trees flashing past as the couple speed towards their cabin in Lars von Trier's *Antichrist* (Von Trier 2009); again in *Devil* (Dowdle 2010), an amusing tale by M. Night Shyamalan of the Devil trapping five people in an elevator: the image is glimpsed on CCTV cameras by a guard.

The Exorcist employs disgust, rather than shock, especially disgust at the body ('Help me', written on Regan's torso), making it a precursor to Body Horror and the work of David Cronenberg (see p. 35). Its legacy is huge, and the movie has left a long shadow. *The Orphan* (Collet-Serra 2009) is a notable attempt ('There is something wrong with Esther') but it has a twist that negates the 'child possession' conceit. *Insidious* (Wan 2011), written by 'Saw' creators Leigh Wannell and James Wan, concerns a couple whose son becomes a vessel for ghosts, and is an 'Exorcist style' horror with a refreshing twist.

There is also *The Last Exorcism* (Stamm 2010), which again explores brilliantly the idea of a man losing his religion. In this, Cotton Marcus, a disillusioned evangelical minister bent on exposing fraudulent exorcisms, gets more than he bargained for.

There are many readings of *The Exorcist*, including ones that claim it to be a misogynistic, homosexual fantasy of the repression of a young girl into a state of virginal innocence. It is very much about puberty, and Regan is certainly surrounded by torturing men. The Evil is explicitly sexual –masturbation with a cross, blasphemy and profanity, and so on – but, all in all, in terms of his power the Devil is a bit lame. The film is no more and no less than that old saw – the threat of female sexuality.

> The Exorcist dispenses with any ambiguity, returning it to a medieval Judeo Christian view of women and in the process inadvertently exploring the idea that the control of woman's bodies is one of organized religions central concerns.
>
> James Marriott, *Virgin Book of Horror Films*

The supernatural: ghosts, hauntings, poltergeists

Ghosts do not exist. Despite this, they hold an enduring popularity in horror and in our imaginations, easily adaptable to comedy, romance, comic books and to Disney in equal measure. From the white-sheeted Scooby Doo ghost to the long-hared wet women of Japanese Horror, they remain a staple of the movies, and long may this continue.

A ghost, apparition, spectre or spook cannot physically harm you. It may shock you so hard that you suffer a heart attack or fall out of a window, but ghosts are the souls or spirits of the dead. They are ethereal beings who are felt more than they appear, often only present in groans, scratches and creaking doors. If seen, they are apparitions, a mist, a blurred shape or an afterimage. The writer of ghost stories must modulate unease and dread throughout the main part of the tale, only bringing horror as a stark result.

The masters of this art were Edgar Allen Poe, H. P. Lovecraft, M. R James,[21] Sheridan LeFanu and Henry James – the gothic tradition being the culturally acceptable face of horror. A ghost will try to drive you out of your mind, and madness is the result of many of these ghost stories, a particularly superb example being M. R James's *Oh Whistle and I'll Come*

---

[21] The BBC/BFI box set of M. R. James's *Ghost Stores for Christmas* is indispensable.

to You, My Lad.[22] This in turn may drive you to suicide and to becoming a ghost yourself.

Ghostly powers extend to haunting and turning up where you least expect it – in mirrors, in water, or right behind you. A ghost defies natural laws, floating, walking through walls and shape shifting. Like cats, they are deemed to have a territory, either bounded by the person whom they are haunting or the place where they died and where their tormented soul resides and craves release (*The Changeling*: Medak 1980). There are two opposing views that co-exist here. Although there have been many horror stories and movies in which the spirit haunts a place – for example *The Innocents* (Clayton 1961), *The Canterville Ghost* (Jules Dassin and Norman Z. McLeod 1944), *The House on Haunted Hill* (Castle,1959), *The Amityville Horror* (Stuart Rosenberg 1979; Andrew Douglas, 2005) and *Poltergeist* (Hooper 1982) – there are just as many in which it is the *person* being haunted.

Ghosts in movies before 1940 used to have a similar function to that of the devil: to provide light relief. The first serious US ghost film was *The Uninvited* (Guard and Guard 1944) in which a brother (Ray Milland) and sister stay in a haunted house in Cornwall. They are a very British thing, ghosts, what with Britain's long history of spooky old houses and Bloody Towers. American ghostly horror tends towards Southern Gothic settings in antebellum houses, or the old states of Massachusetts and also New England. Ghosts from California or Nevada are something of a struggle.

In *The Haunting* (Wise 1963), Eleanor Lance is a spinster who is escaping from her claustrophobic family and is plagued by telekinetic powers. As with *Carrie* (De Palma 1976) and *The Shining* (Kubrick 1980), the real question is, is she the target of the haunting or its source? Are the other people in the house creations of Eleanor's mind? It is made clear that the house wants her. It wants her to be absorbed by its evil. It is a living thing. This movie has subjective angles making us feel as though we are *with* the thing that is spiralling down from its rooftops. There are numerous mismatched shots, door handles, silver reflections and oddly placed mirrors that disrupt the space. Dr Markway, the suave psychic investigator in charge, explains that all the angles are wrong; the doors either won't close or they spring open by themselves, it is all disoriented, with tight spaces and full of heavy cluttered Edwardian furniture. It is fractured, like Eleanor's mind. The multiple mirrors are saying 'Look at yourself, can't you see?' The most frightening thing for Eleanor is Eleanor. Admittedly she is a neurotic, making it hard to identify with her, but her use of the guilt-ridden voiceover is straight out of *Psycho* (Hitchcock 1960).

---

[22] From *Ghost stories of an Antiquary,* 1904.

Ghosts are manifestations of unresolved issues. We cannot see them because they are part of the 'doubling' process of horror. It is no accident that many hauntings and ghost sightings have female or young protagonists, as it is generally held that women and the young are more in tune with their psyche. There is nothing as spooky as the child who 'sees' what we cannot. Unlike much modern-day horror, which can be nihilistic and feral, ghosts promote the idea that there is something beyond the veil, a world greater than our own, containing knowledge untapped and powers beyond time and space, the price of admission being your sanity or physical form. In a sense, this is redemptive. Ghosts can be seen as offering hope, as do the lies propagated by major religions.

The way to be in contact with a spirit, if one has not contacted you already, is to conduct a séance or use a Ouija board. The latter is the horror equivalent of opening Pandora's Box, and is incredibly dumb, as is proven by numerous movies such as *13 Ghosts* (Castle 1960), *Witchboard* (Tenney 1986), *What Lies Beneath* (Zemeckis 2000), *Long Time Dead* (Adams, 2002) and *Paranormal Activity* (Peli 2007). The Ouija board itself was made commercial by businessman Elijah Bond in 1890 and was regarded as a harmless parlour game until spiritualist Pearl Curran used it as a divining tool in World War I. It is of course, as we now know, a tool of Satan.

The séance is a way of receiving hidden (plot) information, but in actuality it is more often than not fraudulent. Nevertheless, séances do make for effectively spooky scenes, especially if they result in releasing unwanted spirits or form part of a magic ritual, as in *The Devil Rides Out* (Fisher 1968) or *The Ninth Gate* (Polanski 1999), or as in *Insidious* (Wan 2010) when they have the psychic wear a gas mask.

Poltergeists are angry (the word means 'noisy ghost'), moving your keys and furniture and, once things get out of hand, throwing the kitchen everywhere. Again, these troublesome spirits tend to haunt a person rather than a place.

Japanese culture and movies are full of restless spirits[23] who have died violently, missing the ceremony that would have reunited them with their ancestors. Drawing on folk tales, kabuki and Noh theatre, the most popular figure is the vengeful female ghost, related to mythic *hannya* (female demons), which we see in *Ringu* (Hideo Nakata 1998), *Ju-on* (DVD, Shimizu 2000), *The Grudge* (Shimizu 2004) and *Dark Water* (Nakata 2002).

---

[23] 'Obake' for ghost, meaning to undergo change, 'Yojai', a bewitching apparition, 'Yurei', faint spirit, and 'Oni', demon or ogre.

Witchcraft

The devil has had quite a part to play in the history of cinema from Georges Melies's early experiments, Paul Wegener's version of Poe's *Student of Prague* (Rye and Wegener 1913) to F. W. Murnau's *Faust* (1926). In *The Black Cat* (Ulmer,1934), Boris Karloff played a high priest of a satanic cult, and later Val Lewton produced *The Seventh Victim* (Robson 1943), which set the template for modern-day devil worshippers who try to convert the sceptic. Jacques Tourneur's excellent *Night of the Demon* (Tourneur 1957) invoked a real-life character familiar to anyone interested in the Black Arts, namely Aleister Crowley, known as 'The Great Beast' (1875–1947). No work on Satanism or witchcraft is complete without some reference to him.

Born in 1875 and the son of a wealthy brewer, Crowley became an influential member of a magical society, the Hermetic order of the Golden Dawn. He was a poet, artist, mountaineer and drug abuser. He was later contacted by a 'Holy Guardian Angel' on his travels in Egypt, who dictated to him The Book of the Law – within it the motto 'Do what thou wilt shall be the whole of the Law' – a call to arms for libertarians everywhere, taken up once again with enthusiasm in the 1960s when he attained posthumous cult status.

Crowley founded his own philosophy and occult society, the OTO (Ordi Templo Orientis), which was pansexual and involved heavy drug use. He became widely notorious in his lifetime, becoming known as the 'Wickedest Man in the World' and even fighting a libel case over a 1932 book that named him as a black magician (he lost). The judge. Mr Justice Swift, said 'I have never heard such dreadful, horrible, blasphemous and abominable stuff as that which has been produced by the man [Crowley]'.

Towards the end of his life he sold 'Dr. Crowley's elixir of life pills', which contained a mixture of chalk and, to quote Dr Pretorious in *Bride of Frankenstein*, 'he made them from seed'. Crowley has been hugely influential, inspiring Somerset Maugham's character The Magician, Le Chiffre in Ian Fleming's 'Casino Royale', and John Fowles's The Magus in literature. In film, *Night of the Demon* (Tourneur 1957) has him as Karswell, and in *The Devil Rides Out* (Fisher 1968), from the novel by Denis Wheatley, he is Mocato. In *Rosemary's Baby* (Polanski 1968) he appears as Adrian Marcato. His most recent appearance was in *A Chemical Wedding* (Doyle 2009), written by Bruce Dickinson of Heavy Metal band Judas Priest. He is your go-to guy for black magic.

In witchcraft movies, the central tenet is the acceptance that white and black magic exists, and the onus is on the protagonist to accept this. Thus, in *Night of the Demon*, sceptical Dr John Holden is in London to attend a convention where the late Mr Harrington intended to expose a cult. On meeting Karswell, the first thing the two do is to mock one another's beliefs.

In *Night of the Eagle* (Hayers 1961), it is an academic's wife who uses witchcraft to further her husband's career – an idea reversed in *Rosemary's Baby* (Polanski 1968) where Guy Woodhouse allows a satanic cult to use his spouse as a vessel in order to further his acting career. *Rosemary's Baby* was a huge success, grossing over $30 million and making it one of horror's first blockbusters. Copulation with the devil is strong stuff, but the story is presented in such a way that it might all simply be Rosemary's changing mental state during pregnancy. The potions given to her are the most obvious witchcraft aspect of the movie, but it avoids any ritualistic spells, and we are not party to the Faustian pact made by Guy. In the late 1960s, interest in devilry and witchcraft was growing. The Rolling Stones had released their album 'Satanic Majesty's Request' and there was an interest in the occult and the esoteric. Roman Polanski had read Professor R. L. Gregory's 'Eye and Brain, The Psychology of Seeing', which stated that we see less than we think and that our perception of reality is filled in by false memories. An agnostic, Polanski stated in his 1984 autobiography that 'the entire story, seen through [Rosemary's] eyes, could have been a chain of only superficially sinister coincidences, a product of feverish fantasies' – shades here of Ebenezer Scrooge's denial of the spirits.[24] Many audience members were convinced they saw cloven hooves and the baby's face at the reveal, when all you can actually see (superimposed) in the final frames are two slightly feline eyes.

Witchfinder General (Reeves 1968) was more about the hunting and burning of witches as sadistic ritual, and Ken Russell's masterpiece *The Devils* (1970) was a political piece concerning trumped-up charges against a priest rather than a witch. Robin Hardy's *Wicker Man* (1973) is the best British folk horror bar none about paganism, and is a marvellous reversal of Judaeo-Christian beliefs. Please ignore any sequels and remakes.[25]

The Witches of Eastwick (Miller 1987), based on a John Updike novel, concerns three women abandoned by their husbands who do not realize they are witches. They form a coven and accidentally summon up the Devil (in the form of Jack Nicholson). The movie was played for laughs with few horror ingredients bar mild disgust and should not trouble us further. *The Craft* (Andrew Fleming 1996) has a coven of three female teenagers who, discovering that a fourth member propagates greater powers, cast spells on their classmates and on each other. Again the Wiccan rites get out of hand as bad girl Nancy leads

---

[24] In Charles Dickens, *A Christmas Carol* (1843).
[25] *Blood on Satan's Claw* (Haggard 1970) is also recommended.

them astray. Eventually they turn on her and protagonist Sarah invokes a 'higher power' which nullifies Nancy (she ends up being committed) and removes the others' powers. This seems to be more about teenage socialization than true witchcraft, with a message that implies it's OK to be different – but not *that* different. That they were all bullied or abused outsiders is interesting, but the revenge motive could have been darker, with perhaps a bit more 'witch' fulfilment.

Witches as adjuncts of Satan or cults were popular in the 1960s Hammer Horror offerings, whereas the portrayal of modern-day witches in movies does not rely on a male mentor. With the rise of feminism we might have expected more movies about witches, but perhaps this is too obvious. Ira Levin's great work, *The Stepford Wives* (Forbes 1975), said a great deal about women's supposed place in society (as automata). There are plenty of countries today that still have a medieval attitude towards women and it may be to them that we look for a new stories.

In terms of period horror, other than the previously mentioned *Witchfinder General* (Reeves 1968) there has been little made about the great European purge of women. In America there is the story of the Salem Witch hunts, written for the stage as *The Crucible* by Arthur Miller (1953) and filmed in 1957 (Rouleau 1957[26]) and then in 1996 (Hytner 1996), but little since.

Werewolves and Body Horror

The transformation of the human body is one of horror's basic template ideas, beginning with R. L. Stevenson's novella, *The Strange case of Doctor Jekyll and Mr. Hyde* (1886). The inner wolf outwardly projected is a being of sexual repression. In Waggner's *Wolf Man* (Waggner 1941) he is a projection of Larry Talbot's sexual frustration in his relationship. Irena's fear of transformation in *Cat People* (Tourneur 1942) is manifested in numerous images of cats. *The Company of Wolves* (Jordan 1984) and the excellent *Ginger Snaps* trilogy (Fawcett 2000; Harvey 2004; Sullivan 2004) are metaphors for the onset of female puberty. In the 1970s and 1980s, transformation scenes came to the fore, partly due to advances in prosthetics and robotics, which allowed Rob Bottin and Rick Baker to produce their best work (*The Howling*: Joe Dante 1981). Once we arrive at Carpenter's *The Thing* (Carpenter 1982), in which the beast can transform into anything, all bets are off.

One director who has consistently explored the vulnerability of the human body is director David Cronenberg, whose early movies *Shivers* (Cronenberg

---

[26]Written by Arthur Miller and Jean-Paul Sartre.

1975), *Rabid* (Cronenberg 1976) and *The Brood* (Cronenberg 1979) concern its transformation at the hands of science, as well as telepathy, sexual disease and mutation. Cronenberg is known as the 'King of venereal horror' or the 'Canadian prince of body horror'. He has developed a new form of cinema, both visceral and literate, adapting works by beat writer William Burroughs (*Naked Lunch*: 1991, from the 1959 novel) and SF master J. G. Ballard (*Crash*: 1996, from the 1973 novel) into a new aesthetic of the body. Cronenberg's early films were prophetic. *Shivers* anticipated AIDS, while *Videodrome* (1983) foresaw the cheapening imagery of the then emerging satellite TV. He studied biochemistry in Toronto, but switched to English Literature and wrote SF stories. His break-through film was *Scanners* (1981), which concerned a corrupted technological future. Cronenberg manipulates disgust with great skill, not merely for pure gross-out. On referring to these excesses, such as the woman with the external womb in *The Brood*, or the man with a vaginal slit in his stomach in *Videodrome*, he states:

> It's fascination but also a willingness to look at what is really there without flinching, and to say that this is what we are made of, as strange and as disgusting as it may seem sometimes.[27]

One of Cronenberg's most often quoted lines is given to Eliot, one of twin gynaecologists in the movie *Dead Ringers*: 'I've often thought that there should be beauty contests for the insides of bodies – you know, best spleen, most perfectly developed kidneys'. He has since moved away from genre movies, but his unique sensibility marks him out as an iconoclastic writer/director.

Bad science

Oh, in the name of God! Now I know what it feels like to be God!
(Frankenstein James Whale 1931)

With this line from Universal's 1931 classic, Frankenstein played out the fear of a generation. There has always been fear of change. The Industrial Revolution in Britain was accompanied by the Luddite movement which smashed the looms in the cotton factories – seeing the advance as a way of making them redundant. Early surgery was kill-or-cure, with Victorian doctors competing over

---

[27] Quoted in Marriott 2004.

how fast they might remove a limb. World War I brought the mechanization of death in vast numbers: it was scientists who created the mustard gas that slaughtered so many; and then, later, the poisons used in World War II extermination camps. It was science that brought us the atom bomb, but also nuclear fission – energy to power the world. It was the use of the atom bomb in 1944 that irrevocably changed the perception of science, which was subsequently reflected in Science Fiction/Horror crossover movies of the 1950s. Never again could a scientist be entirely trustworthy; they often worked at some sinister plant or were in the pockets of some shady covert government department.

Once the iconography of Frankenstein bedded in, there came several variations on the mad doctor theme, including Dr Richard Marlow (played by Bela Lugosi), who used black magic and the souls of kidnapped girls to revitalize his dead wife (*Voodoo Man*: Hook 1944), Dr Peter Blood, who exhumed corpses and put living hearts in them to bring them back to life (*Dr. Blood's Coffin*: Sidney J. Furie 1961) and plastic surgeon Dr Genessier, who disfigured his daughter as a result of his reckless driving then experimented with facial skin grafts that failed to take (*Eyes without a Face [Les Yeux Sans Visages]*: Franju 1960) – masterfully updated as *The Skin I live In [Le Piel que Habito]* (Almodóvar 2011).

The 1980s heralded a proliferation of media, pornography, advertising, video and cable TV (later, satellite and YouTube). An idealized vision of the human body was formed. Critic Naomi Wolf called this the 'Beauty Myth'.[28] This impossible state, she claimed, could not be created without the intervention of plastic surgery or liposuction. The idea of gender transformation also grew, and both are features of Cronenberg's work, which starts to look eerily prescient. The obverse to the rise of the Photoshopped, airbrushed 'ideal' is the explosion in body modifications, tattoos, piercings and scarification, in a revolt against the idea of the perfect body.

Cronenberg reverses received ideas. A plaque on the doctor's wall in *Shivers* (Cronenberg 1975) states that 'Sex is the invention of a clever venereal disease'. Seth Brundle in *The Fly* (Cronenberg 1986) sees himself as having being struck by 'a disease with a purpose'. *The Fly* was Cronenberg's most commercially successful film. This remake introduced a strong love interest, incredible prosthetics and tragic transformations. Brundle begins as a classic mad scientist with sets of identical clothes in his wardrobe so that he does not have to think about what to wear (Einstein did the same). Sanity, or at least logical reasoning, deserts him early on, as the matter transporters prove effective. In the original version (*The Fly*: Kurt Neumann 1958) scientist Andre Delambre pointed out its benefits: 'humanity need never want or fear again';

[28]Naomi Wolf, *The Beauty Myth*. New York: William Morrow and Company, 1991.

but Brundle's interest is to put a woman through the transporter – perhaps chiming with Cronenberg's ideas, as in *VideoDrome*, of combining the sexes. The transformation is an ageing process, a love affair burning through its stages toward tragedy with Brundle's penis pickled in a jar and partner Veronica growing increasingly disillusioned. Finally, she needs rescuing from Brundlefly, who revolts against her ex-boyfriend by dissolving his arm and ankle in acidic fly vomit. The transformation is complete and, having nowhere to ascend to or descend from the human–insect mutation, Brundlefly merges with the Telepod itself. The resultant pathetic creature begs only for release. This man–machine interface anticipates Cronenberg's later work with Ballard's *Crash* (Cronenberg 1996) and was influential in Shin'ya Tsukamoto's *Tetsuo* (Tsukamoto 1989) and *Tetsuo II: Bodyhammer* (Tsukamoto 1992).

Bad science is here to stay. From disasters like Bhopal, nuclear disasters like Chernobyl (*Chernobyl Diaries*: Parker 2012) or the nuclear accident at Three Mile Island,[29] there has been a continual leak of science related fears. The effect of the SARS epidemic in Hong Kong in 2002, which nearly caused a pandemic, can directly be seen in Steven Soderbergh's *Contagion* (Soderbergh 2011). The colourless, odourless chemical weapon, Sarin gas, to which were exposed 5,000 Japanese commuters in 1995, changed a nation.

It is a common plot device now that 'wonder' drugs curing cancer are routinely kept from us by pharmaceutical corporations waiting until the price is right. Scientists are all too aware that research funding can be removed and tenure threatened unless the research is deemed 'sexy'.

In *28 Days Later* (Boyle 2002) the Rage virus has been farmed and tested on animals and takes a heartbeat to turn anyone infected into a feral blood lusting zombie. This can only have been developed as a chemical weapon, as what other function could it possibly serve? A new playground for experimental chemical weaponry was found in the Middle Eastern countries during the last decade, and movies are starting to give nod to these ramifications. As technology becomes nanotechnology, cybernetics become more sophisticated, gender is blurred by surgery and medicine continues to eradicate disease, we are never short of a mad scientist or three. Dr Moreau – prepare your island for more visitors.

Lastly, the body horror canon would be incomplete without mention of its alumni, Frank Henenlotter with *Basket Case* (Henenlotter 1982) and *FrankenHooker* (Henenlotter 1990), Stuart Gordon's *Re-animator* (Gordon 1985) and *Dagon* (Gordon 2001), or Brian Yuzna's *Society* (Yuzna 1989); the majestic

---

[29] The Three Mile Island accident was a partial nuclear meltdown, which occurred at the Three Mile Island power plant in Dauphin County, Pennsylvania, USA, on 28 March 1979. It is the worst accident in US commercial nuclear power plant history to date.

twisted visions of Clive Barker in *Hellraiser* (Barker 1987) and *Nightbreed* (Barker 1990); as well a tip of the scalpel to Lloyd Kaufman, co-founder of Troma Entertainment, the American independent film production and distribution company responsible for *Tromeo and Juliet* (Kaufman and Gunn 1996) and *The Toxic Avenger* (Herz and Kaufman 1984).

Slashers

The Slasher, or Stalk and Slash movie, has the hardest burden to bear of all subgenres. It is the whipping boy, the one that receives the worst notices. It has become clichéd. From its inception in Bob Clark's *Black Christmas* (Bob Clark 1974) to its popularization in Carpenter's *Halloween* (Carpenter 1978), the genre took off in the 1980s with its sequels as well as those of *Nightmare on Elm Street* and *Friday the 13th*. There followed second-rate cash-in franchises such as *Sleepaway Camp* (Hiltik 1983) and *Prom Night* (Lynch 1980), which did nothing to help. The introduction of VCR and VHS tape meant that horror was no longer confined to the first cinema run and could be passed around sororities and sleepovers.

A decade later, along came Kevin S. Williamson with *Scream* (Craven 1996), introducing a new icon, Ghostface, and a post-modern take, bringing deliberate irony to a tired subgenre and killing its 'star' Drew Barrymore, some 15 minutes into the movie in an homage to *Psycho*. It went about gleefully subverting the usual 'scary movie' clichés and nailing them flat in the sequel *Scream II* (Craven 1997). Imitators followed with *I Know What You Did Last Summer* (Gillespie 1997) and *Urban Legend* (Blanks 1998).

Feminist theoretician Carol Clover wrote a treatise on the Slasher genre entitled 'Men, Women and Chainsaws' (Clover 1992) in which she created the 'Final Girl' theory, describing the girl who survives the ordeal as being the investigating consciousness of the movie, the one who displays intelligence, curiosity and vigilance. She has a unisex name (Laurie, Sidney), is often virginal, unavailable or uninterested in sex, as opposed to her colleagues (hence the erroneous idea that sex = death in horror films). She will have a familial or other connection to the killer, and over the course of the action she becomes masculinized by appropriating a phallic weapon with which to dispatch the killer. In order to do this she must appropriate the evil and be subsumed by it, often physically as she enters the charnel house. There will be blood and mud and fluids that replicate the amniotic. There will be a symbolic death and re-birth via a womb or womb-like tunnel. In *Halloween* (Carpenter 1978) the womb is a cupboard with a slatted door: for some reason – as is wittily noted in Scott

Glosserman's *'Behind the Mask*: The Rise of *Leslie Vernon'* (2006) – serial killers are very afraid of slatted wooden cupboard doors.

Our Final Girl has to be feminine because she must endure abject terror, something we would not tolerate in a male lead. In fact her gender is quite fluid. She is something of a tomboy, never a slut, and about as far away from the old 1950s idea of the helpless female as you can get. In this way, Clover states that this fluidity of gender combined with the wrecked masculinity of the killer illustrates the impact of feminism in popular culture.

Most horror writers, directors and producers are well aware of these 'rules', and in the last decade, attempts have been made to try to twist the subgenre to avoid the obvious. *All the Boys Love Mandy Lane* (Levine 2006) is one sterling example, with strong characterization, most plot holes shored up, and a reveal that delights and annoys in equal measure. *Teeth* (Lichetenstein 2007), despite being more of a blackly comic take on the coming-of-age movie (involving vagina dentata), also has a strong female protagonist. In Eli Roth's *Cabin Fever* (Roth 2002) all the characters are intentionally unlikeable, so we mind not a jot when the women get the flesh eating disease first.

The Slasher has gone through its rococo phase and now has seemingly nowhere to go except parody and homage (*Hatchet*: Green 2006). However, two fundamentals still apply: first, that the young, strong, female protagonist is relatable to both sexes; and second, that pretty girls in skimpy white or khaki T-shirts will always attract financiers.

Chapter 4
Staging the Horror: Five Tropes

Setting the mood for horror is deliciously fun and evocative. Darkness and night are obvious locations used in the Gothic tradition, in such early films as *Nosferatu* (Murnau 1922) and *The Old Dark House* (Whale 1932). What we know is there, but cannot see, remains one of the most effective ways to scare the pants off an audience. Small, unlit spaces invoke palpitations, as do crawl-spaces and cupboards and hiding under the covers. Old, dark rooms with cobwebby corners and huge high-ceilinged castles were the mainstay of horror movies in the 1930s and 1940s.

Large, empty places breed uncertainty. No one has yet matched those soulless, endless hotel corridors of *The Shining* (Kubrick 1980), and big old apartment blocks with empty rooms have been put to great use in Polanski's *Repulsion* (Polanski 1965) and *Rosemary's Baby* (Polanski 1968). The dim, foggy streets of old London town are the stamping grounds of *Werewolf of London* (Walker 1935), *Jack the Ripper* (Franco 1976) and *Sweeney Todd* (Tim Burton 2007), as were the foggy moors of northern England in *An American Werewolf in London* (John Landis 1981). Fog was used in every film by the Italian director Mario Bava: it is *the* horror movie cliché, as it creeps slowly across the graveyard, settling at waist height, partially obscuring and changing the shape and perception of the known to something more sinister. Black and white photography was well suited to this, as anything might be hiding in those murky greys and blacks, ready to loom out at us from any angle or any place, as in *Night of the Demon* (Tourneur 1957). Fog and mist are such perennials that they have been awarded their own titular movies, *The Fog* (Carpenter 1980) and Stephen King's *The Mist* (Darabont 2007).

The haunted house is endlessly adaptable. It does not have to be in Amityville or on Elm Street – Ridley Scott placed his haunted house in space in *Alien* (Scott

1979), creating an equally mordant mood with industrial pipes, rattling chains and dripping water ducts. This idea was replicated in *Event Horizon* (Anderson 1997). It can be a scientific outpost, as in *The Thing* (Carpenter 1982) or as small as a log hut as in *The Cabin in the Woods* (Goddard 2012), *The Evil Dead* (Raimi 1981), *Timber Falls* (Giglio 2007) or *Wrong Turn* (Schmidt 2003).

Blackness represents infinity and so too does the endless forest. Greenery, trees, branches, earth and mud all look universally much the same, which is why there are so many movies made with girls in tight-fitting soiled T-shirts running from their antagonists. *The Blair Witch Project* (Myrick and Sánchez 1999) made superb capital out of this sense of 'endless wooded nothing'.

Snow, too, is infinite. At first pristine and crystal clear, but blinding when in storm. It can be a useful – if rarely used due to the cost – device to keep the protagonists apart. Best practice examples include *Misery* (Reiner 1990), *The Shining* (Kubrick 1980) and more recently *Dead Snow* (Wirkola 2009), *The Thing* (van Heijningen Jr. 2011) and *Let the Right One In* (Alfredson 2008), remade in the US as *Let Me In* (Reeves 2010)

Wild desert landscapes work too, as in *Wolf Creek* (McLean 2005) and the *Hills Have Eyes* (Aja 2006), or you can abandon land altogether and set your movie in the ocean. *Jaws* (Spielberg 1976) took a long time to shoot, as water continuously changes colour, but there was a spate of movies set entirely at sea in the mid-2000s, including *Open Water* (Kentis 2003) and *Triangle* (Smith 2009).

The endless human jungle may also be pressed into use. Industrial urban wastelands have long been used in crime movies but the 'projects' (or, in the UK, council estates) are rapidly growing as an alienating and dangerous place to be lost in. Carpenter's *Assault on Precinct 13* (Carpenter 1976) defined the abandoned and uncared-for communal space that bred urban horror. Another was *Candyman* (Bernard Rose 1992), and this particular flaming torch has been taken up by the European horror of *La Horde* (Dahan and Rocher 2009), *Outcast* (McCarthy 2010) and *Attack the Block* (Cornish 2011).

Once we leave town and get down on the farm there is *Black Sheep* (King 2006), *Isolation* (O'Brien 2005) and *Calvaire* (Du Weiz 2004), all bred or mutated out of loneliness, the latter featuring isolation and porcine sex.

Mood in the horror genre is all about grime and dirt and being unable to see what is hiding right in front of you. Directors have become savvy of late, taking the new digital technology that seeks to illuminate everything, and making the blood and gore as filthy as it can be, as in such films as *Hostel* (Roth 2005) and *Saw* (Wan 2004). Movies have also begun to use the opaque qualities of plastic sheeting to cover up a multitude of sins, for example in *H6: Diario de un asesino* (Barón 2005) or *Sick House* (Radclyffe 2008). Both of these used sheets of plastic hung in rooms to create uncanny shapes. So, too, can the plastic curtain that surrounds a hospital bed hide many sins, as in *Saw*, *Planet Terror* (Rodriguez 2007) and of course the obvious progenitor, *Psycho* (Hitchcock 1960)

The writer can help the director here. In the few opportunities you get to describe a place of pain, carnage or the wispy trails of the supernatural, you must use it to best effect. Setting the scene and making us instantly uneasy is a vital tool in these first few pages.

Once achieved, the basic plot of all horror is as follows.

Someone is put under threat by something Unknown. Before they can deal with it they must understand that it *is* the Unknown. They must then come to conceive of how it operates and try to defeat it. They will first try to defeat the horror with what they know, but this will not be enough, as it cannot be defeated in this way. In order to find out what will stop, harm or kill it, the protagonist has to venture into the Unknown's territory. If they can learn to behave as the Unknown does then they will be successful, although sometimes this is not enough and they are defeated. The Unknown then moves on to select another.[30]

The Unknown is at the heart of all horror and this is what drives us to the multiplex, be it the insanity of the psychopathic serial killer, the superhuman strength of the monster or the encroaching madness of paranormal torment. In order to appreciate this (if that is the right word) we must be open to the improbable, the impossible and the fantastic. This is not the exclusive province of the young, but this genre, along with SF and Fantasy, is particularly popular with younger minds.

This is in part because being 'teenage' is a time of great flux: you are not yet fully mature, have not established a working routine and are in that liminal space between living at home and breaking away. You have dispensed with childhood fantasy, where any product of the imagination is seen as valid, but conversely you are still in a state of play as you discover the moral and tangible boundaries in life. You are seeking to understand yourself as an entity apart from the family and establishing your role within your peer group. You are protean, unformed. No wonder the scary monsters can get to you.

The young also have a different relationship with death. Chances are they have not yet lost a family member, partner or friend to the grim reaper, nor have they witnessed a genuine scene of horror, such as a car crash or a building fire. In this they are protected from the world of pain and anguish and from the drawn-out numbing pain of grief and mourning. For those of us who have experienced these feelings, they are things we wish to be rid of. The agony of

---

[30] Adapted from Stephen Cleary's Lecture Notes, *Arista Horror* (2005).

protracted illness or the frustrating physical and mental decline that age pins on all of us is a very real threat, too real for horror, and remains the province of the movie-of-the-week afternoon TV drama.

The young are invincible. This is why they drink to a state of stupefaction or take unnecessary risks near moving sharp objects. It is why they foolishly jump off things into water or ignore safety instructions. They know better. Death isn't coming for them anytime soon, and if he is, he's got a goddam fight on his hands. Their bodies are strong and lithe and will withstand deprivation, intoxication or physical punishment. Not for them the crippling shame of the hangover or aching desire to recover and replenish with hot water, vitamins, wine and chocolate. They can watch death taking its toll over and over again and simply laugh, which is why the *Final Destination* (Wong 2000) series was such a delightful funfair ride. They can watch Victor Crowley tear a man asunder for kicks and Leatherface dismember a fresh kill, and feel nothing. This is not to say the young are sociopathic (not all of them) but their threshold is unsullied by the real stuff of life. We experience a very different reaction when watching intestines torn out in a horror movie to watching an operation in a TV medical soap. Horror places empathy and revulsion into a 'safe play' area where, seemingly, anything goes – from *Cannibal Holocaust* (Deodato 1980), *Martyrs* (Laugier 2008) and to its *reductio ad absurdum*, *The Human Centipede* (Six 2009).

The belief that you can act without consequence is at the heart of many teenage pranks, and this fits neatly into the Slasher mode. Not only is it thrilling to see this in action as perpetrated by the killer (the serial killer as Superman) but we can also enjoy it remotely when our gang of teens behave irresponsibly and condemn them for it. 'I would never pull such an audacious prank as that douchebag', thinks the coolest kid in the auditorium. It is at once a side dish to the main attraction (getting our Final Girl up and running) and an easy way of scapegoating the dumb. They are going to get what's coming on screen. We rejoice as the jock is beheaded, mauled, castrated or otherwise defiled and destroyed, condemning him as a Neanderthal Alpha Male and rewarding ourselves for our superior knowledge and sense of propriety. This is catharsis. If we see the 'practical joker' as a kind of sacrificial lamb, then so be it. If done well, the audience feels a tangible antagonism toward the annoying joker and shouts of delight will accompany his dispatch.

Horror is not entirely the province of the young. Many supernatural horror movies have become breakthrough hits, such as *Paranormal Activity* (Peli 2007), *The Blair Witch Project* (Sanchez 1999), *The Sixth Sense* (Shyamalan 1999), *The Omen* (Donner 1976) and *The Exorcist* (Friedkin 1973). These horrors contain psychological and intellectual depth, ask questions of our existence, of reality and the subconscious world. They feature adults in the lead roles rather than teenagers, a way of encouraging an older demographic to seek them out.

Sometimes, the movie will be marketed as a 'Jodie Foster' or 'Julianne Moore' movie. Ewan MacGregor may feature, or Adrian Brody. Melissa George and Sarah Michelle Gellar have also featured in genre movies. Bruce Willis, from solid beginnings in TV and action movies, has consistently picked interesting projects, many in the science fiction/horror crossover including *The Sixth Sense* (Shyamalan 1999) and *Twelve Monkeys* (Gilliam 1995). However, movie stars in horror – witness Jack Nicholson chewing scenery in *Wolf* (Nichols 1994) or Sir Anthony Hopkins in *The Rite* (Håfström 2011), tend to overbalance the story and undermine any credibility it had in the first place. Like sitcom, horror does better when it makes stars.

Those actors who began in horror are legion. There is no shame in *Attack of the Killer Tomatoes* (De Bello 1978), Mr Clooney, or in being the first teen to die in *Nightmare on Elm Street* (Craven 1984), Mr Depp. Some remain faithful to it (Robert Englund, Christopher Lee) or continue to work in the genre as and when it suits them (Donald and Keifer Sutherland). For actresses, it is one of the few ways to lasso that elusive lead role. Sadly, it is not in the province of the screenwriter to dictate terms when it comes to casting. If you have sold your script and a big name is being touted as star, you may simultaneously rejoice (as it will get a wider release) and moan, as you are likely to be asked to re-write to accommodate the 'new direction in which the script is going'.

The five basic tropes

The experience of being scared is not a simple one, and there are five basic tropes within which the horror movie is modulated. The screenwriter and director must manipulate these effectively in order to achieve the best dramatic effect. They may be delivered in differing amounts, and not all five are necessarily required, but they are so common as to be ubiquitous. The screenwriter/director does two things: writing/telling the story, and delivering the shocks. Often the latter are integral to the story but sometimes, as in the case of false shock, they are an add-on. Ordered in terms of intensity, we must use the following so as to effectively put an audience into a state of apprehension and fear:

Unease
Dread
Terror
Horror
Disgust.

Unease is the tingling in the throat or the heaviness in the limbs when you are beginning to feel ill. It is people acting strangely, remaining silent, muttering behind your back. It is the feeling as you step on board a rickety boat and need to re-orient your sense of balance. It is the map reference that should be there but isn't, a patting of your pockets and finding your wallet or phone missing.

It is a slight upset in nature, a dislocation of reality.

It is the world refusing to conform to your view of it.

Unease

Unease is the first stage in any horror movie and can be triggered by many things: a new environment, a liminal warning, a premonition (*Final Destination*), a new person in your life who has not yet earned your trust (*Orphan*), a mysterious stranger (*Halloween*) whom you cannot quite see. It is the movement in the woods, the creak on the stair, the howling of the wind and the dimming of the lights.

A sense of unease can only be modulated in the first act, as it is a precursor, a delicate feeling that dissipates when the real terror comes along. It is non-specific. Once you reach the point of no return when the Unknown is making its presence felt (by killing or possessing people) then unease has done its work.

In the haunted house movie, there are standard Freudian places which will engender unease. The locked room is one such common example (*The Skeleton Key*: Softley 2005). The great thing about this is that it plays with the forbidden and with our urge to transgress. Tell a child not to go into a room and what does he want more than anything on this earth? The locked room raises questions – why is it locked? What is in there? What is it trying to hide? Where is the key? Is it Alice in Wonderland or the gateway to hell?

You may add to the sense of unease by having sounds emanate from it at night, scraping on the walls and floors, or children's feet running about (*Dark Water*: Salles 2005), light shining under the door or movement within. The doorway is a symbolic barrier preventing ingress and also a portal to the other. It does not even have to be a regular room – it could be a locked cell, a missing or hidden floor of a hospital (*Boo*: Ferrante 2005; *Autopsy*: Gierasch 2008) or a sanatorium wing that is closed for renovation (*Session Nine*: Anderson 2001). This will ramp up the mystery and confirm the unease.

There is the attic room, with all its secrets. Childhood toys, the rocking chair (*Black Christmas*: Clark 1974), the room with the cupboard (*Poltergeist*: Hooper 1982; *The Amityville Horror*: Douglas 2005), locked trunks that contain … who knows what? It is too early to explore the crawl-space just yet, as we have not reached the point of transgression.

There is the cellar. Every self-respecting serial killer has a cellar (*Silence of the Lambs*: Demme 1991), often complete with a well (*The Hole*: Dante 2009), hidden compartments and satanic markings (*The Sect [La seta]*: Soavi 1991). A cellar stands is a useful stand-in for the dungeon – the place down below where the evil is stored. In *Silence of the Lambs*, was it really necessary to keep the psychopaths underground in old-fashioned brick-walled cells with bars? Would it not be more likely to be a pristine white space that could be easily monitored? Hannibal Lecter, the worst of all psychopaths, has a glass-fronted cell: thick but transparent, so that nothing protects us from his hungry gaze ('mmm, liver'). When Dr Chisholm gives Clarice Starling the tour, it is a master class of unease moving towards dread. He warns her as he goes, revealing a handy photograph (which he clearly keeps about his person at all times) of the disfigured nurse whom Hannibal ate. He leads her from the hospital corridor (there is a mad patient glimpsed behind them, just out of focus), descending the stairs to a red-lit hell of locked doors, bars, then a complete 360-degree pan around the guardroom, before facing that dreadful corridor.

'Closer … clo-ser!' ushers Hannibal, spider to her fly.

This is not yet dread, for dread is what comes when you know that something is wrong. Unease is the favoured tool of the writer of ghost stories and the super-natural. Many of the Asian horrors employ this technique well. Unease relates to the future, in that it is concerned with what might happen. It is so effective because it is not rooted to anything. With unease, almost any object selected in close-up will assume a greater meaning than the object itself merits. Two of the greatest horror movies ever – *The Exorcist* (Friedkin 1973) and *The Shining* (Kubrick 1980) – both modulate unease for a sustained period.

Dread

Dread is a tangible feeling that something is wrong and that it pertains to you. Dread is heading home towards your apartment and being passed by fire engines heading in your direction. Dread is a mother losing sight of her child in a shopping mall. Dread is an official-looking envelope in the mail or approaching a meeting with a friend or lover to find a knot of anxious people around them. Dread is fear heading in your direction. Unfounded, uncertain fear, but fear none the less. It is almost the basic unit of currency in a horror movie, in that we must feel for the protagonists as they approach the unknown. If there is no dread then we cannot connect and it will not resonate with an audience.

The great thing here is that you are unsure of what is scaring you and because you do not know what it is, you can invent terrible nightmare scenarios. It's the 'What's the worst that could happen?' scenario – and of course, it will. Once it does, there will be some degree of relief, because at least your fears were founded – even though a chainsaw-wielding madman is chasing you.

In *Don't Look Now* (Roeg 1973) the movie begins straight away with unease and quickly moves to dread. A small girl is playing near a pond; her brother rides his bike over broken glass. There is a GI Joe doll but with a woman's voice. There is a horse, running wild in the distance across the field – all is wrong from the outset. The parents, played by Donald Sutherland and Julie Christie, are inside, having eaten their Sunday dinner (or have they?). He prepares architectural slides on Italian Renaissance churches. There is blood on the slide, something/someone red sitting in a pew. His daughter wears a red coat. Suddenly she is no longer in view. Unease switches to the universal parents' panic. He dashes out, straight into the frozen water. He dives under and comes up with the lifeless body. His wife stumbles out, already collapsing in grief as she emits a terrible howl of anguish. Dread.

Dread can also lead to *rising dread*, which is a more intensified fear. A good example of this is in *The Vanishing* (Sluizer 1988) in which a young couple touring in France pause at a roadside rest stop. Saskia leaves Rex to browse, and then she vanishes, leaving no clue to her whereabouts until three years later,when Rex starts to receive postcards from her abductor. Nearly the whole of this movie works on rising dread. The protagonist Rex has the certainty that all is wrong, but does not know how it is going to play out. He can only stumble forward into the dark, powerless to resist, as he awaits his inevitable, awful fate.

Dread is also well modulated in *The Mist* (Darabont 2007), as the thing in the mist traps the inhabitants of a small town in a local store. Each attempt to get out is met with setbacks and then, once they band together, the tale turns inwards and the true horror is revealed to be among them in the form of the crazy Christian lady, Mrs Carmody. As she starts to gain followers, invoking Biblical texts and damning the rationalists, our hero and his son become aware that the real enemy is the mob mentality of fundamentalism and that the witch hunt will ultimately lead to blood sacrifice – 'Let he who is without sin ...'

Dread is inescapable because it is real; it knows the unspeakable is about to happen but it is unable to do anything about it. This closes the trap on our unsuspecting participants. The writer cannot leave a way out for the protagonist, otherwise credibility sags. The bridge must be out (*The Evil Dead*: Raimi 1981), all money sunk into the property (*The Amityville Horror*: Rosenburg 1979), the map lost (*The Blair Witch Project*: Myrick and Sanchez 1999). It is the darkness descending, the last flickering rays of sunlight as the werewolves and vampires begin to awake.

Dread is the emotive proof that we have identified properly with the protagonist and his or her descent into the world of the unknown.

Terror

Terror is horror's orgasm. If unease and dread are about what is to come, then terror is right in the now. This is the thing we have been worried about suddenly bursting onto the screen. It is seeing the alien in all its acid-dripping, multi-clawed, teeth-chomping terror. Terror is the scream! It is visceral and gory and the characters' only reaction to it is panic. Terror is right in the moment. It is *now*, close up, in your face. Here, a good director will use fast cutting, showing frenzied movement, ripping, tearing, the teeth, the hide, the weapons glimpsed. There is no escape as your heart hammers your chest. It is visceral, straightforward and as uncomplicated as a car chase. The pure adrenaline will make the heroine fight or flee and neither of these will be effective. You cannot keep a story at near hysterical pitch because we cannot exist in that state – we need respite, so it must be used sparingly. Being wholly visual it cannot go on for too long. Think of how a chase scene in an action movie can be overdone once they have mined all variations of leaping, dropping and smashing through windows. Action scenes are pure spectacle, and as such they suspend plot and character development.

Movies that succeed in keeping you on a knife-edge throughout the second and third acts are rare. In *Halloween* (Carpenter 1978), once Michael starts the killing again, he never lets up. Equally effective are *Texas Chainsaw Massacre* (Hooper 1974), *Saw* (Wan 2004), *Feast* (Gulager 2005), *[REC]* (Balaguero and Plaza 2007) and *Eden Lake* (Watkins 2008).

Because it is so hard to keep going for long, you will save up the greatest terrors for a multiple horrorgasm at the end. *Texas Chainsaw Massacre* did this with the dinner party scene and Sally Hardesty's ultimate escape. *Silence of the Lambs* (Demme 1991) does likewise when Clarice drops in on Jame Gumb; and *[REC]* manages to keep us screaming like little girls right until the final frame. Most movies cannot do this, and if persistently terrifying scenes are not where your story is going, then use them sparingly.

They are not complex. Because they are in the moment, they must be written without cutting away, over-description or much character interplay. These kinds of scene require a lot of setting up, so use them wisely and save the actual terror for your lead character.

There is also the convention of the 'double wake-up', best exemplified by *American Werewolf in London* (Landis 1981), where David Kessler awakens from a nightmare running through the woods, only to find his hospital ward overrun by Nazi werewolves before he properly wakes up. This kind of double/false shock (common in *Final Destination*) can only really work if you are writing comedy horror, as an ironic knowingness is part of the experience, that or mainstream fun like *Tremors* (Underwood 1990) or *Piranha 3D* (Aja 2010), the latter ending with a great line and a big scream. This is known as the 'good laugh', in which you set up a scene of terror but deflate it only to then throw the terror right back at us. The audience laughs, as they are unable to differentiate between the serious shock and the false one. Overdone, it will undermine the integrity of the movie; used sparingly, it will add immeasurably to the experience.

The dream ending played as sustained terror worked extremely well in *Carrie* (De Palma 1976), where the 'happy ending', instead of being Carries' funeral, was revealed to be the unending nightmare of her insane tormentor.

Terror is always surprise, whether it is the result of building the tension of unease and rising dread or, indeed, it simply comes out of nowhere. If you use terror in the first act, it ought to be brief, whereas later on you may do all you can to sustain it. The scare delivered by terror is a purely physical one, which is ideal for the horror audience, but there is a deeper fear that lasts longer – and *that* is horror.

Horror

Horror is pictures of Auschwitz. It is the alien autopsy, the opening shots of rotting corpses displayed in a bizarre tableau in the *Texas Chainsaw Massacre* (Hooper 1974). Initially, when the world was made aware of the Holocaust, they could not comprehend the scale of such human carnage. Horror arises from the contemplation of the awful thing or act that has been committed, and in this way it is backward looking instead of being in the now. Because it is less of the now, is it not a prescient kind of fear; it is perhaps less effective immediately than the previous tropes. However, it tends to be the horror that we remember after we leave the movie theatre. It is what we take away with us, and this is hugely important.

Horror is the consideration not only of what the Cenobites (*Hellraiser*: Barker 1987) did to their chosen ones, but the sadomasochistic aspect that they, and by extension, we, *wanted* it in some way – as witnessed by Frank's enraptured expression as he is literally torn apart by chains. It is not only the possession of Regan in *The Exorcist* (Friedkin 1973), but also the increasing scale of the torment it visits upon her. It is looking back after the conclusion of such unforgettable horror movies as *Martyrs* (Laugier 2008), *Audition* (Miike 1999) or *The Wicker Man* (Hardy 1973), the endings of which all combine Terror and Horror.

We are at once thrilled and appalled, as in the autopsy scene or at the scene of a crime. Think of how we rubberneck when there is a motorway crash, and of how, if there is a long tailback, we expect a decent amount of carnage. We can show it in photographs – such as the grainy, blurry ones of the victims in

Se7en and in those glimpsed at the start of *Silence of the Lambs*. We want to see more, always more.

In *Lambs*, Lecter's escape is a sustained sequence of Grand Guignol cinema as shots are heard and the lift indicator wavers from floor to floor. Numerous cops surround the building, rushing to the floor where Lecter is being held in an unnaturally large, caged space. As they break in with guns primed they find, pinned butterfly-like and brightly backlit, a policeman splayed, gutted and presented like a Renaissance crucifix. The horror is captured in one stark image, and it combines with our contemplation of what has occurred. What incredible madness to have engineered such a tableau. And yet ... and yet it is still not over – for Lecter is nowhere to be seen. Sergeant Pembury lies prostrate, his face a bloodied mess, still alive but unable to talk. Pure horror.

You cannot have too much horror, and the longer we spend with the object of our revulsion the more used to it we become: do this and horror loses its power. It must be employed sparingly, sprinkled, like drips of blood.

Black, tainted blood.

Disgust

Remember the first time you stripped the skin from your knees riding a bike or falling from a tree? As soon as the pain was gone and the scab started to form, a slightly fetishistic quasi-medical fascination began to grow. What is this new part of my body? What is this dark encrusted thing? How long will it take to heal? What if I pick it and look underneath? Oh, that's disgusting!

Disgust is what the gore-hounds and splatter fiends of horror crave. Disgust sears itself onto your eyeballs. It is visceral and memorable. It is a highly personal reaction to the abject. It is a universal sense. Having said this, there are variants to some forms of revulsion, for example against unusual foodstuffs in non-Western countries. As they say, one man's cannibal is another man's clown.[31]

In terms of Horror movies, disgust was not employed as a trope until some time after the rubble of World War II had settled. This was partly due to censorship and partly because there had been enough of it in the real world. Before then, vampires were gallant, Frankenstein's Golem was a madman and werewolves were less than visceral. Killing was usually done by strangulation, as in *Rope* (Hitchcock 1948) or a bloodless shooting. *Psycho* (Hitchcock 1960)

---

[31] For more on the emotion of disgust it is worth looking at the work of P. Rozin, J. Haidt and C. R. McCauley, 'Disgust'. In M. Lewis, J. M. Haviland-Jones and L. F. Barrett (eds), *Handbook of Emotions*, 3rd edn (pp. 757–6). New York: Guilford Press, 2008. Rozin, Haidt and McCauley created the 'Disgust Scale' in 1994.

was the first movie to introduce multiple stabbing (no actual penetration) and even so was muted to black and white, with chocolate sauce for blood.

The 'Godfather of Gore' and creator of the splatter movie was Herschall Gordon Lewis with *Blood Feast* (Lewis 1963), a wholly gratuitous and badly acted exercise in flinging gore at the screen. Italians Mario Bava and Dario Argento later took on this mantle, adding violence, moral complexity and penetration by a weapon to the bloodletting.

In the US, disgust flourished in the work of Wes Craven in the extended torture scenes (introducing the chainsaw as weapon for the first time) in *The Last House on the Left* (Craven 1972) and *The Hills have Eyes* (Craven 1977), and let us not forget George Romero's *Night of the Living Dead* (Romero 1968), the precursor to the many people-munching zombie films of the 2000s.

It was the arrival of the Slashers in the 1970s that popularized this sea of gore with *Black Christmas* (Clark 1974), *Texas Chainsaw Massacre* (Hooper 1974) and *Halloween* (Carpenter 1978) leading us willingly into the charnel house.

Rick Baker, as special make-up effects designer on *American Werewolf in London* (Landis 1980), won an Oscar for the gore, and this, along with Rob Bottin's effects in *The Thing* (Carpenter 1982) pushed the boat out for prosthetic special effects, later opening the gates to *Hellraiser* (Barker 1987) and the subdivision of gory films into multiple sub-genres. The new terminology includes Torture Porn, Gorno, Splatstick and Splatterpunk. Since the turn of the century, CGI and the availability of cheaper prosthetics and mechanized automata have allowed splatter movies to thrive and to garner a wider audience. They no longer look 'hokey'.

This is also true of comedy horror. Splatstick is a variant on slapstick in which, instead of the traditional custard or foam pies there is dark humour to be found in messing around in blood and bodily organs – some superb examples of this are to be found in *Bad Taste* (Jackson 1987), *Slither* (Gunn 2006), *Child's Play* (Holland 1988) and *Zombie Strippers* (Lee 2008).

Where we see disgust at its darkest is in Asian Extreme Cinema, in movies such as *Ichi the Killer* (Miike 2001) and *Tokyo Gore Police* (Nishimura 2008), the latter being a ballet of blood. Scenes of disgust are obligatory in splatter and, uniquely, they combine terror with the giddy reaction of disbelieving macabre laughter. Asian Extreme Cinema peaked toward the end of the 2000s and the Europeans took over, most especially the French with *Martyrs* (Laugier 2008), *Frontier(s)* (Gens 2007) and *Inside* (Bustillo and Maury 2007), although it is worth mentioning Danish DOGME founder Lars von Trier's *Antichrist* (2009) and Dutchman Tom Six's *Human Centipede First Sequence* (2009).

Disgust gained bad press with Torture Porn, in particular Eli Roth's *Cabin Fever* (Roth 2002) and *Hostel* (Roth 2005) as well as the *Saw* franchise, for its focus on inventive, cruel and inhuman punishments. This is addressed elsewhere in the book, but it is clear that gore, shit and decay are now expressed on film in ways hitherto impossible, and so we have had in recent years *Tortured* (Lieberman 2010), *The Collector* (Dunstan 2009), *Dead Snow* (Wirkola 2009) and the UK's *Mum & Dad* (Sheil 2008) – all of which are jabbing hard at the disgust button.

There are so many facets of the physical emotion of disgust that are relevant to horror that it is worth examining them in greater detail. In no particular order, they are contamination, bodily functions, injury, torture and slice and dice, unclean or foreign foods, consumption (by or of), splicing by gene or anthropomorphic mating. Disgust, *in extremis*, will cause fainting or vomiting: it is an emotion associated with the inedible, unclean or infectious and, unlike fear anger or sadness, it lowers the heart rate.

- *Contamination.* The idea that an infected person will contaminate us is universal and goes back to leprosy in the middle ages and before. Any kind of physical revolt, open sores, goitres, pus, gigantism, malformation and odd growths are abhorrent to us. In horror this is played out well in *Shivers* (Cronenberg 1975), *Slither* (Gunn 2006), *Contagion* (Soderbergh 2011) and in every single zombie film.

- *Bodily functions.* Smells, excretion, copious bleeding, vomit, mucus coming from orifices. Other people's pus and phlegm. Also foul are the fluids that may emanate from a corpse, plus of course decay in all its forms.

- *Injury (which we are helpless to fix).* Human or animal – put him/it/her out of his misery. It is disgusting to us because we identify strongly with its predicament and, put in this position, we would want our suffering to end.

- *Torture.* The subjection of the human body to excruciating pain. One always empathizes with a character, unless one is a sociopath (doctor, nurse, serial killer). This involves the surgical opening of the body and the abject process of turning us inside out.

- *Slice 'n' dice.* The cutting, severing, wounding, traumatizing or otherwise exposing and damaging our insides. Crushing, pounding, mincing, slicing, stabbing. Also broken bones, limbs and crushed skulls.

- *Unclean or foreign foods.* We are revolted by stale or rotten food, even food that is alien to our palette (because of colour, smell or taste), either dug from the ground (truffles) or animal – especially insect, crustacean or reptile. Muslims believe that the pig is an unclean animal. Some vegetarians believe that meat is tainted and unclean. They are revolted and repulsed by the thought of eating it.

- *Consumption.* By insect, crustacean, reptile, alien or cannibal. We (perhaps hubristically) consider ourselves to be at the top of the food chain. We are revolted by the idea of being consumed, masticated, swallowed and dissolved into the being of another (see, e.g. *Society*: Yusna 1989).

- *Splicing/Anthropomorphism.* The unscientific melding together of humans and animals, making fresh twins or groups of people through surgery (e.g. *Splice*: Natali 2009; *Human Centipede First Sequence*: Six 2009; *Dead Ringers*: Cronenberg 1988; *The Island of Dr. Moreau*: Taylor 1977).

Then there is moral disquiet and disgust. Some people are squeamish about moral behaviour that does not equate to their own. Some are disgusted by homosexuality, race (touching or kissing a member of another race) or alternate sexualities, and yet none of these are contaminants to society nor contagious in any way. One might say, therefore, that disgust plays a role in moral and ethical judgments. It is also tied in with obsessive-compulsive disorders, phobias and extremes of body shape, such as obesity or anorexia, which have so increased of late in the West that they are almost pandemic.

Moral disgust is culturally obtained and ingrained. In *The Hydra's Tale: Imagining Disgust*[32], Robert Rawdon Wilson discusses moral disgust, looking at representations in literature, film and fine art. There are clear characteristic facial expressions (clenched nostrils, pursed lips), as Darwin and others have shown, that can be applied to any set of circumstances. There may even be 'disgust worlds' in which disgust motifs are so dominant that it may seem that entire represented world is in itself disgusting. Wilson argues that contempt is acted out on the basis of the visceral emotion, but is not identical with disgust. It is a 'compound affect' that entails intellectual preparation or formatting, and theatrical techniques. There are many such 'intellectual' compound affects, such as nostalgia and outrage, but disgust is a fundamental and unmistakable example.

Moral disgust is different from visceral disgust, in that it is more conscious and more layered in performance. There are few horror movies that manage to invoke the two, but I would cite *Night of the Living Dead* (Romero 1968) as a brilliant example of this.

Those films that do invoke a sense of moral outrage are few and far between but there has been a subgenre of UK Home Invasion or Hoodie horrors that have managed to do this in recent years, namely James Watkins's *Eden Lake*

---

[32] Robert Rawdon Wilson, *The Hydra's Tale: Imagining Disgust*. Edmonton: University of Alberta Press, 2002.

(Watkins 2008), Paul Andrew Williams's *Cherry Tree Lane* (Williams 2010) and Johannes Roberts's *F* (2010). To the morally thought-provoking we must add Michael Haneke's *Funny Games* (both the 1997 and 2007 versions) and Lucky McKee's *The Woman* (McKee 2011).

There is no denying that disgust works if used well, and there will always be a section of the audience for whom more gore is simply more; but, as with every dish, there is always a point when you have to call a halt. David Cronenberg's early body horror pictures featured disgust, a particular favourite moment being in *The Fly* (Cronenberg 1985) where actor Jeff Goldblum, following his human–fly splicing transformation, begins to mutate into an aphid. Isolated, Seth Brundle has grown so used to vomiting stomach acids onto his sickly sweet doughnuts before consuming them that this appears normal to him. We see this through his shocked girlfriend's reaction. His only reaction is the deadpan observation, 'Oh, that's disgusting.'

There is little disgust in ghostly hauntings, and unease is swiftly dispensed with in any gore-fest of Grand Guignol, but the wise author will use each of the five tropes to build the fear, block by block, leaving his audience wrung out at the end, yet oddly craving more – to watch it again or to tell their friends to see it.

Enjoy responsibly.

Chapter 5
Creating the Nemesis

External monsters become internal fears

At the heart of every horror movie is the monster, whether a literal representation of something monstrous outside of us in the form of a beast, alien, demon, ghost or vampire, or a depiction of the madness that lives within, as in the psychopathic behaviour demonstrated by the serial killer. The original externalized monsters, Nosferatu, the Golem, Dracula, demons or Frankenstein's creation, are easy to categorize, as is the bestial monster in modern horror, the Alien – a visual representation of H. P. Lovecraft's Cthulhu being a perfect example of this.[33] Screenwriter Dan O'Bannon worked up his screenplay for *Alien* over the years (originally entitled *Star Beast*) and gave detailed notes to designer H. R. Giger. It was to have three forms, at first the egg (larval), then the thing that clamps itself to and invades the body (pupal), finally the full-grown adult: metallic yet fleshy, with numerous rows of teeth within teeth, multi-limbed, a vicious predator and killing machine.

In the film, the first sighting of the eggs and then the mothership give glimpses and hints as to the sheer scale of the thing, yet it is what it leaves behind that triggers our awful sense of dread. Following this, the monster begins to encroach on the territory of the shipmates. When Kane (John Hurt) is brought on board with the face-hugger, we find it has parasitically attached/assimilated itself to him, and yet the real danger to the crew is still unrealized. This was subsequently done just as effectively in John Carpenter's remake of *The Thing* (Carpenter 1982) (both he and O'Bannon were fans of the original) where again the intruder was unknowingly brought into camp – the gift on the doorstep, the wooden horse.

It is important at these early stages that the monster be glimpsed only in part. This is what Carpenter calls the Monster problem. You show it all and we can gauge its size. We can begin to conceive of it, to put it into a frame of reference. It is why Michael Myers was created as a vacuum, a nothing, a no-man, without characteristics. Examples of hiding the monster well are legion and include *Feast* (Gulagar 2005 and 2008; Adam 2009), *Cloverfield* (Reeves 2008) and *The Mist* (Darabont 2007).

Early monsters were metaphors for migration, immigration and the power of the masses. Europe underwent a terrible time of change during the twentieth century and, from the pogroms onwards, a vast displaced population was on the move, fleeing Russia and Central Europe. Lovecraft was something of a xenophobe, and his views of the Russian émigrés flooding into Providence, Rhode Island, informed many of his early stories. To the receiving nation they would have been seen to a degree as 'monstrous': all those different cultures and languages, unable to communicate, a mass of unwashed humanity needing to be fed and sheltered. The threat is not merely that they will settle in the ghetto but that they will breed and take us over – like The Blob or the Borg.

---

[33] H. P. Lovecraft wrote 'The Call of Cthulhu' in 1926. A tale of a giant sea monster which slept at the bottom of the ocean until woken by foolish men, it was published in *Weird Tales* in 1928. To describe it, he used many evocative yet non-specific adjectives, so that it could be visualized in myriad ways. Stuart Gordon filmed it as *Dagon* in 2001.

It is interesting to note that, since 9/11, the first real attempt to 'invade' the US, there has been a huge spate of zombie invasion, post-apocalyptic and plague/contagion horror movies; in short, a real expression of a symbolic fear.

Horror is an emotion one feels when faced with something unfamiliar. It is different to being frightened by a spider or a sudden noise; it is something outside of our usual experience. Philosopher of horror Noël Carrol[34] used a term, *category jamming*, to suggest a mismatch. By late childhood our cognitive classification system has locked down, solidifying enough of our day-to-day experiences to make sense of the world. When something comes along that has dissonance, the mismatch makes us uncomfortable and creates fear. We feel disgust when faced by the unknown – especially by impurity, those bodily fluids that we expel that are part of us and yet not part of us: the abject. Many monsters have slime oozing from them, nasty dripping fangs, tentacles, mucus, blood and pus. Lovecraft suggested that 'all human beings have an instinctual awareness of a paltry state of human understanding, especially when compared with the almost limitless domain of the strange and unfamiliar, a kind of cosmic fear.'

The same year that Lovecraft published 'Supernatural Horror in Literature',[35] German philosopher Martin Heidegger wrote of a radical dread he called *angst*, separating it from fear because fear is a definable threat.

> When the horror genre pushes past the simple fear-based narrative of a monster chasing a victim and instead constructs an eerie world of foreboding, it seems to cross over into this more metaphysical pessimism of cosmic absurdity.[36]

Emmanuel Kant spoke of a cosmic fear (an inability to grasp the extent of the cosmos), which he called the sublime, hence the subliminal and from it liminal, as discussed elsewhere in this book. He spoke of experiences that were both pleasurable and painful. If we try to imagine the universe (or indeed a giant monster) in its entirety, we cannot. We can have some idea of it, but imagination fails us. This displeasure is a sheer annoyance at our inadequacy, but it is also pleasing because 'in presenting the sublime in nature the mind feels agitated, while in aesthetic judgment about the beautiful in nature it is in restful contemplation.' The philosopher's view was a pessimistic one, furthered by Schopenhauer and Nietzsche, who saw our drives as being solely towards power, towards the will over nature. They were concerned with man at odds with a cruel, ambivalent universe. It was pure Darwin – 'nature, red in tooth and claw'.

---

[34] In Asma 2009 (p. 184).
[35] In 1927, in a one-off magazine, *The Recluse*.
[36] In Asma 2009 (p. 186).

Come the twentieth century, there was something of a sea change. Freud moved on from this cosmic metaphysical form to suggest that our fears are born of the human experience, and it has been his views that have predominated ever since, as Asma puts it: 'The unconscious becomes the 20th century home of the monsters. Having worn out their welcome in religion, natural history and travellers tales, the monsters settled into their new abode of human psychology.'[37]

In 1919 Freud wrote an essay called '*Das Unheimliche*' [The Uncanny], in which he describes elements of horror: severed limbs, disembodied spirits, the fear of being buried alive, evil twins and doppelgangers. He argues that the evil twin is another version of yourself that wishes to extend its life. This fantasy of eternal life – because life will soon bring us up short – will be proven to be untrue. In order to mature we must negate this urge to live forever and it must therefore be repressed. In this repression the desire is turned from a positive to negative, but it is still there. These feelings of the uncanny can therefore be expressed as zombies, the undead, or those super-monsters that cannot be killed. We have this same uncanny feeling when it comes to robotics or computer generated simulacra of man (virtual humans). Japanese robot scientist Masahiro Mori noticed a common feeling he called 'Uncanny Valley' concerning the feelings we have towards virtual protagonists.[38]

This is true of animated cartoons as well. The more stylized they are, the more comfortable we feel with the portrayal, but if a drawing is almost human, an avatar, it is deeply unsettling. This chasm of mysterious emotion has been explored well in the early works of David Lynch – especially in *Eraserhead* (Lynch 1977) and *The Elephant Man* (Lynch 1980). The former, being too bizarre to be considered a genre movie, certainly contains plenty of the *unheimliche*. Influenced by Dalí and Buñuel, the *Eraserhead* universe offers us a man weaning a baby goat, a severed head whittled into pencils, and a lady living behind a radiator who steps on giant gloopy sperms. Kubrick screened it for the cast of *The Shining* (Kubrick 1980) to put them in the mood.

Commonly in the early movies, the monster would be vanquished, a heroic triumph, which has come to be short-lived. The monster outside or inside of us cannot die. There is still a legion of unstoppable monsters over the brow of the hill ... As horror grew up, and as modern psychology and the realism of the 1970s horror brats took shape, we began to accept that there is no moral fabric to the universe. There is no stopping them.

---

[37] In Asma 2009 (p. 188).
[38] Masahiro Mori, 'Bukimi no tani' [The uncanny valley]. Trans K. F. MacDorman and T. Minato. *Energy*, 7(4). 1970; 33–5.

Serial killers real and fictional

Freudian readings of character psychoanalysis developed in the 1960s. The term 'psycho' refers to either the mind or the soul, but it was Alfred Hitchcock's 1960 masterpiece that changed its meaning for us to an argot for the psychotic or psychopathic. Inextricably linked to this was the publicity surrounding the deeds of serial killers Ed Gein and later John Wayne Gacy and Charles Manson. Gein was responsible for major horror icons Leatherface, Norman Bates, John Doe and Hannibal Lecter, but there have always been serial killers. The public fascination with and hysteria about them began with Jack the Ripper and a letter to the *London Illustrated News* in 1888, from someone claiming to be the murderer (possibly a journalist), which led to extensive newspaper coverage. 'Jack' was also known as the 'Whitechapel Murderer' or 'Leather Apron'. He is not the first to be publicized. Since then there has been much publicity surrounding the Leopold and Loeb case, involving the kidnap and murder of a child without remorse; and in Britain, there were Christie, Haig and Nielson, Hindley and Brady, Harold Shipman, the Wests, and, in 1992, Venables and Thompson, two children who killed another child – the final taboo.

Asma concludes his excellent chapter on inner monsters thus:

> Monsters make up a significant part of the frightening underbelly of modernity, whether they are only hinted at in the uncanny experience or are chasing us with chainsaws. Monsters of contemporary horror are not like their medieval counterparts who were more like God's henchmen. That older paradigm held out the inevitability of monstrous defeat by divine justice, but the contemporary monster is often a reminder of theological abandonment and the accompanying angst.[39]

According to Dr Kent A. Kiehl, of the Olin Neuropsychiatry Research Center in Connecticut, psychopaths do not fail cognitively so much as emotionally.

> Psychopaths do know right from wrong, they can tell you right from wrong. They just don't care.[40]

---

[39] Asma 2009.
[40] In Matt Crenson, *Dark Minds*, Associated Press, 11 September 2005.

Human monsters

Norman Bates (*Psycho*: Hitchcock 1960)

Norman Bates has his origins in a farmer, Ed Gein, of Plainsfield, Wisconsin, whose inhuman crimes stemmed from a controlling mother who abused him. After her death he tried to recreate his relationship with her, going so far as to attempt to disinter her body, and when this failed he dug up other women and made suits of their skins before starting on live ones. Robert Bloch's novelization of these crimes[41] was sold to Hitchcock for $5,000.

  Psycho popularized psychological horror in movies. The final scene in which detective and psychologist discuss the boundaries of the new talking science can be seen as a regression to exposition-led drama where the scientist/detective explains away the motive of the killer: an easy way out and a sop to those who have been utterly horrified by this new terror. Despite the explanation, can we ever know what goes on in poor Norman's deluded mind? It is an effective advertisement for the new pseudo-science of psychiatry. As the camera drifts down the corridor into Norman's cell, we get a final chill as we hear 'mother's' internal monologue ('Why she wouldn't even harm a fly') contrasted with Norman's (no-man) insane leer, before seeing his mother's skull superimposed on his face. This is 'doubling' – a visual representation of the duality of man. Another excellent example appears earlier in the movie when Norman brings Marion Crane her supper. At the very moment his reflection appears in the motel window, he says the line 'Mother isn't quite herself today'. This is not an accident (cinematographers have to be very careful around reflections) and the fact that Gus Van Sant's shot-for-shot 1998 colour remake of *Psycho* omits this, speaks volumes.

  The use of the word 'psycho' itself, too, is open-ended, as for most of the movie we do not know to whom it refers. At the start, the camera's attitude towards our protagonist is quite ambivalent. Here is a young woman, Marion Crane, making love at 2.43 p.m. in an anonymous hotel room. This is shocking to an audience used to Doris Day and married couples in separate beds.[42] Furthermore she is an opportunist who later takes the money on a whim and then is wracked with guilt for doing so. The 'voices' she hears when driving out of Phoenix may be incipient schizophrenia. Is *she* the psycho? Unusually for the time, she is a strong, independent woman, and for this she is punished. There are no strong father figures in the story, merely ineffective men: her nervous boss

---

[41] Robert Bloch, *Psycho*. New York: Simon & Schuster, 1959.
[42] Under the Hays Code a man and a woman were not allowed to appear in bed together.

Lowery, the drunken spendthrift Cassidy, the spooky patrolman, the yapping salesman, and finally our Mommy's boy, Norman. Nowadays, we are alert to the idea of the insane protagonist, and we are looking for it, but back then the audience was more trusting. Marlon Brando and James Dean may have been rebels but they were still essentially decent. Norman isn't.

But we don't get to Norman yet. If the psycho is not a woman, then might it be the leering Cassidy, who pays her far too much attention? The older man who senses the sin on her? Or the patrolman who re-appears time and time again, stalking her, his eyes invisible under his obsidian Aviator shades? When the rain finally subsides and Marion slinks into the Bates Motel we feel nothing but relief. It is only when Mother is introduced (and then only as a disembodied voice and a shadow at the window) do we have a possibility for a real antagonist.

Norman Bates is responsible for some horror tropes that have echoed down the decades: the basing of crime on real events, the use of psychological and internal motivations that are complex aspects of the human mind, the idea that the boy-next-door could be a murderer, and that of the rural backwoods horror. The Bates Motel stays, but the highway moves away. The modern world disassociates itself from its roots, abandoning those left behind to their stuffed toys, to their birds and their barbaric murderous ways.

As Norman says, 'We all go a little mad sometimes.'

Leatherface (*Texas Chain Saw Massacre*: Hooper 1974)

Leatherface introduces us to the mask of human skin, which was again based on Gein's crimes. In the original *Texas Chain Saw Massacre* (Hooper 1974) he had three masks, the 'killing' mask, the 'old lady' mask and the 'pretty woman' mask. According to Tobe Hooper and writer Kim Henkel, the mask he wore determined who he would be on that day. Gunnar Hansen, who played Leatherface, added: 'There is no personality under the mask. That was the idea in talking with Tobe and Kim. When they created the character, they said he has to put on masks to express himself because he can't do it. The way we tried to create him, there is nothing under the mask, which is what makes him so frightening.'

In Tobe Hooper's 1974 version Leatherface is scared of strangers and of having his family invaded. In Marcus Nispels' 2003 reboot (*Texas Chainsaw Massacre*: Nispel 2003) he is given more backstory (should we choose to accept it). He has a name, Thomas Brown Hewitt. His mother died giving birth to him at the Blair Meat Company. He is found in a dumpster and raised by Luda May Hewitt. The Hewitt family lose their jobs when the plant closes and take to kidnapping and butchering humans; one family member says he got the idea for eating human flesh when he was a POW in the Korean War. Leatherface has a facial disfigurement and a skin disease, and so wears a leather mask to cover it up, later making masks of human skin by slicing off the faces of his victims. Although Leatherface's family still manipulate him, they show themselves as being more caring and less abusive than in the original film. Before killing the sheriff, his brother/uncle Charlie even defends him by saying, 'He's not retarded – he's misunderstood'.

Vim vimmm …

Michael Myers (*Halloween*: Carpenter 1978)

Independent producer Irwin Yablans and financier Moustapha Akkad saw John Carpenter's *Assault on Precinct 13* and asked him to write a movie about a psychotic killer who stalked babysitters. Carpenter and then-girlfriend Debra Hill drafted a story called 'The Babysitter Murders' and Yablans suggested setting it at Halloween. Debra Hill said: 'The idea was that you couldn't kill evil, and that was how we came about the story. We went back to the old idea of Samhain, that Halloween was the night when all the souls are let out to wreak havoc on the living, and then came up with the story about the most evil kid who ever lived. And when John came up with this fable of a town with a dark secret of someone who once lived there, and now that evil has come back, that's what made Halloween work.'[43]

Hill wrote most of the female parts while Carpenter wrote Loomis's dialogue. There are many nods to *Psycho* – actor John Gavin's character was named Sam Loomis, and Jamie Lee Curtis is Janet Leigh's daughter. Carpenter's use of handheld camera establishing the killer's point of view (although too high for the POV of a small boy) echoes the opening of *Psycho* as voyeuristically we watch Loomis and Crane in their hotel room. Halloween is also light on gore but peppered with false shocks, another feature of Hitchcock's work. With the killer, however, there is one main difference. Whereas Norman is ungainly but with a little charm, a kind of Ichabod Crane, Michael Myers has no personality at all. Nick Castle, Carpenter's friend who played the grown-up Michael, was given no direction and merely told to hit his marks to add the air of anonymity. The only thing he was permitted to add was a slight tilt of the head after one slaying.

At the age of six, Michael sees his older sister Judith with a boyfriend and kills her with a kitchen knife. He is put away in Smith's Grove Sanatorium, where he becomes catatonic. Fifteen years later, on the eve of a court hearing (coincidentally the anniversary of the slaughter), he escapes and returns to Haddonfield

---

[43] Interview in *Fangoria*, 19 April 2006.

where he removes Judith's gravestone and places it on the bed in their old home. Having killed a truck driver, he now wears the driver's blue overalls and has obtained a mask from what must presumably be a Star Trek fan store (it was William Shatner's face, painted white). He then proceeds to slaughter teens until he is shot six times at point blank range by Loomis, after which he gets up and disappears. There is no explanation here, no rationalization. Loomis merely points out emotionlessly that 'He was the Boogeyman'.

A lot of fuss was made about *Halloween*'s apparent sexism and degradation of the women until Clover's Final Girl[44] theory made some redress. Others saw it as a morality play, but Carpenter has denied this, saying that the critics 'completely missed the point there. The one girl who is the most sexually uptight just keeps stabbing this guy with a long knife. She's the most sexually frustrated. She's the one that's killed him. Not because she's a virgin but because all that sexually repressed energy starts coming out. She uses all those phallic symbols on the guy.'[45] The mask is blank, furthering the earlier argument that the psychopath is utterly devoid of emotion, a blank canvas of a man – with no remorse, a force of nature.

Jason Voorhees (*Friday the 13th*: Cunningham 1980)

Jason Voorhees was inspired directly by Michael Myers. Writer Victor Miller says: 'The success of the film *Halloween* gave me the impetus to write a screenplay in the same style, appealing to the same audience. I was in no way an aficionado of the horror genre. I had loved *Psycho*, but I simply studied the structure of *Halloween* in a single viewing and learned most of what I used in the structure of my screenplay. Carpenter and (Debra) Hill had made it very clear.'[46] The concept began with Miller's title, *A long night at Camp Blood*, but producer/director Sean S. Cunningham preferred *Friday the 13th*, and rushed to get an advertisement out so as to claim the rights. It was a huge hit and, unusually, we have a mother killing to avenge the death of her son. Miller says: 'Mrs Voorhees was crucial to the success of my film. To quote a producer in Hollywood at the time, "This kid took Mom and apple pie and turned them upside down." A mother avenging the death of her challenged son is a meaningful mythic narrative even if her methods are wretchedly homicidal. I wish my own mother had been as strongly motivated.'[47]

---

[44] Clover 1992.
[45] In Jones 2005.
[46] Taken from an interview with Victor Miller by the authors, March 2012.
[47] Ibid.

In the real world to date there has been no comparable female serial killer. There was Aileen Wuornos, who slew nine men in Florida in 1989–90, as portrayed by Charlize Theron in *Monster* (Jenkins 2003); and in the UK Myra Hindley and Rosemary West – but they were, as it were, working for their men and lacked clear motivation. In the movies, the closest we have is *Carrie* (De Palma 1976) but her telekinetic killing spree was a revenge for being bullied (and for having a psychotic mother). It is hard to create a female serial killer – though there have been transvestite ones – *Dressed to Kill* (De Palma 1985) – and those of 'confused' sexuality such as Jame Gumb/Buffalo Bill in *Silence of the Lambs* ('What skirt should I wear this woman's skin with?). It is a stretch. The state of 'woman' is too associated with birth and nurturing, and the giving of life rather than taking it away. Women using phallic objects to destroy their oppressors is such a deeply imbedded trope of the genre that it's hard to turn that around. Ripley in *Alien* is faced with a monstrous feminine, and that bitch fight did not end well for anyone.

For the sequel to *Friday the 13th,* Paramount's initial idea was for a series of discontinuous movies released at the same time each year (as later happened with 'Saw'). However, Phil Scuderi, co-owner of Esquire Theaters, along with the producers of the original film, insisted that the sequel should have Jason Voorhees in it even though his surprise appearance at the end was only meant to be a joke. Part Three introduced the iconographic hockey mask, and Jason ploughed on through differing locations and sequels to a total of 12 movies, including a remake of the original and a monster mash-up, *Freddie Vs. Jason*. It has spawned a TV series, novels, graphic novelizations, and a lot of merchandize.

Jason Voorhees has none of the complexity of Norman Bates and no psychological resonance. He too is an empty man in a mask, bereft of the humanity of Lon Chaney's Phantom (*Phantom of the Opera*: Julian, Chaney, Sedgwick and Laemmle 1925) or Leatherface's desire to be part of the family. S. T. Karnick, editor of *American Culture* noted that *Friday the 13th* did not try to emulate the cleverness of *Halloween* but 'codified the formula of *Halloween* and boiled it down to its essentials', so that it might be copied by other film-makers. *Friday the 13th* changed the Slasher genre by not providing back-stories for characters, so when an audience witnesses a character's death they are quite unaffected. It goes on to focus on the history and motivation of a killer who exacts revenge not on those responsible for his own predicament, but on innocent people. This is a template which has been replicated in *Nightmare on Elm Street* (Craven 1984), *Child's Play* (Holland 1988), *Scream* (Craven 1996), *I Know What You Did Last Summer* (Gillespie 1997), *Saw* (Wan 2004) and the 'Halloween' franchise.

This act of collusion is pertinent. Film critic Roger Ebert wrote that during *Friday the 13th Part 2*, he noticed the audience had no sympathy for the victims and cheered during death scenes. S. T. Karnick explains that Ebert's remarks show how the film series forces 'audiences to experience the very thing that motivates the murders: a lack of compassion'. He concludes by saying that these films were not puritanical, but proved that audiences 'could be just as indifferent and callous as the characters in the films.'[48]

In this way we are removed from and absolved of responsibility, rather in the way that true-life serial killers dehumanize their victims and often convince themselves that their victims are culpable in creating their own fate. Perhaps the Freddie and Jason movies were made cartoonish and abstracted in order to deal with the fact that the 1980s was a time of social change and upheaval. Eli Roth, director of *Hostel* (2005), believed that the Clinton era produced fewer violent movies, but, as for the 2000s, he cites the example of a soldier in Iraq who wrote to him saying that *Hostel* was extremely popular in the military. 'I asked – Why on earth would you watch *Hostel* after what you see in a day? He wrote back and said that when he was out in the day with his friends, they saw somebody's face get blown off and then they watched the movie that night they were all screaming. But when you are on the battlefield, you have to be a machine. You can't react emotionally … it all gets stored up, and its got to come out. When they watch *Hostel* it's basically saying for the next 90 minutes not only are you allowed to be scared, you are encouraged to be scared because its okay to be terrified.'[49]

Freddie Krueger (*A Nightmare on Elm Street*: Craven 1984)

Set in the fictional town of Springwood, Ohio,[50] the concept of 'nightmare' is that, if the teenagers fall asleep they will be killed in their dreams. The film was based on a number of newspaper articles for the *LA Times* about Khmer refugees who escaped from Cambodia but were having such awful nightmares they refused to sleep. Some actually died of this, and it was subsequently named Asian Death Syndrome.

Krueger is drawn heavily from director Wes Craven's childhood. One night he saw an elderly man walk past his bedroom and stop and stare at him. The young Craven never forgot this strange occurrence. Krueger was intended to be a child molester, but Craven changed it to a child *murderer* to avoid a highly publicized spate of child molestations happening in California at that time. He

---

[48] S. T. Karnick, 'Babes in the Wood, A Franchise of Fear'. National Review Online.
[49] Eli Roth. Interview: Capone and Eli Roth discuss Horror Movies. Ain't It Cool News, 3 June 2007.
[50] Elm Street was also the location of John F. Kennedy's assassination.

named Freddie in a delicious act of revenge that only a writer could make, after his school bully, Fred Krueger (in *The Last House on the Left*, the villain's name was shortened to Krug). The iconic sweater was based on DC Comics' Plastic Man, choosing red and green as those colours 'flash' with the most irritating dissonance. It was rejected by every studio until independent New Line bought it. They made such a success of it that the studio is to this day referred to as 'The house that Freddy built'.

Hannibal Lecter (*Silence of the Lambs*: Demme 1991)

Thomas Harris's story *The Silence of the Lambs* is brilliantly simple in its conceit. It is the old saw – 'It takes a thief to catch a thief' – with the added moral that if you make a deal with the devil you will get burned. It was originally made by Michael Mann as *Manhunter* (Mann 1986), starring Brian Cox as Lecter, a movie some consider to be the better of the two. However, it is the Jodie Foster/ Anthony Hopkins remake we remember best. Indeed, *Lambs* is to date the only real thriller/horror crossover to sweep the board at the Oscars.

It is startlingly original, in that it introduces us to the monster within 15 minutes of the opening, leading us to wonder 'If Lecter is that bad, what's Bill like?' The lead-in is superbly modulated. Clarice Starling is shown from the opening credits as a loner, a woman in a man's world, slight, bird-like ('fly, fly away little Starling'), desperately seeking a father-figure to replace her lost parent, an orphan with whom we can easily sympathize. She is surrounded by hulking men (in the elevator at Quantico, at the autopsy in West Virginia) and must symbolically grow a set of balls. As she is summoned to Jack Crawford's office we already start to pick up information from the notice and the blackboards: 'Bill skins fifth'.

Crawford, a father- or mentor-figure, reads out her impressive resumé, which she modestly demeans, her shyness inappropriate for such a job and her status as 'trainee' wholly insulting to the king of the monsters she is to face. Starling is told outright *not* to tell Lecter anything personal, otherwise he will get inside her head. The cannibal is assigned superhuman powers. He can read her mind and smell her fear, perfume and skin cream through thick glass, a sense more usually attributed to the blind. He has the power to will others to perform terrible acts (as does Dracula with Renfield), and later convinces Miggs to swallow his tongue merely by 'whispering' to him. Even his name, Lecter, a pun on Lectern or Lecture, is a sign of impending conundrums, anagrams, puzzles and clues. This is the thriller side to the plot, the game of discovery. Later, the tension will increase sharply as the ticking clock is introduced in order to discover the whereabouts of the Senator's daughter. Lecter shows no concern: his psychopathology does not permit empathy, but he does give out clues when they are most needed in order to serve his own needs of escaping his prison.

And what a gaol it is. Its gatekeeper Dr Chiltern is introduced as slimy and lecherous ('it can be quite a fun town'), another possible killer in the way that the cop is portrayed in *Psycho*. He is lustful and discourteous, in contrast to Hannibal Lecter who is portrayed as a southern gentleman with courtesy and manners (Hopkins based him partly on Katherine Hepburn).[51] There is an obsession with rules and order. Crawford and Chiltern have them, and so does Lecter. Everything is a test for Starling, the honor student. The trust exercises and mentoring by Crawford and Lecter are all part of the *quid pro quo*.

Chiltern, a man with no real power, delights in his petty tortures. He leads Clarice down to hell and, as they sink lower, the lighting turning fiery red; suddenly there are industrial noises and guttural scrapings. Chiltern takes time to show Starling a photograph of what Hannibal the Cannibal did to a nurse's face. Clarice walks past the insane and the perverts and comes face to face with the king of the psychopaths – who is the very opposite of all she has been told. Controlled, and polite to a fault, he is the ideal father-figure to unravel those messy teenage feelings that Starling has tried so hard to hide. The job? To engage him in a hunt for a killer whose psychopathology is 'one thousand times worse'. In order to proceed, she cannot move forwards; instead she has to go back home, both physically to the rural locations and mentally to undergo Lecter's psychoanalysis: back to where she must address the central question – What is the Silence of the Lambs?

In fact Lecter is preposterous. A real psychopath would not be nearly so charming. He would have no empathy with people and certainly not with a child-like detective. Why take a shine to her?

Clever writing makes us believe the lie. The delineation seems real. No one would do a deal with someone such as he. And why would he want to tell Clarice anything about Benjamin Raspail? It is so well set up that, when we are salaciously fed the information about what he has done, it overwhelmingly colours our perception of him.

Author Thomas Harris has spoken little about Lecter's genesis, claiming it was a collage of his court reporting in the 1960s. He did, however, attend the court hearing of Petro Pacciani, said to be the 'Monster of Florence', perpetrator of 16 murders in Italy. Hannibal Lecter remains one of the most potent serial killers of our times, a worthy reincarnation of Dracula in all his urbanity and carnal needs.

Jigsaw (*Saw*: Wan 2004)

James Wan met Leigh Whannell when they were fresh out of high school and had just started studying media arts at university. 'We knew we wanted to make

---

[51] Interview: 'Inside the Actors Studio', Season 4, Episode 7, 4 October 1998.

a super low budget movie that we could finance with our hard earned money, so the idea had to be small and doable. I called Leigh up one day and said:

'"Listen, I don't quite know what I have here but see if you like it. The whole movie takes place in a bathroom. There are two people chained to the opposite sides of the room, and lying in between them is a dead body. In the corpse's hands are a gun and a tape recorder. Our guys realize that they're put in this predicament to kill each other and all the while someone is watching them. You think this voyeur is the villain of the piece, but at the end … the dead body gets up off the floor and walks out!" After I finished pitching that, I was expecting Leigh to blow it off, but he really loved the concept. So we went off for an entire year to write the first draft, and brought in all the serial killer element of Jigsaw and the traps.'[52]

Note here that the concept is not born out of character, but by an unusual situation. The character of Jigsaw did not come until months later when Whannell was working at a job he was unhappy with and began having migraines. Convinced it was a brain tumour he went to have an MRI, and while sitting in the waiting room he thought: 'What if you were given the news that you had a tumor and you were going to die soon? How would you react to that?' He imagined the character Jigsaw having been given one or two years to live, and combined that with the idea of Jigsaw putting others in a literal version of the situation, but only giving them a few minutes to choose their fate.[53]

The first *Saw* movie was a huge hit in 2004, but by the time of Sequels II and III (directed by Bousman 2005, 2006) the emphasis was leaning towards the kills. For this, the franchise was tagged alongside *Hostel*, *Haute tension*, *Wolf Creek* and *The Devil's Rejects* as being emblematic of the new torture porn or 'gorno'. That *Hostel* (Roth 2005) is a critique of American foreign policy and was inspired by real events in Thailand escaped the critics, but one ought to never let the truth get in the way of a good story. By the third episode in the 'Saw' series a more elaborate backstory had been fleshed out for John Kramer (Jigsaw) whose apprentice (Amanda) kidnapped a doctor in order to try to keep him alive as another victim went about his testing. What marks out Kramer/Jigsaw from the accusations of torture porn is that he is an avenging angel attempting to place a new moral compass on Western society. His point, made to his victims, is quite clear. You are morally bankrupt, therefore you are dead already. If you can prove

---

[52] Email Interview with Axelle Carolyn, April 2008. In Carolyn 2009.
[53] From an interview between Scott Tobias and Leigh Whannell. AVClub, 29 October 2010.

that you are worthy of life (via extreme physical sacrifice) you may then win the prize of your freedom. Admittedly the dice are loaded in Jigsaw's favour, and as the series progresses we are left in little doubt as to the outcome of each fresh victim, but at the outset it had a clear parallel to the dilemma faced by Sergeant David Mills and the other six victims in *Se7en* (Fincher 1995).

This kind of avenging serial killer is not a new idea, as psychopaths who believed they were doing the world a service by removing those unworthy of life include Stalin and Hitler. Intriguingly, whilst we would never side with genocidal maniacs, we do with Jigsaw, as with other fictional killers – because in the safe confines of a movie theatre, we can give vent to our unrestrained and quite amoral *Id*.

Kramer earns our sympathy too as he is near to death, a state of grace which has traditionally been associated with prophetic gifts of clarity (as in *Martyrs*: Laugier 2008). It also encourages the deathbed confession, which is often considered to be an ultimate 'truth' because of its final incontrovertibility. In addition, he asserts a moral authority that was considered lacking in the American political arena at that time (the Bush Era of buying a Presidency). Third, the victims he selected are those we deem unacceptable, such as bankers, liars, addicts, adulterers, Republicans, etc.

Kramer/Jigsaw, as with all serial killers, has a doppelganger: the two faces, the mask. There is the old dying man in reality, but it is contrasted with the child's toy, the painted doll, a ventriloquist's dummy: a clear example of the dualism within man as he fights *Id* over *Ego* and wrestles his inner demons. Dolls have often been used in horror as totemic images. A doll is a fetish object, simultaneously an inanimate toy and a simulacrum. It has that *unheimliche* feel of the robot in 'Uncanny Valley'. It is of life but not life. The more lifelike a doll is (especially those that talk or weep or wet themselves or grow hair), the more uneasy we feel – no wonder they have been so useful in horror movies; and how many more times are we going to see a deadly doll, whilst hearing mad versions of 'Momma's gonna buy you a mockingbird'?

Poltergeist (Hooper 1982) made great use of the evil doll, as did *Chucky* (aka *Child's Play*: Holland 1988) and its sequels, but also there is the ventriloquist's dummy. *Dead of Night* (Cavalcanti, Crichton, Dearden and Hamer 1945) introduced the killer doll, which did for Michael Redgrave as Maxwell Frere (meaning brother) and was later employed in *Magic* (Attenborough 1978) with Anthony Hopkins, *Devil Doll* (Shonteff 1964) and the wonderful portmanteau *Asylum* (Baker 1972). More recently, in *The Hills Run Red* (Parker 2009) the killer wears a mask of a cracked doll's face – make what you will of the psychology there.

The point with *Saw* (Wan 2004) is that the killer was bolted on to an idea. Methodology takes precedence over motivation. The 'Saws' are enjoyable and stylish movies in the main, but, as with most franchises, they became diluted once the killer's motives are revealed. Where *Saw* does win out is in the psychopathologies of his followers. His wife Jill is drawn inexorably in. Police Lieutenant Mark Hoffman has close ties with Kramer. Amanda Young, his first surviving victim, idolizes him as her 'saviour' and becomes his protégé. It is interesting to ask 'What might make you follow someone who kills?'

Where next?

With the greatest of respect to Penny-wise the dancing clown (*IT*, TV mini-series, Wallace 1990), *Candyman* (Rose 1992) and Pinhead (*Hellraiser*: Barker 1985) who are more fantastical creatures, the monster has of late been confined inside us. We have an enduringly narcissistic love of analysis, and though we can define psychosis better today (and treat it with medication) we still are no closer to curing or fully understanding it.

When it comes to good old-fashioned monsters there has been a trend, post Ghostface in *Scream* (Craven 1996), towards the post-modern ironic take, for example in *Hatchet* (Green 2006), with the creation of Victor Crowley. The movie poster tagline reads 'Old school American horror. It's not a remake, it's not a sequel and it's not based on a Japanese one.' About halfway into the movie, trapped and faced with the swamp-living monster, local cutie Marybeth dumps (in flashback) a whole bunch of exposition on us. Victor Crowley was born hideous deformed. Daddy brung him up. He was bullied by local kids. One Halloween night the kids were throwing firecrackers at him to get him out but they done set light to the shack. Daddy come back and tried to beat down the door with an ax, but Victor was behind the door and the ax done gone in his head, killing him. Daddy died of a broken heart ten years later. Victor roams the forest swamp as a vengeful spirit.

And lo, Victor subsequently appears for some head ripping, axe-splitting fun. And fun it is, but the sequel ran out of steam.

When configuring the monster, you have to look inside, deep down. There is a term still used in American law and that is the *malignant heart*. We conclude with another quote from Stephen T. Asma:

The State of California retains the language of 'malice aforethought' but under section 188 of the Californian Penal Code malice is divided into two forms: express and implied. Express Malice insists 'When there is manifested a deliberate intention to unlawfully to take away the life of a fellow creature.'

Malice may be implied by a judge or jury, 'when no considerable provocation appears or when the circumstances attending the killing show an abandoned and malignant heart.'[54]

Find the rotten heart and you'll find your killer.

---

[54] Asma 2009 (p. 228).

Chapter 6

The First Act: Unease and Dread, Character and Milieu

As we examine the tropes associated with the horror screenplay, please do not take these notes as prescriptive. We will make some particular reference to those embedded in Slasher or Serial Killer movies, as they have held market dominance since their inception in the late 1970s. There is, however, a good argument to be made that, now the Zombie phase has run its course, the supernatural is returning as market leader (though Thai, Japanese J-Horror and Korean K-horror are in abeyance). Horror is cyclical; witness the continual re-birth of Frankenstein, vampires, wolfmen and ghostly presences. Whatever subgenre is chosen, the astute writer will absorb the structure and lay down his own fresh take on the template.

The first act in a horror movie has a great deal of work to do. Like a travelling salesman or a fairground barker it must announce its presence immediately and make its product and intentions clear. The trailer, poster and advertising (viral and internet) will have done much of the work in establishing in the minds of audiences what kind of feature they have paid to see, but the subgenre must be made clear, as well as the 'feel' of the film. Many Slasher, Gorno or Zombie flicks will open with a kill, which are an easy way to shock but also something of a cliché. Of course, inventive kills are a mainstay of good Slasher – *Wrong Turn II* (Lynch 2007) opens with a doozy – but how do you rise above the norm?

What if your movie is a supernatural horror or relies upon a lot of backstory? Ever since Carl Laemmle Jr came to the front of the stage in *Frankenstein* (Whale 1931) to warn us 'what you are about to see may thrill you, it may shock you. You have been warned', we have enjoyed the futile last minute warning. In *The Texas Chain Saw Massacre* (Hooper 1974), a stentorian voiceover establishes that not only has there been a terrible discovery, but also that these awful deeds had been going on for a considerable period of time. A pre-credits sequence, involving a chase and kill or incarceration and imminent torture, is enough to have the audience on the edge of their seats. In the case of the supernatural, the power of the Unknown is hinted at and a mordant atmosphere created.

A horror movie must engage from the start. An action movie will often use a high-octane chase sequence, and a crime drama will introduce a murder: Horror can use these tropes, but it must also introduce the insane, the paranormal, the amoral, death, disease or decay. It is not a fantasy world, but ours gone awry.

The credit sequence is a useful way of avoiding clumsy exposition. Instead of having some ham-fisted scientist or local police chief explain what has transpired, it is hugely effective to show a montage of newspaper reports (*Amityville*, *TCM*[55]) serial killer diaries (*Se7en*) or grainy 8mm footage of the horrific nature of what happened before. Although it may look creaky now, one of the great horror movies, *The Haunting* (Wise 1963), has a pitch perfect opening. Dr Markham explains the hanging of Mrs Crane. We do not see it and nor do we need to. The camera winds its way up a spiral staircase and drops down so suddenly that we are in no confusion as to what occurred. As the tale unfolds, the camera takes on the persona of the spirit, swooping down from the gothic ramparts like a murderous black crow. We are drawn into the haunted house. It is not a place where we would wish to spend the night, in the dark. It is understated and chilling and the stage is set.

Due to the pace of videogames, today's audience is visually sophisticated and used to reading and collating information at incredible speed. Horror can employ fast cutting to show as little as possible but leaving us wanting more. The credit sequence can be, at once, a potted trailer for the movie and a great way for the writer to get across the backstory without resorting to dialogue-heavy scenes. It is, however, most often the choice of the directors/producers as to their eventual placing, but the writer does himself a favour by using these opening pages as a 'grabber'.

Bookending or framing the narrative is a writers' device that never fails to work. You may introduce the killer by simply showing the event about which the movie will revolve. In *Halloween* (Carpenter 1978) we are placed immediately in the killer's eyes. The massacre is shown and the resulting shock reveal. Fifteen years pass as the credits roll, and here we are again in Haddonfield, Illinois, knowing that the return of the evil is inevitable. In the *Texas Chainsaw Massacre* remake (Nispel 2003) we have all the paraphernalia of the killer: the newspaper clippings of the murders, the shutting down of the meatpacking plant, the gritty milieu of this backwoods country slaughterhouse. The original *TCM* was more inventive, using tantalizing peeks of rotting underground human

---

[55] TCM = Texas Chain Saw Massacre.

carcasses (with those high-pitched flashbulb shrieks), a radio broadcast to describe the bizarre artwork of corpses, and a boiling Texan day with clouds of dust blowing past. The next shot, accompanied by deafening atonal noise, is the red heat of a sunspot (Hooper used stock footage). This is horror in a heat wave.

In the opening to *Se7en* (Fincher 1995) the unseen killer shaves off his finger-prints and assembles a scrapbook of medical illustrations, minute lettering and religious iconography. It is interesting to note that it is common wisdom that the serial killer must keep trophies, things in jars, a mad diary or a scrapbook of his activities, plus he needs good sewing skills for bookbinding and human flesh. It's become a mandatory part of the serial killing profession.

Once the credits are over, there is more heavy lifting to do in establishing credibility in the minds of the audience. It is often believed that the first act is the easiest. In plotting terms, it is relatively straightforward. Here is the cast and their fractured relationships – the newlyweds, the lone female, the gang of teens: the victim(s). Here is the danger they are getting themselves into and here – with a few false shocks on the way – is how they are becoming entangled and ensnared in a world of which they have no knowledge. There are movies in which it seems little is happening at all in terms of actual horror (*Teeth*: Lichetenstein 2007; *The Wicker Man*: Hardy 1973; *The Last Exorcism*: Stamm 2010; *Paranormal Activity*: Peli 2007), but this is deceptive. The most resonant kinds of horror are those in which we are so drawn to the character and their world that we lose the urge to anticipate or hurry it along to the slaughterhouse.

Character identification is vital, even with – and indeed *especially* with – the dumb teenage Jocks we love to hate. Granted, the outsider's view of the 'horror movie' is still trapped in the 1980s, somewhere on a loop in the middle sequels of *Friday the 13th* (Cunningham 1980), *Nightmare on Elm Street* (Craven 1984) and *Prom Night* (McCormick 2008), a scenario where a group of spoilt teenage brats clearly deserve to die for their hubristic and atavistic pleasures; but this is fallacy. The 'Scream' franchise smartened this up considerably in the 1990s and the slashers of the last decade have become decidedly post-modern and ironic (*Piranha 3D*: Aja 2010; *Sorority Row*: Hendler 2009; *All the boys love Mandy Lane*: Levine 2006) in their approach to a much-loved form. Putting aside zombies, horror has latterly become much more real, a return to the golden age of New Horror of the 1970s.[56] We need to believe. We need to learn about our characters' exterior and inner lives. They must be three-dimensional people.

---

[56]Jason Zinoman has written an excellent treatise on the genesis of the works of Romero, Craven, Carpenter, O'Bannon, De Palma and Hooper in *Shock Value*. London: Penguin, 2011.

If you are writing a Slasher, there must be empathy with the Final Girl from the start.[57] We must be able to identify the one who will survive the ordeal. Although it's fun to play games with this (as in *Behind the Mask: The Rise of Leslie Vernon*), in general she will be the voice of reason amongst her peer group. She is female but not overly feminine – something of an outsider, the Goth chick, Emo or Tomboy (Jamie Lee Curtis in *Halloween*). She's introspective. She is the one who questions. She might even be bookish. She may be sexually active but it's clear she's not the one who gives it up easily. Her boyfriend, if she has one, will be inconsequential, lost in his own solipsistic world, unsuitable. Why? Because boys must also be able to identify with her. If she were too overtly sexualized she would become a lust object, if too immature she'd be the bratty sister. She may often have a bratty sister, or sluttier friend, in order to paint her in a better light. All this must be portrayed simply and efficiently and without resort to cliché.

Where do they live – and with whom? If we begin at high school, a sorority house or on spring break, there's an easy set of markers, but if the characters live at home there is going to be a parental figure. Parents and authority figures do not loom large in teen horror. They are adjuncts that need to be dispensed with, often only appearing in the first act, if at all. Their role is as a signifier of the real world which is to be left behind. They are useful to us in establishing how they see our protagonists. Parents tend to typecast their children – the good girl, the rebellious teen, the wallflower – which gives them a chance to bloom into something else with their peer group. This 'being two people at the same time' mirrors the duality in horror, from Jekyll and Hyde to Frankenstein and his Monster. Recently, the double life of country lawyer Chris Creek, as shown in *The Woman* (McGee 2011), was a shocking reveal. Mum may be strict, smothering or a religious nut (*Carrie*: De Palma 1976). Another option is step-parents. They may be loving or malevolent, but theirs is a functional and thankless role unless they are at the root of the story (*The Stepfather*: McCormick 2009; *The Orphan*: Collet-Serra 2009), in which case it's not a 'teen horror' at all but a family one (*Insidious*: Wan 2011).

In the supernatural genre, identification with the lead character is paramount. If we do not care, we will not go on the journey. We must engage fully with the main character, and the first act is seeded to show us what might turn into full-blown madness or possession. *Rosemary's Baby* (Polanski 1968), *Repulsion* (Polanski 1965) and *The Shining* (Kubrick 1980) all do this admirably. We move slowly from the real to the unreal. Often, in writing the first draft, we find things later on which we may then reincorporate in the first act, so don't worry too much about getting it first time. Write from the page.

---

[57] Clover 1992.

The real world

In Act One the quotidian world is sketched in, but we aren't staying for long. In rural horror, the principals have left town and are barrelling towards the impenetrable forest – cue expensive helicopter shot of expansive woodlands. Backwoods horror is a subgenre now, harking back to the Australian New Wave 1970s cult movie, *Long Weekend* (Eggleston 1978), through to the 1980s Sam Raimi camp classic *The Evil Dead* (Raimi 1981), then *The Blair Witch Project* (Myrick and Sanchez 1999) and more recently *Cabin Fever* (Roth 2002), *Timber Falls* (Giflio 2007) and *Wrong Turn* (Schmidt 2003). The forest is just as effective a horror device as the haunted house, in that it is simultaneously real and yet filled with potential dangers: hidden places, lost bearings and danger awaiting you at every step – plus it is cheap to film there.

Families starting out on new life are also a common trope and feature in Tobe Hooper's *Toolbox Murders* (2004) and *Mortuary* (2005). *The Shining* (Kubrick 1980) and *The Orphanage* (Bayona 2007) both commence with a new endeavour and in *Panic Room* (Fincher 2002) it is the purchase of a new home after a difficult divorce. The move to an idyllic suburban home (*Insidious*: Wan 2011) is typical of the diaspora of American life. Deep down in the psyche there is a sense of the frontier spirit, the ability to up sticks and move to another state and start all over again. Elsewhere in the world this is not so simple, there are immigration and passport issues, language problems, cultural, religious or social barriers to overcome. Whereas this mobility is a benefit to Americans, this optimism of the horizon, it is also fraught with danger. What will the new environment bring? Peace and happiness? Or challenges, obstacles and more pain? Horror thrives on the fear inherent in this kind of change, even if it's only temporary, such as with the family vacation (*The Hills Have Eyes*: Aja 2006) or the gap year trip (*Hostel*: Roth 2005; *The Ruins*: Smith 2008).

The most potent example of this is *The Amityville Horror* (Rosenberg 1979). You buy the perfect new home and it turns out to have a past. This Norman Rockwell, Andrew Wyeth idyll of the clapboard antebellum home with the wraparound porch set in fertile land is a seductive one, but it comes with a price. It's haunted and the previous inhabitants aren't keen on the new arrivals.

We must quickly reduce the real world to the possessions lashed to the family car, or to what we can carry in a backpack. Within a quarter of an hour of the start we are survivalists, living on our wits: alive, alert and adrenalized. However, we cannot go directly into the realm of the unknown, for first there must be a liminal scene.

The liminal scene

The liminal scene is the threshold scene. It is the point at which we move from the normal world into the world of horror, and there is no turning back. This is where the warning is given to our participants not to proceed. It is the old guy at the gas station, the janitor or the housekeeper, the real estate agent's advice not to buy. It is the local villagers in *American Werewolf in London* ('Keep to the road lads, and beware the moon!'). It is challenge and transition.

The warning adds a further element of danger to proceedings. Thrills without risk is all part of the rollercoaster ride, but if you were warned within a few feet of the gate to the ride, would you stop? Of course not. You have paid your money and the ride has begun. You cannot climb down now, as that would invite humiliation and shame. The horror movie is a challenge to the teenage audience. It is deliberately provocative. 'Who will survive and what will be left of them?' asks the *Texas Chainsaw Massacre* (Hooper, 1974). The 'Saw' franchise and Eli Roth's *Hostel* were accused of spearheading the pornography of gore, but the element of challenging an audience to endure these movies was no different to that of Herschel Gordon Lewis's *Blood Feast* of 1963 or the Video Nasties of the late 1970s and early 1980s (such as *Driller Killer*: Ferrara 1979; *I Spit on your Grave*: Zarchi 1978; or *Cannibal Holocaust*: Ruggero Deodato 1980). If horror is about confronting our fears then this is the last moment to refuse.

The annoying villager or gas station attendant is the gatekeeper to another realm, that of the subliminal, the subconscious and the bizarre. It is no accident that he is old, ugly and spitting out his tobacco. The crypt keeper in *Tales from the Crypt*[58] was ancient, a skeleton with bony fingers and empty eye sockets. The message is clear: Abandon hope all ye who enter here. The state of being old is the contrast to all that young, unsullied flesh. Age is wisdom and experience, elements our protagonists do not possess, because the function of the tale is to educate them into these things.

We spend our youth being told how the world operates, by teachers, parents and elders, but we have not seen it at first hand. We know there is no substitute for experience and so experience we must. We need to be forged in that flame. The gatekeeper is the first to give a scare, but his warning goes unheeded. He has no power, only threat – one that he is powerless to carry out, the only exception to this being when the gatekeeper is part of the conspiracy. Here, he has a dual role, for he is hiding the real horror on his property and the

---

[58] Max Gaines, *Tales from the Crypt* (1944–55), *Entertaining Comic* (EC). EC was a seminal influence on many horror directors and writers and was later made into portmanteau movie *Creepshow* (Romero 1982), with screenplay and guest appearance by Stephen King.

protagonists have unwittingly stumbled upon it, thus providing a catalyst for the next spate of killings. Fresh meat, if you will.

'Don't say I didn't warn you' is the tenet, but the novice blunders blindly on. 'Stay in your homes. They're coming!' proclaimed 1950s schlock horror SF blends, but we cannot resist a peep through the curtains.

Unease and dread

Allowing for a teaser fright, the first act is composed of modulating the tropes of unease and dread (see Chapter 4), and the longer you can go without a proper scare the better. It is quite common not to show the monster until at least halfway through the movie. The true scale of the Alien in *Alien* (Scott 1979) or *Cloverfield* (Reeves 2008) must be held off until the last possible moment. If not, as in *The Host* (Bong 2006), once the thing emerges from the Han River in Seoul it is no longer frightening, like showing Bigfoot or the Loch Ness Monster in the first reel (for this see *Loch Ness Terror*: Ziller 2007). Something is wrong and it is coming our way. Don't show your hand yet.

Context and exposition

The supernatural must be clearly signposted and this is the point of the liminal scene. Once this has taken place, there is often a need for exposition. This used to be done heavy-handedly, as in the 1950s Horror/SF B-movies (*Them!*: Douglas 1954; or *Invaders from Mars*: Menzies 1953) where a scientist would give a spurious reason for the nuclear cloud or giant insects or zombie-like replacement of hitherto-sensible townsfolk. Today there is no such obvious figure to turn to. In *Paranormal Activity* (Peli 2007) and *The Last Exorcism* (Stamm 2010) it is a man of the church, a psychic practitioner, or both. In possession movies it is often a renegade member of the church, in hauntings a ghost hunter/buster. In slashers it will be the nearest cop, but by now the victims are out of cellphone range. The local cop is too old, drunk or uninterested to care anyway, or else he is involved himself in the kidnapping shenanigans. The point here is that our protagonist must not be believed. In any case, the amassing supernatural faces are so great that the authority is powerless to deal with them ('We're going to need a bigger boat'). Effectively, they are infantilized, children begging to be heard and believed.

Act One isolates our protagonist; from their home, school or daily life, partners and close relatives. They cross the threshold to unexplored realms, to the inner and outer lands of the unknown.

Realism

Horror is essentially risible. You have to buy into it. The astute horror fan knows that a serial killer would not behave in the way depicted (they are extremely rare and nowhere near as intellectual as they are portrayed); or that paranormal entities cannot act with the kinds of force shown; also that there is no Devil or God. But they are willing to allow the possibility of these things. This is why the expository part of introducing the tale must be handled with care. It has to have credence. It has to be either someone who has already experienced it and more than in an 'Urban Myth' kind of way. Someone who has a real connection to the place, the entity or its victims, as in the early vox pops with the fishermen in *The Blair Witch Project* (Myrick and Sanchez 1999).

A liminal character will do this, one who is marginalized by society or whose worth is not recognized. A janitor, an eccentric academic, a down and out who has lived in the area long enough to have witnessed the original events. The character may be male or female but he is an adult who *connects*. In John Carpenter's *The Fog* (1980), the movie opens with salty old seadog John Houseman telling an entranced bunch of children the tale of how the sailors returned to Spivey Point in the fog to claim what was rightfully theirs, 'a hundred years ago to this very day ...'

Chronological happenstance is a common catalyst for horror, most especially in the slasher. *Black Christmas* (Clark 1974) introduced the idea of horror based around a festival or holiday event, and Carpenter's *Halloween* nails it as Michael Myers returns on the anniversary of his first murder. Halloween is not universally celebrated, but many cultures have similar festivals around the same time to mark the beginning of winter. It is both a pagan festival and a day of honouring the dead. Indeed, All Hallows Day (1 November) is a day for All Saints. An anniversary gives us a time and place. In the teenage calendar there is also Spring Break (*Piranha 3D*: Aja 2010; *Jaws*: Spielberg 1975) and Prom Night (*Carrie*: De Palma 1976; *Sorority Row*: Hendler 2009; *Prom Night*: McCormick 2008).

When writing ensemble horror there will perhaps be one member of the party who scoffs at the tale. Instead of being the voice of reason, he is often the one who has been instrumental in planning the practical jokes or a seduction. We've all been there.

Exploration

There is still some time for looking around the haunted forest/house in the daylight. The night has not yet come, so we can tour Castle Dracula for he is still abed. It is new territory and there are things to behold. There is age and decay, the mortuary, the vine-covered ruins (*The Ruins*: Smith 2009) or the odd passages and the old dilapidated cells of the former mental hospital (*Session Nine*: Anderson 2001). As the characters explore, this invites yet more unease. You might want to point out burnt or scarred things or marks on the walls – objects that may later become significant but for now are merely incongruous.

The curse of the cellphone

The advent of cellular communications gave rise to the logistical problem of the cellphone. As soon as our protagonists get into trouble, the sensible thing to do is immediately to call the authorities or home, or to warn your friends that the unknown is coming. If this were to happen the story would be sunk, so the scriptwriter customarily places them in an area with no reception (all areas of woodland, apparently) or make sure they have low batteries or the phone has been destroyed or lost or left behind: any strategy to remove this pesky problem. Most of these solutions have become as clichéd as the hot babe punching at her useless phone, but they do seem – at least in the most pedantic of Slashers – to be almost obligatory, a nod to the audience to say that yes, we are dealing with this one.

When you do come across this, I suggest going one of two ways. Either, as in the opening of *Dead Mary* (Wilson 2008), have a wordless scene wherein the protagonist waves the phone in the air so we know it's out of range, or find some way of making it a positive feature, as in *Scream*, where each time the phone rang it was the killer delivering threats. In some remakes of late, the stories have been set as period pieces, which avoids the issue. If your tale is current, why not use the technological problems to your advantage? Often the signal can be distorted, intermittent, or can cut out when we are travelling. Sometimes all you get is an odd robotic sound when the person speaks at the other end. What about other strange noises or the perennial problem of only getting through to voice mail?

If you are writing contemporary horror, you have to include cellphones, Facebook, Twitter or whatever social networking systems are current, otherwise your credibility is undermined. As with the gremlin on the wing in *The Twilight Zone: The Movie* (Dante, Landis, Miller and Spielberg 1983), it can be a huge opportunity instead of a drudge. Facebook can be hacked if you leave your account open, and your identity may be stolen. Who would pay attention to a Twitter feed about some mysterious goings-on in your home? The intermittently operating cellphone has to be a blessing and not a curse.

False shocks

It is good to have a couple of jumps in Act One, as a kind of aperitif. It is the film-makers tipping us the wink that the game has begun in earnest, and preparing us for the real carnage. However, too many, and credibility will disappear. One judicious use of the 'Lewton Bus'[59] scene and we jump in our seats, overuse it and we become inured to the real horror, too hyperaware of the form. It is difficult to use comedic irony or superior position in horror. It has only been effective, in my view, in the 'Scream' (Craven 1996) franchise and *Behind the Mask* (Glosserman 2006), in which we are complicit in the analysis of the genre but still do not guess what is coming. Horror must always be played straight, unless it is horror comedy (*Black Sheep*: King 2006; *Brain Dead*: Jackson 1992). Playing games, rather than teasing, becomes tiresome and infantile after a while.

The Cabin in the Woods (Whedon 2012) is not scary because we are taken out of the story from the start. We are acutely aware of the form, and no matter how clever and convoluted it gets, the contravention of tropes puts us at a remove. This is a common error made by directors who are 'too good' for the form. We admire the craft and, as with *Buffy the Vampire Slayer* (TV series, 1997–2003), all the in-jokes. There is nothing innately wrong with a vanity project. Surely, *Citizen Kane* (Welles 1941) was one, but until you are considered an auteur, it might be better to just tell the story and pepper it with enticing scares.

By the end of Act One, we have crossed the threshold. This new world is to be our dark playground or slaughterhouse. We have crossed the bridge and we are cut off. We cannot go back. The tension is racked up, the characters are trapped and the descent into hell or madness has begun.

---

[59] See Chapter 2.

Chapter 7

The Second Act: Modulating Fear, Terror and Horror

The Second Act is a complex unit, embodying the bulk of the action. It is often here that script readers comment that the pace 'flags' or the story has come adrift. Act One offers anticipation and Act Three resolution, but the Second Act has to grip us by the neck and not let go. It is sustained conflict but it is not enough to pile on shock after shock, as the fear must be modulated. There must be exploration, investigation, experimentation, campfire scenes where events are configured, information collated and decisions made before the beast is faced again.

As previously stated, it is important to hold off the reveal of the monster until the last moment. In Universal Studios' *Frankenstein* (Whale 1931) we are almost halfway through the movie before Karloff's monster is seen in full face, and even then he enters the scene backwards. In *The Exorcist* (Friedkin 1974) we only ever see what the possessing demon does to little Regan McNeil. In *Rosemary's Baby* (Polanski 1967) the true horror of what she has birthed is not revealed until the penultimate scene. Even then it is but a few brief frames of its eyes, shown in similar fashion to the superimposition of Norman Bates's face and his mother's skull at the end of *Psycho* (Hitchcock 1960). In *The Blair Witch Project* (Myrick and Sanchez 1999) the witch is never seen. In the 'Final Destination' franchise (2000–11), Death is only evident via his plan. This is incredibly powerful, because it lets our imagination do all the work.

We don't want the audience to be let down by the monster. 'Bruce' in *Jaws* was shown late because it was quite obviously a big rubber shark. Putting aside creature features and focusing on killers or man monsters, once exposed, we are dealing with a man in a hockey/William Shatner mask chasing teenagers. He may be impossible to kill but he is human and can be wounded. He may be horribly disfigured (Victor Crowley in *Hatchet*, Leatherface in *TCM*, the cannibal hillbillies of *The Hills have Eyes*) but, once seen, we are admiring the prosthetics. If non-human, it is the abilities of the CGI team.

Although CGI has improved immensely from the ham-fisted *Mummy* (Sommers 1999, 2001) to the suave excess of *Prometheus* (Scott 2012), it is not generally scary. There is something in our psyche that recognizes it as plastic and, though we may feel revulsion (the 'penis' monster who swallows Andy Serkis's head in *King Kong*: Jackson 2005), we stare as well as cringe. Keeping the monster in your mind is what has the more sensitive among us cowering behind the cushions. The vampire must be of the dark, the serial killer only glimpsed as he goes about his sick trade (John Doe in *Se7en*, Buffalo Bill in *Silence of the Lambs*). This is what made *Cloverfield* (Reeves 2008) so successful: the subsequent reveal was a bit of let down towards the end.

Establishing that the reveal must be delayed as long as possible (the sexual analogy is not wasted here) we have the bulk of an act in which the villain/antagonist does not appear. We see his trail, what he has done (horror), what he is doing (terror), and flashes of fragments – the limbs, the fangs or tentacles (I hate tentacles). His weapons and armoury are an extension of his body; the sharp long bladed knife is most commonly used, but there have been all manner of effective killing tools, from hammers and hatchets to the humble chainsaw.

Character must carry story

Once the Unknown becomes tangible we can begin to comprehend it and therefore to configure the evil. Our initial revulsion gives way to curiosity. As the antagonist is a minimal presence, we have no one to carry the story but the protagonist. For a horror film to be successful we must empathize fully with both them and their situation. To do this, it means modulating horror and terror (plus the judicious use of gore) in a series of escalations until we reach the climax.

Some viewers were frustrated by the three protagonists of *The Blair Witch Project* (Myrick and Sanchez 1999), finding Heather to be shrill and self-serving, Josh the cameraman petty and Michael the sound guy oafish and idiotic; but they acted with huge conviction. They were *real* (it was semi-improvised) and part of the success of this movie was due to the fact they were not acting as if they were in a horror movie.

Act Two begins at the point at which there is no escape physically (isolated location, injury) or psychologically and our protagonist is beginning to understand that he or she is the one being stalked, haunted, possessed or invaded. This recognition and acceptance propels us towards investigation and Act Two immediately throws up many questions.

- What is it? Why is it doing this to us?
- Why us, why here and now?
- What did we do to attract it? Are we therefore morally suspect?
- If we cannot escape it/this place, what are our options?
- Does it have a greater knowledge about us than we do ourselves?
- Can we fight it? If so, with what?

Before we can begin to act on these, it is important to nullify the authorities unless they are instrumental to the tale – the later reappearance of a hitherto-forgotten minor character being common and yet so effective. The clichés are legion: The Southern deputy who doesn't want to know (dang those city folks!), the overworked City Cop, the disbelieving doctor, and the blind priest are all important to increase the sense of isolation. The police will not investigate a 'crime' which is not part of their everyday business. Scientists will deny such a leak or genetic mutation could happen. Doctors, psychiatrists and hospital staff will be deaf to your pleas of bodily invasion or possession – that's if you can even get to these people, as most horror takes place in a rural location far from the purlieu of the local County sheriff (spits tobacco). Be it Southern gothic or the endless forest, the horror movie is mainly set in the drive-thru states, off the disused highway, far from prying eyes.

If it is a city location, it will most likely be in a soulless apartment block, either empty and due for demolition or peopled by unfriendly neighbours who will not open the door to strangers or axe-wielding maniacs. The end result is the same: our protagonist must go it alone. This is liberating, as it allows them total freedom to act without consequence. In essence, your characters are returned to a frontier mentality where they are cop, bounty hunter, judge and jury. They are in pursuit of what they believe to be evil because this external force has threatened the tribe or family unit.

Sometimes our protagonists have trespassed on another's domain, but despite this they continue to see themselves as innocents (*The Hills Have Eyes*, *Hostel*) and morally correct, rather than catalysts or even participants. The evil will engage them against their will. A good horror movie suggests that we are complicit in the evil and that it is a part of us, no matter how vehemently we deny it.

In this way, the protagonist is behind the audience. Often the inciting incident, say the killing of a secondary character or reveal of the newly reborn monster, is not known to them. Laurie Strode in *Halloween* (Carpenter 1978) does not know about Michael Myers's escape or what he did in the deserted house, or even that he is watching her. In the 'Final Destination' franchise, none of the protagonists are aware that they have been selected until it is too late, but we have had a superior position for the whole of Act One. This now begins to disappear, so as we are in alignment with the characters. We now know as much as them and no more. Later, when we head towards Act Three, information will be hidden from us so that we are *behind* the action, a vital situation in order for the protagonist to surprise us when she finally finds a way to overcome the beast. If not, we guess it, and the plot is sunk.

Portals

On the bridge between Acts One and Two there is often a portal from the real world to another. This is the Wardrobe containing the Lion and the Witch (never a good combination), the result of evoking the *Candyman* (Rose 1992) or the reading of the Necronomicon, as in *Evil Dead* (Raimi 1981). There are often physical objects with magical connotations, such as the mirror.

The mirror represents duality: the balance between good and evil, light and darkness, the duality of man's existence. This doubling can be seen as Frankenstein attempts to duck away from his creation in the climax at the windmill in *Frankenstein* (Whale 1931), when the *Wolfman* (Waggner 1941) shies away from the glass, or when, in *Psycho* (Hitchcock 1960), Norman Bates is seen in reflection. In the portmanteau horror, *Dead of Night* (Cavalcanti 1945), one story is based on a mirror bought as a wedding present, one that reflects a whole other world – a gothic bedroom that lures the viewer inside. In the 1970s, David Warner met a similar end in *From Beyond the Grave* (Connor 1974), this too with an antique mirror. More recently, Sean Ellis wrote and directed *The Broken* (Ellis 2008) starring Lena Headey, who finds a doppelganger threatening her family as a result of a broken mirror. In Alexandra Aja's *Mirrors* (Aja 2008), Keifer Sutherland is a guard in an old hotel dominated by vast dark mirrors – many secrets lay behind and within and they soon leak out to ensnare him.

A mirror or looking glass is an object that reflects light or sound. Whether made of gold leaf, lead or silver/mercury, they have existed since the first century – and we have always had pools of water, as Narcissus knew all too well. In the Renaissance a way was found of coating glass with a tin–mercury alloy, and it was highly sought after. In literature we have Lewis Carroll (*Alice's Adventures through the Looking Glass*) and the Brothers Grimm's 1812 creation, the Queen in *Snow White*, such powerful mythological narratives that they have been repeated ever since, the latest Hollywood version being *Snow White and the Huntsman* (Sanders 2012). Mirrors traditionally reflect the soul, which is why vampires cannot see themselves. To break one will incur seven years bad luck – the time taken, it is said, for the soul to regenerate itself (although this is also true of human skin). In some European countries, if a newborn child sees a mirror before the age of one it will supposedly die, not having yet been able to form a soul. In witchcraft mirrors were used as scrying tools or to cast spells. In the US Southern states, mirrors were routinely covered during a wake for fear that the soul of the deceased might be trapped inside them – a practice still carried out in Romania.

Then there is the summoning ritual in the slumber party game 'Bloody Mary', which has echoes of *Candyman* (Rose 1992), and was made into a superb Indy horror, *Dead Mary* (Wilson 2007). The game was originally a method of divination for young unmarried women, who were told to walk up a flight of stairs backwards holding a candle and a hand mirror in a darkened house. It was said that they would see their future husband in the mirror. If they saw a skull or the grim reaper, they would die before they were married. Of late, the ritual has changed to looking at your own face in a mirror, whilst repeating Bloody Mary three times as you spin around, adding 'I've got your baby' – a reference to Queen Mary I (known as Bloody Mary) who had several miscarriages. Mary then appears as a witch, a ghost or a corpse, usually to teenagers.

The mirror does not lie – or does it? A mirror image is not a true one, as it is reversed in the left/right horizontal axis but not the vertical one. We are aware that we look different in a mirror as opposed to in a photograph. A mirror has the twin associations of vanity and ruthless self-examination. To place two mirrors opposite one another creates a seemingly endless dimension of reflections and counter-reflections, as in the fun house. Things may flit behind us or be caught in our peripheral vision. The danger of mirrors has been well captured in the novel 'Apartment 16' by British horror author Adam Nevill. Use them to your advantage.

Another portal is a book – for example the Necronomicon in *Evil Dead* (Raimi 1981). Books are both real and symbolic, in that they contain knowledge which, once released, has the power to do good or evil as in a Bible or the Koran. Knowledge is power, and a book of spells is a common magical item. The words form incantations or catechisms that either protect or damn. As with the repetition of the Prayer of Exorcism there are, in black Magic or satanic rituals, spoken invocations to the dead or deadly – prerequisites of any demon-raising story. What lies beyond the veil of human experience is something to be feared and yet craved. When we are prepared to do anything to find a magical object to get us there, we are in the realm of the box in *Hellraiser* (Barker 1987).

Pandora's Box (Hesiod's *Works and Days*: 700 BC) was a large jar given to Pandora – the first woman on Earth. Entrusted to her by the gods, she could not stop herself from opening the box and thus releasing all the evils in the world. When she tried to close it she found the box was empty but for one thing, the spirit of Hope or Elpis. A symbolic item such as a box or container plays on this classic story trope. It was employed in the tale of *Possession* (Bordenal 2012), where a girl buys an antique box containing a *Dybbuk*, a Jewish demon, at a yard sale.

Other portals are doors to a locked room (*The Skeleton Key*: Softly 2005), cellar or attic. As we know from childhood, the denial of something makes us want it even more, especially when there are ominous noises, scrapings and whisperings coming from within. As in Pandora's Box, once the evil is released, it is too late.

Investigation

After the first attack by the unknown or agents of the unknown, refuge must be sought. Once safe ground is secured, it is time to investigate the phenomenon and attempt to understand it. This will be ultimately futile because, as Hannibal Lecter says of Buffalo Bill, 'his psychopathology is a thousand times worse than you could ever imagine.' You can, however, seek to comprehend its modus operandi. This is difficult, because the characters have hitherto been in a tense physical state of fight or flight, and are now being asked to switch to sedentary study and research.

This tension is worth noting, as the writer might now employ the device of the ticking clock (it's coming …) to accelerate the investigation process. In this way we can get across exposition without annoying the audience, because it's being done 'on the hoof'.

This is a time for re-grouping, possibly the only time the group will get to do this. Later, they will be divided, dead, or both. It is time to deepen characterization. First, the Alpha Male or Female will attempt to dominate. Those more pensive participants who may possess a skill that might lead to understanding or undermining the evil will likely not be heard. During this exchange our 'Final Girl' is likely to remain mute or in abeyance: she has not yet developed the cognitive or physical strengths she will later need.

Democracy is the first victim. Those who wish to fight force with force will have their say or be instrumental in planning an escape. Perhaps a breakaway faction is formed and alliances are fractured. This is not solely the province of Slasher films, as families or couples may too be seen to splinter and crack in the presence of ghosts or evil doings.

When untrammelled force comes across a greater enemy it will, by the nature of the transaction, fail. This will result in injury or, most likely, another character killed off (this is usually when the black dude dies). It is important to the integrity of these kinds of stories to remove the person with the strongest chance of defeating the enemy or of rationalizing the situation, that is to say any paternal figure or one of maturity. It is not his journey. It is that of the immature, yet more resourceful character who combines smartness with feats of endurance and great stamina. If not a group, then the male half of the couple may become injured (*Eden Lake*: Watkins 2008) or otherwise incapacitated. If the tale concerns a lone female she may come up against an insurmountable physical barrier. Once the option of fighting back is removed, there is no choice but to turn to reasoned approach – to strategy.

The investigation scene is the one with the microfiche in the library where every local newspaper is scoured for 40 years into the past until at the last minute a clue is discovered. It is the unearthing of the history of the house or the root of the curse. The clues may be visual – an old photograph of a child can be the catalyst for the protagonist to join up the drips of blood – or it could take the form of the occult, unearthing a Ouija board, talisman or cursed object.

Investigation also encompasses the autopsy scene. The *Silence of the Lambs* (Demme 1991) and *The Thing* (2011 remake) illustrate two versions of this. In *Lambs*, there is a detailed forensic examination of Buffalo Bill's latest 'hump'. It registers strongly on the disgust scale, but it is rookie Clarice who spots that the corpse has a death's head butterfly cocoon inserted in its throat – a vital piece of the puzzle. In *The Thing* (van Heijningen Jr. 2011) the alien is killed before it can regenerate, and female crewmember palaeontologist Kate Lloyd is asked to participate in opening up the carcass. Inside, amidst all the gloop and intestines, is an amniotic sac containing a half-formed replication of another crewmember. These investigation scenes are hugely important plot points and, if used well, can push our heroine beyond her personal boundaries and reveal necessary exposition. Once new knowledge has been brought to light, it is time to proceed to experimentation.

Experimentation

Experimentation is dropping a stone down a well to see how deep it is. It is rattling a stick in the wasps' nest. It is trying to contact the spirit via the Ouija board to ascertain what it wants. By now the protagonist will have discovered that they have a connection to the horror. Although there are numerous horror movies that involve the random brutal killing of teenage hikers who have ventured beyond their comfort zones (life is nasty, brutish and short), in other forms of horror there is often a relative or ancestor who was the progenitor of the evil.

In a haunting, this is almost inviolate, and it is rare to find a spirit which randomly chooses its victims. In general it is people who are haunted, not places, no matter what we have been led to believe (see Chapter 3). In Asian horror, the vengeful spirit, as in *Ringu* (Nakata 1998) and *The Grudge* (Shimizu 2004) is out to harm or hurt those whom it feels have disrespected it. This connection is redemptive. It is the saving of the family name. It is curing 'the sins of the fathers' via a trial or an ordeal by fire.

If your movie involves transformation (body horror, contagion, zombification or werewolves), now is the time for the subject/victim to ask questions of his new abilities. When David Kessler in *American Werewolf* (Landis 1981) is bitten for the first time, the rules are unclear. How often do I change, and for how long? What happens when I do, and why am I unaware of my state of mind after I do? What if I were to be restrained during this process? Added to this, his recently dead buddy, Jack, is popping back at inappropriate times to tell him to kill himself before the next full moon. If it is a zombie film, we must ask how much of the world has already been affected (try contact by radio, semaphore or smoke signal). Is it airborne, waterborne, or does the virus only affect those who have been bitten? *28 Days Later* (Boyle 2002) introduced the Undead that run. Instead of shambling, brain dead, easy to kill walking dead, we have a vicious, feral strain of Undead, able to outrun all but the athletic. New rules come into play. Fortifications must be stronger, higher. Weapons must be more powerful to stop them in their tracks.

The advantage of this is that it clarifies for us who the antagonist is. We are still ahead of the protagonist (we have seen things she is unaware of), which means we know they will underestimate their nemesis. Since *Love at First Bite* (Dragoti 1979), most attempts in going after Dracula with a stake, a crucifix and Holy Water have met with derision at best and have been fatal at worst. In Coppola's *Dracula* (Coppola 1992) the Count modified the myth that vampires could not go out in the day by saying that yes, they could, but they were low on power – thus introducing a chink in their armour.

Reasoning

In order to understand the beast, the protagonist will use rational evidence-gathering and an intellectual approach, something that has stood the human race in good stead for millennia. However, what guarantee is there that the hypothesis/experiment/conclusion model is going to work when dealing with something instinctual? It is something the protagonists have experienced physically but whose nature has been understood primarily by intuition and not by the rational self. Their understanding of it has been in a counterintuitive manner. In debating the way forward, the choice has to be made: use the rational and scientific/pseudo-scientific, or go for an untested approach.

Most likely they will try the reasoned approach first, and it is here where the expert, the policeman, scientist, doctor, medium, priest or psychiatrist will act and fail, and this will make things worse. They have stirred the hornet's nest. The beast will bare its claws. This leads us to the first big moment of terror when we see what we are up against, and the audience and protagonist are working as one.

Both audience and protagonist are asking how to deal with the monster. Up to now we have been ahead of the game, knowing that the cabin/old house/forest where we were headed was filled with dark creatures. Now we are scared for the heroine. She must lead us deeper into the cave, bringing us to the midpoint.

The midpoint

A note first about some unusual movies that break with storytelling tradition and change protagonists halfway through: the industry standard here is *Psycho* (Hitchcock 1960). We are invited to follow Marion Crane and to sympathize with her as she steals the money and then avoids a number of men who may be the 'psycho' of the title. Her guilt propels her ever onwards until inclement weather forces her to the Bates Motel. Norman is the first man to be kind to her, and for a moment we are relieved, until we hear, but do not see, the screeches of 'mother'. We know what happens next but, after the shower scene, we are left with no protagonist.

This is jaw dropping. Who do we root for now?, we ask, as we follow Norman's actions in a protracted nine-minute sequence. 'Mother' did it and Norman is clearing up after her. After he places Marion's body in the trunk, a car glides past and its headlights play on skittish, terrified Norman. It is now *he* with whom we sympathize. He is our new protagonist. Hitchcock has played a magnificent trick on us. *The Sixth Sense* (Shyamalan 1999) contained a big reveal too, as did *The Others* (Amenábar 2001), but these were more akin to Act Three revelations, as in *Don't Look Now* (Roeg 1973).

To change horses in midstream is a hard one to pull off. A contemporary of *Psycho* was *The City of the Dead* (Moxey 1960), a low budget witchcraft chiller whose screenplay by George Baxt was too short at 60 minutes (movies then were only 70 minutes long, as an 'A' and a 'B' movie were released together as a double bill). Producer Milton Subotsky said: 'When I found that the Baxt script was only 60 minutes long, I added the boyfriend that goes to look for Nan after her disappearance, and I thought it looked seamless in the finished film. It had a classic structure and what is interesting is we had the heroine get killed off halfway through and another girl going to look for her who finds herself in the same situation. This was similar to *Psycho* but we did it first.'[60],[61]

Since then, the idea has appeared in *[REC] 2* (Balagueró and Paco Plaza 2009) where we follow the fireman until he dies and then spool back to the kids outside, replacing his story with theirs; and also in *Martyrs* (Laugier 2008) in which the heroine is killed and her friend is gradually revealed to have been the chosen victim all along. These are rare examples, but if you can pull it off, you have found something truly memorable.

New skills

Before we become proficient in a new language, we must first learn the grammar and make sense of the alphabet and pronunciation. These are rules of competence and, once mastered, will lead to the rules of performance – for example the difference between learning to drive a car and driving in a foreign country.

Here, the heroine has to learn what to do to survive in the world of the unknown. This means encounters in which she must fail but from which she can learn. In *Hellraiser* (Barker 1987), Uncle Frank's mistress Julia is inveigled by him to solicit strangers and to kill them in order to put flesh on his bones. In any zombie movie the hero has to learn that, if you dismember zombies, the parts continue to function and they will keep coming until you shoot them in the head.

At this point the heroine is often tempted to join the ranks of the Undead or the dark side. The vampire is a seductive creature. Power unlimited is offered, or some arcane knowledge such as the key to life and death and all its mysteries (as sought by Kenneth Cranham's character Dr Channard in *Hellraiser II*: Tony Randel 1988). The temptation will be stated in terms of whatever the protagonist is repressing, so it represents their darkest, deepest desires. By contrast, the antagonist has not yet revealed his weakness. The only way to discover this will be by the use of intuition.

---

[60] While the authors hesitate to contradict producer Milton Subotsky, *Psycho* (June 1960) was released four months before *The City of the Dead* (September 1960).

[61] Allan Bryce (ed.), *Amicus: The Studio that Dripped Blood*. Plymouth: Stray Cat Publishing, 2000.

Intuition

As the heroine explores the unknown, she also tests the antagonist for its qualities, strengths and weaknesses. It may seem as though the demon or evil force is playing games with the victim, but it, too, is unfurling its powers, which have perhaps lain untested for centuries.

Here, if you have room for subplots involving other characters, these may kick in. These extra characters can either be possible rescuers or aides for the heroine, or, on the flipside, acolytes of the demon creature. These acolytes may now attack the hero (the buxom naked female vampires in *Dracula*: Coppola 1992) or minor members of hillbilly families, as in *The Hills have Eyes* and *Wrong Turn*. They may also be younger, untested wannabes who wish to have their first kill, for example Charlie Creed's son in *The Woman* (McKee 2011).

In this way, the story has now become a dance of death. The protagonist is not yet learning a strategy but feeling his or her way blindly and taking leaps, as must each heroine in the 'Nightmare on Elm Street' series.

This is also where the complex machinery and scientific equipment for the detection of the paranormal entity must prove incapable of the task and be abandoned. It is where the plan to trap the monster fails, succeeding only in enraging it. This is the point at which Clarice Starling finds herself by chance outside Buffalo Bill's home in *Silence of the Lambs*. Intuition has proven correct and has led them once more to the gateway of the evil. Ideally some kind of plan has been mustered, even if it is makeshift.

Plan into action

Now that the evil has revealed itself the heroine has no choice but to take it on, using her newfound powers of instinct. These are the rules of competence. This conflict comes at a point where the heroine is in command of enough knowledge about the antagonist to hopefully stall it, imprison it, or kill it. The aim, on a grander scale, is to destroy or control it, or to send it back to where it came from. In order to do this, the heroine must now absorb the evil.

Absorbing the evil

This is the herald of Act Three, which will lead to the resolution. For the heroine to overcome the evil and to face what it is she is lacking – most evident in slashers such as *Halloween* (Carpenter 1978) – she must almost become part of it. The inner conflict of Laurie Strode is that she is sensible, tomboyish and repressed, the girl who babysits, who doesn't 'get any', who is prissy and bookish – she is as terrified of her subconscious as was Carrie White in *Carrie* (De Palma 1976). Neither of them could control their lives – Laurie's lack of ability to side with her peers and Carrie's maturation and supernatural powers. Both girls must overcome by using what they learn from the monster(s), namely spontaneity and immediate action – in effect, freedom from their *Ego* and the release of the *Id*.

Here they will often be seen to perish. This is a messy, wet death as they are drowned underwater or in mud, perhaps buried alive or stuck inside a house as it burns. They may be trapped under the monster, enveloped by it, swallowed or subsumed in gore or body parts – all of this being a metaphor for death and rebirth as the anxious seconds pass. Then, inevitably, they emerge, covered in amniotic fluid, but breathing now, alive.

According to Syd Field in his book 'Screenplay'[62] (the screenwriters bible), this kind of crisis point often comes at page 75 in the screenplay, but in a horror movie, which is often shorter at only 95 or even 90 minutes/pages, it is compressed, thus propelling us forward into Act Three.

---

[62] Field 2005.

Chapter 8
The Third Act: Tragic and Redemptive Endings

The third act in any movie is of huge importance, in that the ending is what the audience takes with them and blogs/shares with their friends.

Horror is ideally placed for this, as by its nature it will often end on a horrific reveal. Who can forget the conclusion to *Psycho* (Hitchcock 1960), the bleak pagan horror of *The Wicker Man* (Hardy 1973) or the awful nihilism of *Night of the Living Dead* (Romero 1968)?

It is almost a requirement of the genre that the best is saved until last – from the slow build and modulation of unease and dread in the first act to the thrill-packed rollercoaster ride of the second. Act Three has to top them all, and in classics of the genre like *Texas Chainsaw Massacre* (Hooper 1974) it does. Sally Hardesty, having been captured by Leatherface and family, is subjected to such naked brutality in the party sequence that she seems to be going insane right before our very eyes. Once 'Grandpa' fails to kill her with a hammer – as a virtual corpse, he is too weak – she grabs her moment and leaps from a window, running off into the dawn, pursued by Leatherface (dander up, chainsaw priapic) and his hitchhiker brother. She manages to flag down a truck, which then runs over the brother. Leatherface attacks the truck and the driver hits him with a big wrench. Sally finally escapes in a pick-up, soaked in blood and laughing with insane glee, as Leatherface impotently swings his saw around in the fume-filled morning air.

They don't make 'em like that anymore.

Both this and *Halloween* (Carpenter 1978) gifted us with an indestructible serial killer. Later, Freddy Krueger and Jason Voorhees took up the mantle and in the 1980s horrors, mainly slashers or derivatives thereof, the killer was vanquished temporarily while the protagonists survived. This too was true of Wes Craven and Kevin Williamson's 1990s *Scream* franchise. In these audience-friendly pleasers, it was not possible to kill off your heroine. 'Middle America can't take it', cried nervous network executives, and in these high budget tales the desire for box office booty and DVD residual sales wins out.

If this was a truism of the last century, it has now clearly changed, as witness the 'Final Destination' franchise (2000–11) in which death comes to all no matter how clever or pretty we may be. Likewise in the 'Saw' franchise and *Hostel* (Roth 2005), no one gets out alive, or, if they do, they are as physically and mentally damaged as Sally Hardesty.

We have entered an era in which the choice between tragic or redemptive ending has veered towards the former. Deeply unsettling and truly 'awful' conclusions, such as those of *Witchfinder General* (in the US, *The Conqueror Worm*: Reeves 1968) or *The Vanishing* (Sluizer 1988) have become the norm, as too in *Martyrs* (Laugier 2008) and *Eden Lake* (Watkins 2008). Here, the protagonists end up mad, dead, trapped or dismembered; even in ghost stories such as *The Woman in Black* (Watkins 2012) or the *Paranormal Activity* franchise, the dark side wins over. The norm has shifted from survival to defeat and a vision of a kind of dystopian hell, a trope that has been hammered home in every zombie/undead movie of the last decade. In these, it is almost impossible to find an example in which the humans achieve a clear victory, expect perhaps in *Zombie Strippers* (Lee 2008). Perhaps we as a society are simultaneously comfortable enough to contemplate our inner fears yet convinced of the moral bankruptcy of Western capitalism's values. In order to see where the horror genre is going (and therefore what might inform your Act Three denouement) it might be prudent to look briefly at how it has changed over 80 years or so as popular family entertainment.

Safety valve or pressure cooker? Horror, society and censorship

Horror has always acted as a safety valve for society, for if we can know our fears then we can contain them. The fear of the monster was once a metaphor for fear of the outsider, of the invading army or of the principles of a 'different' philosophical or political system. Our fears during this, the first age of modernism, were those of the advance of technology and the loss of individuality, thus *Metropolis* (Lang 1930) portrayed the individual subsumed by the great machine.

Man's attempts to play God took us from Frankenstein's monster to the truly monstrous release of the atom and its power. For the decade following World War II, nuclear fallout was the predominant fear, along with that of the newly risen ideology of Russian and Chinese Communism ('aliens' were portrayed as short yellow/green men with slanting eyes – not a million miles away from the cartoon view of an Asian character). The endings to invasion of the earth movies (via bug, alien, entropy or pod) were warnings to a cowed American public that they were not as safe as they believed, best exemplified in *Invasion of The Body Snatchers* (Siegel 1958).

The 1960s and 1970s turned the fear inwards to human psychosis. What if the monster was insidious, masquerading as a normal citizen, as in *Peeping Tom* (Powell 1960), *Psycho* (Hitchcock 1960) or *The Boston Strangler* (Fleischer 1968)? Once we were liberated from our buttoned-down existence and began to experiment with hypnotism, drugs and psychiatry, then who knew what might result once the *Id* was released? *Forbidden Planet* (Wilcox 1956) was a literal illustration of this concept, and the idea of the lone mind turning mad became a common trope in Rod Serling's superb *Twilight Zone* TV series (1959–64). It was played out in the female mind in *Repulsion* (Polanski 1965) and again in *Rosemary's Baby* (1968), a movie that introduced not only the devil but also the birth of modern horror, filmed as it was not in a studio, but in the day, on the streets of Manhattan.

By 1968, the MPAA film rating system had superseded Hollywood's self-censoring body, the Motion Picture Production Code. However, explicit gore and violence in movies such as *Poltergeist* and *Gremlins* (as well as the early 'Indiana Jones' movies) caused a parental uproar and a call to regulate the 'PG' rating. Spielberg himself lobbied for a 'PG-13' rating, and this was introduced in 1984. The horror genre, by its nature of extremity, has always drawn the attention of censorship bodies and furious parents. In the UK in the 1980s, the distribution of video cassettes was unregulated for home viewing (though not in theatres), thus drawing the wrath of the Press and the self-appointed watchdog Mary Whitehouse. As a result of lobbying, a 'Video Nasties' list was compiled to protect against obscenity, leading to the (UK) Video Recordings Act of 1984. Seventy-four movies were banned and 39 distributors were prosecuted in a cultural witch hunt. All the banned movies have subsequently been able to secure a release; notorious amongst them were Abel Ferrara's *Driller Killer* (1979), *Blood Feast* (Lewis 1963), *I Spit on your Grave* (Zarchi 1978), *The Last House on the Left* (Craven 1972) and *SS Experiment Camp* (Sergio Garrone 1976).

Films that escaped the cull were Sam Raimi's *Evil Dead* (1981), passed but with two minutes cut in 1990, and *The Exorcist* (Friedkin 1974), which was never submitted to the BBFC. The Board's head at the time, James Ferman, stated that if it were to be submitted, it would be rejected. After Ferman retired in 1999 it was passed uncut and re-released, as were *Straw Dogs* (Sam Peckinpah 1971) and *The Texas Chainsaw Massacre* (Hooper 1974). Tastes have clearly changed, and new technology and delivery platforms throw up new challenges, permissions and questions about regulation, as is happening on the Internet right now.

After the groundbreaking work of Romero, Craven, Hooper, Carpenter, O'Bannon and De Palma, horror reverted to pure escapism in the big-haired 1980s. The *Nightmare on Elm Street* and *Friday the 13th* franchises were more reminiscent of the old Universal days than any desire to push the form. There were some ground-breaking films such as *Hellraiser* (Barker 1987), *The Shining* (Kubrick 1980) and *An American Werewolf in London* (Landis 1981), but in general this was a time of great public uncertainty and political upheaval. The concept of mutually assured destruction (MAD) had been examined dramatically in *Fail Safe* (Lumet 1964) and satirically in *Dr. Strangelove* (Kubrick 1964), but despite Thatcher's and Reagan's fingers on the button, the Soviet sickle was beginning to fall, tumbling against the unstoppable greed of the West's free market economy. The monster, for the time being, could no longer be 'over there'.

Despite the overt censorship of the Video Recordings Act of 1984 in the UK, this was the decade that popularized horror, as it came to be watched at home via video recorder with groups of teenagers circulating tapes and making them a feature of slumber parties and Friday nights.

The 1990s kicked off with the horror/thriller blend of *Silence of the Lambs* (Demme 1991), one of the few genre films to win Oscars across the board. It seemed that, despite Romero's (*Dawn of the Dead*: 1978) and Carpenter's (*They Live*: 1988) warnings that consumerism was going to turn us all into the undead, it was not going to happen. Instead, the election of the Democrats (US) and the ersatz Socialists (UK) brought a degree of security and we began to get ironic. *Scream* (Craven 1994) was box office gold, taking the familiar horror movie tropes and laughing at them, while still being a hugely entertaining whodunit. Toward the end of the decade, the Internet threw up its first viral success. *The Blair Witch Project* (Myrick and Sanchez 1999) launched myriad copycat shaky handheld camera movies that are still in demand today.

The new millennium was characterized by a rebirth of supernatural horror in M. Night Shyamalan's *The Sixth Sense* (1999) and Hollywood remakes of Asian horror hits such as Hideo Nikata's *Ringu* (1998). So too was there a commercial explosion. New technology drove down the cost of making movies and, by the end of the decade, CGI and Photoshop were available on your laptop, meaning that a movie could be made on your home computer, as in the case of *Monsters* (Edwards 2010), which allegedly cost no more than 50 dollars.

One world event changed everything. 9/11 bred metaphorical horrors such as *Cloverfield* (Reeves 2008) and *Right at Your Door* (Gorak 2006) but did not result in a slew of 'terrorist' movies. It was in 2012 that *Ozombie* (Lyde 2012) was released, more than a decade since the World Trade Centre bombings and a year after Bin Laden had been assassinated. The invasion of Middle Eastern countries and the implications of the whirlwind this has yet to reap has in the main been relayed back to us in zombie movies. The message seems to be that we are not paying attention. We have not paid heed to the lessons of the past. Perhaps we are all the undead, shuffling along, consuming mindlessly, glaring at our smartphones, plugged into our technology, blissfully unaware of the single shot to the head that might put us out of our misery.

The 2000s also saw 'torture porn' horrors such as *Hostel* (Roth 2005) and *Saw* (Wan 2004). The *Saw* franchise (2004–10) began with the compelling premise that we are unaware of what we have and of how indolent we are. So inured are we to the values of being human that it is only by being put in a life-or-death situation that we can truly know what it is to be alive. Admittedly, in later sequels the die was loaded and most of the characters were fated to meet a gory end from the get-go, but Jigsaw's heart was seemingly in the right place. His acolytes and followers – perhaps as in all cults and religions – either misinterpreted his words or adapted them to their own self-serving ends, resulting in more carnage in the name of the 'cause'. Perhaps this too is a comment on the nature of fundamentalist belief?

In *Hostel* (2005), Eli Roth laments the superiority of the ugly American abroad. The characters are Dionysian, foolish, seemingly invulnerable, but the Eastern bloc is about to show them different – that life is worthless. It is worth noting that in the storyline of *Hostel II* (Roth 2007), despite the indignity visited on the female victims, there is precious little actual torture. It transpires that the torturers are not brutish Slavs: far from it. The winners of the auction to take the lives of these pretty American princesses are two wealthy American businessmen.

We have of late come to see many similar odysseys of teenage gap year stupidity. Australia provided us with the particularly nasty *Wolf Creek* (McLean 2005), and there are thrills and gore galore to be had with *Captivity* (Joffe 2007) and *The Ruins* (Smith 2008). From the UK there is *Donkey Punch* (Oliver Blackburn 2008) and potholing fun in the superb *The Descent* (Marshall 2005). Teen anniversaries/celebratory times have often been popular loci for horror from Halloween (*Trick R Treat*: Dougherty 2007) and Spring Break (*Piranha 3D*: Aja 2010) to Prom Night (*Sorority Row*: Hendler 2009; *Carrie*: De Palma 1976). The gap year phenomenon is an ideal situation in which to get a bunch of attractive teens together in a beautiful location and then kill them. It takes the urban myth, for example the 'guy/girl who went drinking in (choose Central American country) and woke up in a bath of ice cubes missing their kidneys', at its literal best. The gap year horror is as much a fixture on the teen calendar as Prom Night.

One element, which surprises the rest of the world, who are outsiders to these rituals, is just how wealthy these teens are. They live in huge houses with every modern convenience. They own cars even before they can legally have sex and none of them has ever had to do without a cellphone, laptop or any item of fashionable clothing. Comparatively, they have no worries at all – perfect skin, an abundance of beautiful slender partners, and a sense of entitlement that assures them that, if they are not going to become a Master of the Universe, then at least Daddy might buy one for them. No wonder the rest of us poor schlubs are happy to see them killed off. The portrayal of beautiful teens is very much a case of 'same as it ever was' – and its reality, or lack of, troubles the studios not on whit. We have to ask, though, why moviegoers are consuming the death of young adults in horrible ways in increasing numbers. Is this a lesson to them? Is it a new puritanical streak that is in effect saying 'Stop thinking you own the world or else it will come back and bite you on your perfectly formed ass'? What are the values here? There is little interracial mixing in horror, and what there is smacks of tokenism. If you are writing about teenagers, then what are you saying about them? A writer should never preach – Sam Goldwyn said that if you want to send a message then use Western Union – but horror is supposed to speak to our deepest fears.

Mark that the US is a deeply Christian country with Christian values, and this remains in evidence even in the horror industry. Movies about exorcism or black magic always necessitate a reaction against God, thus accepting the existence of a deity. They are rarely atheist, and it's surprising how even the most twisted of nihilistic serial killers often clings to some bizarrely twisted aspect of Catholicism; mind you, if you've been raised by priests, you'd know why. Although it is primarily a ratings issue, note how little actual profanity is used in horror movies. Time and time again I have seen full-on gore scenes and my reaction is a LOT more potty-mouthed than that of the cast. Hell, the F-word is pretty much my go-to cussword when I merely stub my toe.

In the UK, there have been two strains of horror in recent years, the 'hoodie' horror and a resurgence of the home-invasion thriller. The latter has a noble antecedent in *Straw Dogs* (Peckinpah 1971) and re-emerged with a nasty taste in its mouth in Michael Hanake's *Funny Games* (1997, 2007), which was so good he made it twice.

It's easy to see where the fear lies, namely in the violation of the physical objects we hold dear. It is literally 'too close to home'. The French thriller, *Ils* [*Them*] (David Moreau and Xavier Palud 2006) played on this hoodie fear, and *Strangers* (Bertino 2008), its American parallel, contained a chilling riposte to the line 'Why are you doing this to us?':

'Because you were at home.'

These movies sure get the blood boiling among the property-owning classes. In England there is a fear of feral youth that began with the Teddy Boys of the

1950s, graduating to the Punks of the mid-1970s, and that has resurfaced in an urban youth that imitates US gangsta style by wearing anonymous hoodies and mall-bought clothing (no doubt in order to escape the prying eyes of ubiquitous CCTV cameras). These faceless scum are every bit as frightening as the fast-running zombies of *La Horde* (Dahan and Rocher 2009) or *28 Days Later* (Boyle 2002) – a mindless destructive force that respects nothing (all the work you have done to build, maintain and secure your property) and devours all in its path. This is a UK urban threat, one that is perhaps denying itself a bigger audience, since it is too real for a nation that experienced a youth riot in the summer of 2011 (Los Angeles suffered a similar race riot in 1992). After all, you don't go to the movie house to see what is going on right around you – it precludes the aspect of escapism.

Horror cinema is veering towards the tragic end of the scale; redemptive endings are few and far between now. Sure there are still Final Girls who escape their killers and tormentors. Sure, there are families who are brought closer together by the attack of the unknown (*Possession*: 2012), but it seems pretty bleak out there. Writing this now means that it will change, and it is likely to have done so by the time this book is barely in its second edition (☺).

In science fiction, too, dystopian visions are bread and butter. No one is envisioning a happy future here. It is perhaps why horror is aimed at the young, because they have not known any true disasters in their lives and are therefore content to experience it in a staged and caged form. For them it is at once catharsis of their unformed fears and something of a training film. It offers the very worst solutions to the questions 'What might happen to me and my peer group if we go on that camping trip?' and 'Who shall I allow into my home?'

We mature, and time does its dastardly work, stealing our youth and our hair and replacing it with fat, wrinkles, aches and pains. We lose loved ones and, if we are very unlucky, our own progeny (many horror movies concern the loss of a child). We age and decay and go slightly mad. We worry less about the screaming man or the bag lady with a shopping cart and more about when we will become the screaming man/bag lady with a shopping cart. Our organs fail us; we suffer the indignities of age; and we become invisible to the young. We become at first vulnerable then unwanted, and biscuits and alcohol get a lot more important. Horror movies ignore a lot of this, but if you are looking for a deeply unsettling third-act resolution, go for something that terrifies *you* – and by extension your main character. For me, the most effective horrors are those which tell us something about the bleak amoral nothingness of the human condition: films like *Eden Lake* (Watkins 2008) or *Martyrs* (Laugier 2008), or big spooky reveals like that of *The Shining* (Kubrick 1980); but maybe that's because I've always been the caretaker.

Brevity

The third act cannot afford to waste time. Once the monster is fully revealed and cornered, the tension must be at breaking point. Once the hero or heroine has absorbed the evil and entered into that final encounter that will trick, defeat or send the evil back to whence it came, things must move faster than in any other part of the movie. Now is the time for action not character. No backstory or exposition. All thoughts or reflections are banished as the protagonist executes the plan. We are directly in the moment and we want her to succeed or to die trying. It is a huge relief, therefore, when the beast is banished and sent back to hell for the time being. Don't keep this going; we are all elated and spent and we need to lie back and smoke that metaphorical cigarette. Now you are ready for ...

False endings

The innovative shock ending was pioneered in *Carrie* (De Palma 1976), in which Sue, the only surviving member of the carnage, dreams of visiting Carrie's grave. Suddenly, Carrie's hand reaches out to grab her. She awakens screaming in the arms of her mother and now we realize that she is in fact insane. There have been attempts to imitate this, so much so that, amongst the horror community, the double death is quite the cliché (not dead, not dead).

If you are adding a coda to your movie it is better to create not an opportunity for a sequel, which is after all the due province of the producer, but instead the suggestion that the horror, far from being over, will go on and on and on ...

Best practice is in Zack Snyder's remake of *Dawn of the Dead* (2004) in which the survivors of the zombie holocaust escape to a nearby island, only to find it already overrun with the undead. A camcorder records their last desperate moments as the horde attacks. Another tragic twist to the tale is in *The Mist* (Darabont 2007) where in a world overrun by vast tentacled monsters looming out of the mist, family man David Drayton is all out of choices. There are five people in the car and only four bullets. The adults decide that hope has abandoned them and life is not worth continuing. Drayton then shoots the car's occupants, including his own son. Moments later, a deafening rumbling noise turns out to be, not more monsters, but an artillery vehicle followed by a squad of soldiers and civilians. As he comes to realize that they were moments from being saved, David is left screaming in agony. This is tragic and effective, and the fact that Darabont managed to get this version on screen is testament to his tenacity.

Whether tragic or redemptive, Act Three must provide a degree of resolution. This is not to say that everything has to be spelled out – indeed, leaving us wanting to repeat the experience in order to figure it out can be powerful. Both *The Exorcist III* (Blatty 1990) and *Kill List* (Wheatley 2011) achieved this, as did *The Blair Witch Project* (Myrick and Sanchez 1999), and it is often the supernatural genre that is tasked with leaving us with more questions than answers. *[REC]* (Balagueró and Plaza 2007), *Night of the Demon* (Tourneur 1957) and *The Innocents* (Clayton 1961) were hugely effective in leaving us to wonder. For some, this is antithetical to the experience, as there is as much joy to be had in a clear and clever resolution, say, as in the one provided so elegantly in *Final Destination 5* (Quale 2011). However, it is good perhaps to leave some loose ends – not plot holes or shoddy writing, but something that reflects the fact that we must continue to explore and fear the unknown because, when it boils down to it, there really aren't any answers.

Chapter 9
Prequels, Sequels and Franchises

The rules for a horror-movie sequel are: One, The death total is always greater, and Two, The murder scenes are always much more elaborate, with more blood and gore. Three, Never, ever under any circumstance assume that the killer is dead.

Kevin Williamson, screenwriter, *Scream 2* (Craven 1997)

Dracula and Frankenstein are the most reworked stories of the last two centuries, spawning over 50 remakes each in theatre and cinema. These enduring myths, along with those of Jekyll and Hyde (Stevenson 1886) and Scrooge in *A Christmas Carol* (Dickens 1843), are as endlessly adaptable and repeatable as Grimm's Fairy Tales or the story of Cinderella. The sequel and franchise are endemic to the genre. James Whale's 1932 *Frankenstein* was so popular it led to *Bride of Frankenstein* (Whale 1935) then *Son of Frankenstein* (Lee 1939), after which Boris Karloff quit the series. It lumbered on with Lon Chaney Jnr. as the Monster in *Frankenstein meets the Wolf Man* (Neill 1943) and then *House of Frankenstein* (Kenton 1944) before descending into parody in the hands of Abbot and Costello. It was reborn in 1957 in Herbert J Strock's *I was a Teenage Frankenstein*, but the cycle really began again in earnest with Terence Fisher's *The Curse of Frankenstein* (1957) from the UK's Hammer studios. If Universal was the first major studio to see the potential of the sequel, then Hammer was to strip-mine it with *The Revenge of Frankenstein* (Fisher 1958), *Frankenstein Created Woman* (Fisher 1967) and *The Horror of Frankenstein* (Sangster 1970) as well as numerous versions of the Mummy, Jekyll and Hyde and Christopher Lee's *Dracula* (Fisher 1958).

You can't keep a good undead body down. The 1960s threw up the TV series *The Munsters* and the 1970s brought Paul Morrissey's *Flesh for Frankenstein* with Margheriti (1973) and Mel Brooks's *Young Frankenstein* (1974), which spoofed the old Universal movies. Then there was *Re-animator* (Gordon 1985) and *Bride of Re-animator* (Yuzna 1990) and even *Frankenhooker* (Frank Henenlotter) in 1990. The decade brought more literary adaptations with Kenneth Branagh making *Mary Shelley's Frankenstein* in 1994. More recently there has been *Frankenfish* (Dippe 2004) as well as Vincenzo Natali's *Splice* (2009). Latterly, Danny Boyle directed Johnny Miller and Benedict Cumberbatch in *Frankenstein* (2012) on stage at London's National Theatre.

The Frankenstein monster story is not the only story to be re-versioned. John Wyndham's 'The Midwich Cuckoos', a tale of alien children with psychic and telekinetic powers, was made into the superb *Village of the Damned* by Wolf Rilla in 1955 for MGM. A sequel, *Children of the Damned* was produced in 1964 (Leader) in which six super-intelligent children are identified across the world by UNESCO and brought to London. There they develop telekinetic powers but, threatened by the military, they escape to a London church where they construct a sonic weapon. Unlike in the original movie (and its 1995 John Carpenter remake), these children are not malevolent, but far advanced humans, and the sacrifice they choose at the end has Christian overtones.

In the same year that Roman Polanski kicked off a new age of realism in horror, George Romero created an equally groundbreaking movie, *Night of the Living Dead* (Romero 1968). Whilst *Rosemary's Baby* offered no sequel,[63] a decade later Romero came along with *Dawn of the Dead* (1978), which took the undead into the malls of America and made some pertinent social comment. He made it a trilogy with *Day of the Dead* (1985), and continues to develop it, being the writer of Zack Synder's *Dawn of the Dead* remake in 2004, and continuing the franchise with *Land of the Dead* (2005), *Diary of the Dead* (2008) and *Survival of the Dead* (2009).

Horror suits the sequel, regardless of the quality or lack thereof. It paints a big canvas, blood-splattered, melodramatic and full of Grand Guignol. Once the stalk and slash movie got underway in the late 1970s, three serial killers opened up the lucrative vein of repeatable business, Michael (*Halloween*) Myers, Freddie (*Nightmare on Elm Street*) Krueger and Jason (*Friday the 13th*) Voorhees (and his mom).

Wes Craven's *Elm Street* (1984) spawned six sequels including the arch *New Nightmare* (1994) and latterly a remake of the first film itself. *Halloween* (Carpenter 1978), the archetypal slasher, has had seven sequels, a remake by

---

[63] Except on TV: *Look What's Happened to Rosemary's Baby* (Sam O'Steen 1976).

Rob Zombie in 2007 and a sequel to the remake in 2009. Carpenter and Hill wrote *Halloween II* (Rosenthal 1981), having the story follow on immediately from the first film. They intended to wrap up the story, and indeed the next in line – *Halloween III, Season of the Witch* (Wallace 1982), penned by Quatermass writer Nigel Kneale who later had his name taken off the credits – had nothing to do with Michael Myers at all. This tale featured androids in Jack 'o' Lantern masks intent on killing children at Samhain (Halloween), and rather than being a slasher it is more a horror–SF blend, perhaps an homage to *Invasion of the Body Snatchers* (Siegal 1956).

Sean S. Cunningham's *Friday the 13th* is the *reductio ad absurdum* of the stalk and slash genre with 12 sequels to its name, plus novels, TV series and comic books. An interview with writer Victor Miller can be found later in this book. Neither he nor Cunningham returned to write or direct any of the others, and to date the franchise has grossed over $465 million.

Wes Craven struck gold in the post-modern ironic 1990s with *Scream* (Williamson 1996). The film is a fresh take that played merry hell with the form and has led to three sequels, each garnering financial and critical success as they exploit the tropes and clichés of the form.

It is a truism commonly held that if a film makes a certain amount of money it automatically triggers a sequel. Hollywood, in the last decade, has become particularly risk averse as studios collapse or battle to stay afloat in a changing digital/technological marketplace. Superhero movies are being reinvented, cloned and remade as they chase a younger demographic which has no concept of paying for music or movies. To combat this, movies have returned to big special effects, spectacle, Imax, the big tent. In horror terms, this means fewer originations.

The advantages of the sequel to the studio are myriad. First you have built a brand and an identifiable product; second, there is a proven audience for it. Spin-offs and merchandizing turn more revenue than untried product. Yes, you increase the budget, but there is less risk. Often, a new writer or director can be brought in to cut their teeth. James Cameron was hired to do special effects on *Piranha Part Two: The Spawning* (1981) but when creative differences led to director Miller Drake walking, Cameron was hired to step in. Chuck Russell, director of Dream Warriors (*A Nightmare on Elm Street 3*: 1987) had previously been a producer. Remakes too are financially viable, if not always a wise decision. Gus van Sant's shot-for-shot take on *Psycho* (1998) is considered a failure and the less said about the *Wicker Man* (LaBute 2006) reboot the better. Having said this, some remakes are excellent, even surpassing the originals. Adam Gierasch's retread of humdrum 1980s haunted house number, *Night of the Demons* (2009), is high on sex and shocks. French Director Alexander Aja's work on *The Hills have Eyes* (2006) was exemplary, as was Brit Director

Andrew Douglas's *Amityville Horror* (2005) with a pumped-up Ryan Reynolds and reliable Aussie scream queen Melissa George in the lead roles.

The last decade has seen new franchises, most notably that of Leigh Wannell and James Wan's *Saw* which span out seven sequels. *Paranormal Activity*, Oren Peli's low budget treat, has reached its trilogy, as has the Spanish supernatural rage virus horror *[REC]*. Even backwoods chop 'em up *Wrong Turn* (O'Brien 2012) is going for its fifth, aptly entitled *Bloodbath*

So too has the notion of the prequel been gaining momentum. *Hannibal* (Scott 2001) was one of the early movies to examine the origins of the great psychopath, along with Paul Shrader's *Dominion: Prequel to the Exorcist* (2005). Rob Zombie's *Halloween* remake spent much of the first act getting reacquainted with the development of Michael Myers, as did the *TCM* remake (Nispel 2003), focusing on how the Leatherface family became cannibals. It is debatable as to how effective these have been or whether they add to the canon. The precursors of this movement are George Lucas's *Star Wars* origins series of movies and TV shows like *Smallville* (Gough and Millar 2001–), retelling the story of a young Clark Kent, which has run to 10 seasons and 218 episodes. Rather than 'Superman', the original intent was to mine the DC Comics 'Batman' origins but the idea failed to garner interest at Warner Bros. Christopher Nolan subsequently took this on in his 'Dark Knight' trilogy.

It is a given that to write a sequel or prequel will come out of a commission and it would be pointless for a writer to attempt one on spec unless it is a writing exercise. In the main, sequels have tended to come out of the stalk and slash date movies, but these have been spoofed comprehensively in *Behind the Mask: The Rise of Leslie Vernon* (2006), *Scream* (1996) and *Scary Movie I–IV* (2000–) so that until there is a revisionist take on the subgenre, all bets are off. As William Goldman famously said, 'Nobody knows anything.'

Before we address the structural problems inherent in a screenplay based on an existing story, it is worth looking at some of the psychology.

Psychology

Teen horror is a coming-of-age story, one in which the protagonist has both inner and outer needs as they progress through the rite of passage from adolescence to adulthood. Outwardly they need to survive; inwardly they need to achieve maturity, which is exemplified by the monster facing them.

One important facet of the teenage experience to keep in mind as you write is transgression. Teenagers seek to cross boundaries, disobey warnings, unearth what they are not supposed to, meddle in forces more powerful than they are, fall for someone they shouldn't (like a vampire); and they are content to live in filth and depravity.

In creating a strong storyline for a sequel it is vital to carve out a strong and psychologically resonant tale, otherwise it really is just another bunch of kids heading for the sawmill. *A Nightmare on Elm Street 3: Dream Warriors* (Russell 1987) has such resonance, in that Patricia Arquette's character Kristen Parker is one of the last of the 'Elm Street children' (the offspring of the vigilantes who killed Freddie Krueger). A lonely child, she needs her peer group at Westin Hills Psychiatric Hospital in order to piece together the reasons for her stunted adolescence. Nancy Thompson, the new staff research scientist, is none other than Freddie's original victim, at once trying to examine her neuroses using professional means and failing to confront it by taking the pills that will subdue her dreams. Both young women are arrested in a pre-Oedipal state, kept there by the monster (Krueger) as a Freudian *Superego*.

In most stalk and slash movies it is the drug-taking stoners and the sexually active kids who bite it first. They are being punished, not for the sex, but for daring to act like adults. There is also a huge tension between the teenagers and the adults. Mothers and fathers are both oppressive and repressive in trying to infantilize their offspring. This battle is what makes these movies so seductive to its target audience: it is the fight between naivety and experience, safety and risk, childhood and adulthood, *Ego* and *Superego*. Freud is a hell of a template for teenage horror, in that much of his work concerns what happens before maturity.

In a possession story, when a child is at the centre, the Oedipal battle is waged over the child's soul, pulling them between dependence and independence.

In rural backwoods horror – an increasingly popular subgenre – there is not only the psychologically repressed but also the economically repressed. There is violent juxtaposition between wealthy middle-class city kids and the disenfranchised products of an urbanized society. Far from being an abundant fruit/bread basket, the larder for the world, the American countryside has been raped of its goodness and left to dry out and die. Its inhabitants are financially barren and educationally stunted: no wonder, then, that when some 'purty city boy come along 'n their jalopy break down', there's an opportunity for some good old time killin' (*Trailer Park of Terror*: Goldmann 2008).

The lesson of teen horror is the induction into the adult world, which requires going into dangerous and painful territory. The monster represents aspects of the turbulent psyche of the protagonist; this is shown most especially in the attitude to sex. There is often a teasing flirtatious relationship between the Final Girl and the killer. This is because the story is all about initiation into adult responsibilities and a fully sexualized world.

It is interesting to note that in the *Texas Chainsaw Massacre* remake (Nispel 2003), protagonist Erin rescues a baby from the Leatherface family, thus symbolically proving her capable of motherhood and its demands, a clear symbol of maturation – the successful journey into adulthood; a redemptive ending as opposed to the insanity of the original.

Teen horror is also Darwinian, in that those most suited to adulthood will survive. The qualities of childhood and inexperience will prove useless and it will only be adult qualities – restraint, common sense, caution, selflessness, courage and loyalty – that will enable them to come out at the other end. We must be concerned that they do, and, if not, we are invited to dismiss the infantile ones. I recall my attitude to the disposal of the whiney demanding gutbucket Franklin in the original *Texas Chainsaw Massacre* (Hooper 1974). It was neither sympathy nor horror but repressed glee, which was perhaps Hooper's intention all along.

Put simply, in order to write a sequel there is the problem of the law of diminishing returns. The protagonist (or her replica in a fresh Final Girl) has survived but is caught in perpetual adolescence. The initiation ritual has been frustrated and negated, as we see in the increasingly histrionic *Friday the 13th* and *Freddy's Nightmare* series. Events become increasingly nihilistic, as in *Saw*, where the hero is unable to break free of the pre-Oedipal monster. She has discovered that the adult world is irredeemably corrupt. There is no escape from the monster, which is rapidly becoming the default setting for modern horror. In some movies this information destroys the characters. This is both pertinent and resonant to a Western society wherein the state of adolescence has been arrested and where we have no clear rites of passage.

In writing a sequel, the writer is faced, too, with what film historian Thomas Schatz calls the baroque phase of genre evolution.[64] In the first experimental stage, themes and conventions are established, defining the genre or subgenre. In the second, classic, stage film-makers and audiences understand them. Thirdly, there is refinement, the baroque stage. Here, the iconography and formulas are self-consciously examined or introverted to the point where 'they themselves become the substance or content of the work.'[65]

In essence, the viewer is no longer scared, as he has assimilated all the tricks. He recognizes them and wants to see something more complex. We have become over-familiar with the false scare (accompanied by a violin shriek or a musical stab) as a figure passes between the protagonist and audience, the double death or the argument that requires the splitting up of the group.

Writing the sequel is a challenging task, in that we are working with so much existing material and within certain parameters. There is a given antagonist who must return and be at the centre of the narrative. There may be a specific location such as a haunted house or forest. There may be a requirement to

---

[64]Thomas Schatz, *Hollywood Genres: Formulas, film-making and the studio system.* New York: Random House, 1981; pp. 37–8.
[65]Carolyn 2009 (p. 16).

keep the undead monster alive for the next part of the series. There may be pre-existing characters or the need to create a backstory to an existing situation. In short, the writer is being asked to replicate the first film but to add something new and exciting. The issues he is likely to confront include:

- Structural problems
- Backstory and exposition
- Set pieces
- Comedy and camp.

The structural problem

The structural problem with a sequel is that the Unknown has become known. An original story has the bulk of the first and second acts to build up the tale and to hold off the reveal, but now we are faced with an enemy whom we partially understand. We know Dracula is affected by sunlight, holy water and crucifixes, and can be impaled on a stake; that he can only cross running water at low or high tide, can transfer his condition of immortality by biting (but only the jugular vein), and that he requires Transylvanian soil to rest properly. The source material sets down these rules. They may be bent but not broken.

It also means that the audience has a clear idea of his flaws, and superior knowledge as to how he will be defeated. A horror movie is only as good as its villain, and most go to a 'Dracula', 'Hannibal Lecter' or 'Saw' sequel to cheer on their antihero. This weights the sympathy on the side of the antagonist, so right away we are offered a mixed message. We are simultaneously rooting for the monster as well as being asked to identify with the teens that are out to kill him. This means the sequel is always working on an ironic level, because of our greater degree of cognizance. Thus, as with Joss Whedon's *The Cabin in the Woods* (2012), you may get a good movie but you don't get a scary one.

Backstory and exposition

The writer will also need to cater for a new audience which does not necessarily know the provenance of the monster. This means the dreaded exposition, which must be conveyed in Act One or else the audience will be lost. It is also a reminder to the audience who may have forgotten that Dracula bites necks or that Jigsaw kills everyone (for their sins).

The easiest option for this is to tell all in the credit sequence, as in the *Texas Chainsaw Massacre* remake (Nispel 2003); or perhaps with a voice-over narration delivered by an old survivor as the new incumbents are brought in.

Another problematic and page consuming aspect is the book ending. Whereas your Act One may necessitate a retelling of the story, Act Three may have to set up the next part. In effect this means that you'll have five to ten pages that deal with pre-existing business, which is extraneous to the new story. At least you'll be getting paid well for it.

Set pieces

In order to make it scary you are going to have to ramp up the tension, which means more gory deaths and inventive kills. This is certainly true of *Hostel II* (Roth 2007) as well as all of the *Wrong Turn*, *Saw* and *Final Destination* franchises. Since a significant part of your screenwriting job is devoted to inventing these, this means plot over character.

Characterization goes out of the window once the chase begins, and this is the thorn in the flesh of most sequels. They simply rack up the effects and the tension, and hope that no one will notice that there is precious little story.

Because you know what you are getting, the monster has to be bigger and bolder and show more cunning in his evil plans or in executing his long-term revenge. This is evinced when Freddie Krueger becomes ever stronger in the dream world or when Jigsaw dies but his followers continue to carry out his plans. The concept of promoting an acolyte or adding a second monster is a beneficial one. In *Hellraiser II* (Randel 1988), not only did Kirsty have to battle Pinhead and the Cenobites but also the maniacal Dr Channard. Multiplication is a common route, and it is the one taken by Universal Studios once they started combining their monster movies. In contrast, Hammer studios changed the sex of their fiends (*Dracula's Daughter*) or swapped the actors' roles so that amiable Peter Cushing (Van Helsing) became Dr Frankenstein and evil Christopher Lee (Dracula) was able to play the urbane Duc de Richlieu in *The Devil Rides Out* (Fisher 1968). That virtue and evil personified might be reversed was testament to these actors' prowess.

You can also add more to the cast. Wes Craven said about *A Nightmare on Elm Street 3: Dream Warriors* (Russell 1987), 'We decided it could no longer be one person fighting Freddie. It has to be a group because the souls of his victims have made Freddy's stronger.' The Director backs up the whole love/hate claim, saying 'We are never quite sure if we are scared to death or cheering him on.'

Big set pieces rely on budget and there is no harm in letting loose your inner maniac here. In the chapter on writing exercises, we invite you to think of what horrifies you and take it further. Eat some cheese and have those bad dreams. Tease us too. Show us an obvious location like a haunted house or a funfair, or someone looking in a bathroom mirror, but don't go the obvious way. Watch the gymnasium scene in *Final Destination 5* (Quale 2011) for a masterstroke of delayed tension.

Overall, the better approach is to write a story with resonant characterization. The *Amityville* (Douglas 2005) remake worked well because the husband, wife and elder son had real issues that just happened to focus around a haunted house they had stupidly bought. It is always a good idea to look at other horrors around the world for inspiration. There are many suggestions for you in the following chapters.

Comedy and camp

What often happens in a sequel is that comedy creeps in. Because of the extreme nature of this genre, it is not hard to parody, and many sequels have gone this route; working on the ironic level where the audience 'knows' it's a horror movie allows us to play with the form.

When this is bad, it is parodic or has weak gags layered onto formulaic situations (Freddie quips 'Tongue-tied?'); that or it is reliant upon the stupidity of the disposable members of the gang. If however, comedy is used well, it provides the good laugh, which flatters the audience, for example in the undead victims of Werewolf David Kessler suggesting ways of killing himself in *An American Werewolf in London* (Landis 1980). It is all of *Slither* (Gunn 2006), *Brain Dead* (Jackson 1992), *Black Sheep* (King 2006) and *Young Frankenstein* (Brooks 1960), each of which displays a fine comedic sensibility.

Some subgenres fall apart when faced with comedy, such as the exorcism of children or supernatural horror, but the familiar monster is easier to attack because it is so clearly externalized. Comedy is best used as seasoning, but if you smother it in sauce, it turns into camp, as in *The Rocky Horror Picture Show* (Sharman 1975), or every aficionado's favourite Vincent Price movie, *The Theatre of Blood* (Hickox 1973). Camp is 'an aesthetic sensibility that regards something as appealing or humorous because of its ridiculousness to the viewer'[66] and is derived from the French *se camper*, meaning to pose in an exaggerated fashion. Susan Sontag's 1964 essay 'Notes on "Camp"'[67] is worth reading as a study in how the tools of arch irony and wit may be employed to create the artifice that is camp horror/comedy.

In comedy, extreme violence and killing are rendered safe because parameters are drawn and we know it is comedy from the start. This is why Laurel

---

[66] Jack Babuscio, 'Camp and the Gay Sensibility', in *Camp Grounds: Style and Homosexuality*, David Bergman (ed.). Amherst: University of Massachusetts Press, 1993; p. 19.
[67] http://www9.georgetown.edu/faculty/irvinem/theory/sontag-notesoncamp-1964.html/

and Hardy can hit one another with all forms of implements, mechanical or otherwise, and we laugh at them instead of being concerned by the trauma, contusions, lesions or other physical damage that would put any normal person in a coma. This is why the extremes of Itchy and Scratchy (a cartoon within a cartoon) in 'The Simpsons' are hilarious to Bart and Lisa. It is why Lionel Cosgrove in *Brain-dead* (Jackson 1992) will go to any lengths to preserve dignity (ear in custard, severing limbs) until he has no option but to plough through the zombies with a rotary mower.

The comedy must come out of the situation, rather than being imposed on the characters. They must never think for one moment they are in a horror movie or try to be funny. Comedy must in these instances always be played straight.

The first sequel: *Bride of Frankenstein*

Camp has long been allied to the sequel, and its origins lie in James Whale's 1934 picture, *Bride of Frankenstein*.

James Whale, riding high on the success of his first Universal film *Waterloo Bridge* (1931), chose Frankenstein as his next project. It wasn't something he was madly interested in, considering it to be the pick of a bad bunch. He worked on a screenplay based on Peggy Wheeler's 1927 stage play, and wanted the film to share the look of German expressionist classics. To that end he screened *The Cabinet of Doctor Caligari* (Weine 1920) and Paul Leni's *The Cat and the Canary* (1927) for the art director.

Frankenstein caused a sensation, with newspapers refusing to run advertisements, along with censors ordering multiple cuts – and the British censors in particular demanding the loss of a hanging scene. The most notable edit was Frankenstein's/Colin Clive's classic line, 'Now I know what it's like to be God', which was cut or covered by a clap of thunder and not fully reinstated until 1999. All this pulled in the punters (Carl Laemmle Jr's front-of-cloth warning was added after the film was shot) and the film earned over $1 million, twice that of *Dracula*. The publicity department defined the genre by naming it a 'horror picture', and Universal decided on a sequel.

The original ended with the monster dead and the Baron celebrating his son Henry's recovery. Universal began to circulate prints excising this scene, and this epilogue was lost until its American TV release in 1957. Whale rejected the first script, which had Henry and Elizabeth running away to a circus to become puppeteers. Other early treatments had Frankenstein trying to sell a death ray to the League of Nations and Elizabeth being killed and her brain being put into the body of the bride. Whale insisted on a framing device in order to present it clearly as a fantasy, and set it in an unnamed location. Many writers were employed, including Robert Florey, with final credits going to William Huribut with adaptation by William Huribut and John L. Balderston.

The sequel was shot under the titles of *The Return of Frankenstein* or *Frankenstein Lives Again* and took 46 days, reuniting many of the original British cast: Colin Clive, Boris Karloff, Dwight Frye (as the assistant); and bringing in Ernest Thesinger. Elsa Lanchester was first choice for the Monster's mate; and the laboratory was now up and running with Tesla coils, a Van der Graff Generator and lots of flying sparks, thus cementing the image of the mad scientist's lair.

Neither Karloff nor the studio approved of Whale's attempts to humanize the monster, allowing him to speak, smoke, laugh, eat and drink, and in the next sequel, *Son of Frankenstein*, the Monster was again rendered mute. Fifteen minutes of footage were removed after test screenings of *Bride*, including references to the scandalous behaviour of the three writers in the prologue and a sequence where the Monster beats up the Burgomaster, prompting the village idiot to murder his uncle and steal his life savings. The original ending had Henry and Elizabeth dying in the explosion in the castle (they survive in the film), but you can still spot Henry being crushed by the rubble in the lab. Whereas the original film had no scored music at all, the sequel has music all the way through, written by Franz Waxman for a symphony orchestra. It was complex, with signature pieces for each character, including wedding bells for the 'bride', and was rewarded with an Academy Award Nomination for Best Sound Recording (parts of the score were later used for *Buck Rodgers* and *Flash Gordon*).

The story is rooted in a subplot of the original novel by Mary Shelley, where Henry Frankenstein is approached by his old mentor, Dr Pretorius, who has created several homunculi 'from seed'. Pretorius shows him a King and Queen (with helium voices), an Archbishop, a Devil, a ballerina and a mermaid, all in jars. He wants him to create a mate for the monster, and they drink a toast 'to Gods and Monsters'.

Meanwhile, the escaped Monster saves a young shepherdess, but is injured by hunters and trapped in a dungeon from which he escapes. He later encounters an old blind man who befriends him (spoofed in *Young Frankenstein*) and is the only positive relationship shown in the entire movie. The hunters find the cottage and it is burnt down. The Monster flees to a crypt where Pretorius invites him to join him in supping and drinking with the dead as he explains that a mate is being created for him.

Henry and Elizabeth have married, but Pretorius returns to urge him to aid in the experiment. When Henry refuses, Pretorius has the Monster kidnap Elizabeth.

Henry complies, and in his electricity-filled laboratory he brings the bandage-bound bride to life. The excited monster reaches out to her, asking 'Friend?' But she screams in fear and hatred 'like the others'. Heartbroken and enraged, the Monster tells Henry and Elizabeth to leave but that he, Pretorius and the Bride must stay.

'We belong dead', he intones mordantly as both laboratory and tower are destroyed.

The film has long been noted as having clear homosexual undertones. Notwithstanding the fact that Whale, Clive and Thesinger were all gay, Pretorius is hardly portrayed as a quarterback, more like a gay Mephistopheles. There are lines in the script that are hardly open to interpretation, especially when he is introduced as a 'queer gentleman'. It explores sexual deviancy in nods towards necrophilia when he wines and dines the corpses in the crypt. There is the idea that the Monster and his mate are to procreate to make a new race – or maybe the Bride is being made as a sexual playmate for Frankenstein himself?

All fun and frolics, but the women do not fare well. Elizabeth is nagging and screechy to her betrothed, with lines like 'Don't say those things. Don't think those things. It's blasphemous and wicked.' Minnie (Una O'Connor) is a local fishwife who tries to raise the alarm, but she is a shrill type who tips the movie into pantomime. Elsa Lanchester is the only exception, pert as Mary Shelley in the prelude and terrified as the birdlike Bride in her final glory. While *Frankenstein* had so many memorable images, the Bride only has shock-haired Elsa with her famous Malin streak, based on Nefertiti.

Bride of Frankenstein exemplifies for me all that is wrong with sequels. In humanizing the Monster we are invited to sympathize, thus placing him in the role of protagonist. Henry is a chinless unsympathetic character, easily bullied into the dark side by his mentor and unable to defend his new wife or his honour. Whale cast him again because he liked his 'hysterical quality'. Giving the Monster more to do was perhaps inevitable, but Karloff objected strongly to it (Whale and the studio psychiatrist had chosen 44 words that he might say from a test given to 10-year-olds). The acting is hammy and knowing, and the storyline loses much of its integrity. The supporting cast is caricatured and, aside from a deepening of the Monster's psyche (a prelude to our later obsession with the psychopathic brain), all we are left with are bigger set pieces, a lot of repetition (back to the lab again) and the big reveal. It works because it is a template, but first does not necessarily mean best.

Writing the sequel is an unenviable task fraught with problems and pitfalls. Grit your teeth and enjoy the money.

Chapter 10

Adaptation: From Page to Screen

From the beginnings of cinema, adaptation has been a feature of the horror movie. Both *Frankenstein* and *Dracula* were freely adapted from the novels even when permission had not been sought, as was R. L. Stevenson's novella, *Dr. Jekyll and Mr. Hyde* – an endlessly adaptable story that has echoes in Oscar Wilde's *The Picture of Dorian Gray*. Horror movies of these classic texts have been constantly made and remade, as well as the stories of M. R. James, H. P. Lovecraft, Edgar Allan Poe, Clive Barker and the endlessly prolific Stephen King.

Ted Tally, who adapted Thomas Harris's novel *The Silence of the Lambs* for the screen, was on board from the beginning. 'As soon as I read it I knew it would make a great film. I assumed that somebody like Bo Goldman [*One Flew Over the Cuckoo's Nest, Scent of a Woman*] was already writing the screenplay'.[68] He discovered, however, that the screenplay hadn't been assigned. 'At that time, Gene Hackman was going to star and direct it, so I met with him and got him to agree to let me do the screenplay.' (Ibid)[69] As it ended up, Hackman dropped out of the project and then Jonathan Demme was brought on board by Orion to direct. Demme met Tally and they agreed to work together. There were other potential issues. Writing the screenplay of a novel when the author is still alive can prove difficult, if not explosive. In the same interview, Syd Field asks Ted Tally if Thomas Harris had read the screenplay.

'No', he replied. 'Tom pretty much keeps a distance from Hollywood. Since he was already working on another book, he didn't want our vision of this thing rattling around in his head. He was extremely supportive and very

---

[68] Field 2005.
[69] Ibid.

sweet; he even volunteered to open up his files for me, but I preferred to do it just on my own. And I think he was very happy with that.' What did he think of the film? 'I don't think he's seen it to this day.'[70]

Adaptation is not always a marriage made in heaven. Stephen King disliked intensely what Stanley Kubrick did to *The Shining*:

> I'd admired Kubrick for a long time and had great expectations for the project, but I was deeply disappointed in the end result ... Kubrick just couldn't grasp the sheer inhuman evil of The Overlook Hotel. So he looked, instead, for evil in the characters and made the film into a domestic tragedy with only vaguely supernatural overtones. That was the basic flaw: because he couldn't believe, he couldn't make the film believable to others.[71]

King was also unhappy with Jack Nicholson's performance – he wanted it to be clear that Jack Torrance wasn't crazy until he got to the hotel, and he felt that Nicholson made the character unsettling from the start. With director Mick Garris, King ended up working on another version of *The Shining,* which aired on ABC in 1997 as a TV mini-series. At over four and half hours it becomes clear why the author isn't always the right person to adapt their novel.

A problem is in being too close to the source material. In order to make a movie, the story has to be deconstructed. The backstory and inner workings of the principal characters must be known but not shown, or else we end up with clumsy backstory, flashbacks and overwrought exposition. The advantage of prose is that it allows the exploration of the inner thoughts, and attempting to do this in a movie rarely works. One solution is via voiceover, but this is distancing to the audience, unless it is a bookending device to introduce a story. Otherwise, the rubric of all movies is always show not tell.

King has agreed that his elephantine writing is a problem, but Hollywood has made a lot of capital out of his short stories (*Stand by Me*, *The Mist*, *1408*, *The Shawshank Redemption*, etc.). It is easier to adapt a shorter piece, not merely as there is less of it (allowing the screenwriter freer rein) but because there are often only two acts. In a short story we are thrown in at the point of catalyst even if we do not at first realize it – and from there we proceed to denouement. Many of H. P. Lovecraft's finest prose pieces barely reached a thousand words – for example *The Outsider* or *Dagon*, which, combined with *The Shadow over Innsmouth*, formed the basis for the sopping wet Spanish horror *Dagon* (Gordon 2001), but there is enough shocking imagery in the 'Cthulhu Leviathan' for several features.

---

[70] Ibid.
[71] Ibid.

Author as source

John Ajvide Lindqvist's vampire tale, *Let the Right One In*, was published in 2004. Later that same year, John Nordling, a producer at EFTI, contacted Lindqvist's publisher for the rights to the novel. He was not the first to see the potential for a movie. The publishers told him he was 48th on the list. Undeterred, Nordling called Lindqvist and they found that they shared a common vision. Once director Thomas Alfredson had read the novel, he too came on board. Unusually, Lindqvist was allowed to write the screenplay, having insisted on it. Alfredson was initially unsure of this decision, but found the end result satisfying. Many of the minor characters and events from the book were removed and its focus directed primarily on the love story between the two children. In particular, many aspects of the character Hakan (Eli's 'father/keeper'), which had included his being a paedophile, were removed, and their relationship was left open to interpretation. Alfredson felt the film could not deal with such a serious issue as paedophilia and that to include it would distract from the story of the children and their relationship. For Alfredson it was this and the aspect of bullying that interested him. 'It's very hard and very down-to-earth, unsentimental ... I had some periods when I grew up when I had hard times in school. ...so it really shook me.'[72]

The novel presents Eli as an androgynous boy, castrated centuries before by a sadistic vampire nobleman. The film handles the issue of Eli's gender ambiguously: a brief scene in which Eli changes into a dress offers a glimpse of a suggestive scar but has no elaboration or explicitness. When Oskar asks Eli to be his girlfriend, Eli tells him 'I'm not a girl', although a female actress plays the part of Eli. In the original screenplay there were flashback scenes to explain Eli's past, but Alfredson cut these scenes. In the end, Lindqvist admitted, Alfredson 'didn't do it the way I wanted in every respect. He could obviously never do that. The film is his creative process.'[73]

The understanding that adaptation is a team game is essential for the writer. A film may be the vision of a director but, as Jane Goldman says in her interview at the end of this chapter (see p. 127), 'films are such a collaborative venture.'

Let the Right One In was hugely successful, winning several awards, including Gothenburg Film Festival's Nordic Film Prize and The Tribeca Film Festival's Best Narrative Feature, 2008. At Tribeca, the film attracted the interest of Hammer Studios which was looking to re-launch. Alfredson expressed reservations: 'Remakes should be made of movies that aren't very good, that gives you the

---

[72] Interview, Los Angeles *Times*, 14 March 2009.
[73] Ibid.

chance to fix whatever has gone wrong.' He was also worried that the film would be made too mainstream. *Cloverfield* director Matt Reeves was signed-on to write and direct the new version. Lindqvist's reaction was more positive. He had heard that Reeves would make a new film based on the book, not on the Swedish film.

Reeves' version moved further away from the book than the original film. The protagonist's names were changed to Owen and Abby (thus removing any ambiguity regarding the gender of the Eli character) and the setting was moved from a Stockholm suburb to Los Alamos, a small town in New Mexico. Reeves was asked by the studio to change the ages of the characters, but he refused. Reeves admitted to keeping pretty close to the original film, although he forbade the actors from watching the film beforehand, so they could make their own version. He stated that 'There are things that [Lindqvist] adapted so brilliantly in the movie and I borrowed from that because I thought he did a great adaptation. But there are some things that hopefully don't detract and fit into the context of the story. It's a mixture of details from the book, the original film and things that grew out of adapting it.'[74] Lindqvist's response was enthusiastic. He praised both films, saying: 'I might just be the luckiest writer alive. To have not only one, but two excellent versions of my debut novel done for the screen feels unreal ... *Let the Right One In* is a great Swedish movie. *Let Me In* is a great America movie. There are notable similarities and the spirit of Tomas Alfredson is present. But *Let Me In* puts the emotional pressure in different places and stands firmly on its own legs. Like the Swedish movie, it made me cry, but not at the same points. *Let Me In* is a dark and violent love story, a beautiful and respectful rendering of my novel, for which I am grateful.'[75]

Not all authors are given the opportunity to participate in the adaptation of their work, but what is interesting about the twin versions of Lindqvist's book is how the clues in their different interpretations are there right in the titles.

'There is a key passage in the book 'Let the Right One In' which Lindqvist wanted included and that Alfredson had misgivings about. The title alludes to the tradition that a vampire cannot enter your home unless he or she is invited in. Alfredson and Lindqvist shape this trope into something else: an expression of love and commitment. Eli loves Oskar, but must be 'invited in' to his life. When Oskar refuses ritually to invite Eli over the threshold of his mother's flat, her emotional pain expresses itself horribly in bleeding from her eyes, ears and pores: a haemophilia of rejection.'[76] The film links us directly with that darker side

---

[74] Ibid.
[75] http://moviesblog.mtv.com/2010/10/04/let-me-in-let-the-right-one-in-john-lindqvist-note-matt-reeves/
[76] http://www.guardian.co.uk/film/2009/apr/10/let-the-right-one-in-vampires-film-review/

of human emotion and vampirism. Eli is bound by rules, and to breach them causes physical pain. It is reflective of the film as a whole. The Swedish version is more visceral than Reeves's.

Let Me In is more of a request instead of a sentence that invites retribution. It also implies that the request is more than mere permission to enter a room. It is an emotional plea – let me into your life. It plays towards the love story element of the book in a more direct way. There is no ambiguity or sense of androgyny in Reeves's vision of the text. Eli is represented as a girl, and was played by the same actress who starred in *Kick-Ass*, cast because 'she showed how beautifully vulnerable she could be, and how tough she could be.[77] She is a tomboy but still definitely a girl. Perhaps it was felt that American audiences would not respond favourably to sexual ambiguity, particularly in children. As it turned out, despite the film having such great credentials and the blessing of the makers of the original and its author, it didn't do so well at the box office, and was fifth amongst the 10 lowest grossing releases of 2010.

Real life as source

Though the majority of horror adaptations have come from novels or short stories, there are several that have been influenced by real life/true crime stories. Historically, the first serial killer to create publicity was London's Jack the Ripper who, over the summer and autumn of 1888, killed 12 women, disembowelling most of them. His spree lasted but a few months, and by November no more was heard of his gruesome activities. His identity remains a mystery and has given rise to much speculation and many adaptations of the tale (*From Hell*: Hughes 2001).

Wisconsin-born Ed Gein lived on a farm with his mother. A short while after she died, Bernice Worden, a local hardware store owner, disappeared. Suspecting Gein's involvement, police searched his property and found her decapitated body in the shed. She had been hung upside down like a deer with her wrists tied and a crossbar at her ankles. On searching Gein's home the police later discovered:

- Four noses
- Whole human bones and bone fragments
- Nine masks made of human skin

---

[77] http://entertainment.ie/movie/feature/Interview-with-Let-Me-In-director-Matt-Reeves/202/937.htm/

- Bowls made from human skulls
- Ten female heads with the tops of the skulls sawn off
- Chairs covered with human skin
- Mary Hogan's head in a paper bag (a woman he killed in 1954)
- Bernice Worden's head in a sack
- Nine vulvae in a shoe box
- A belt made from human nipples
- Skulls on the bedpost
- A pair of lips on a string for the window shade
- A lampshade made from the skin of a human face.

These activities and Gein's somewhat extreme psychopathology acted as a blueprint for *Psycho*, *The Texas Chain Saw Massacre* and *Silence of the Lambs*, as well as providing the template for many others. Gein was the go-to guy for the serial killer despite the mass murder of others such as 'Killer clown' John Wayne Gacy, Charles Manson, Jeffrey Dahmer, Ted Bundy, Albert Fish and Dennis Rader (the BTK Killer).

The novel *Psycho* by Robert Bloch (1959) was based on the events of the case. Bloch was living 35 miles away when Gein was arrested in Plainfield. 'Familiar with the Gein case but not the specific details, Bloch began writing', wrote Paula Guran in 1999,[78] reviewing Bloch's book *Behind the Bates Motel*, 'with "the notion that the man next door may be a monster unsuspected even in the gossip-ridden microcosm of small-town life." Bloch was surprised years later when he "discovered how closely the imaginary character [he'd] created resembled the real Ed Gein both in overt act and apparent motivation."'

For this, Bloch won the prestigious SF Hugo award in 1959. He had in fact written an earlier short story involving split personalities, *The Real Bad Friend*, which appeared in the February 1957 and foreshadowed his 1959 novel, *Psycho*.

Norman Bates was loosely based on two people. First Gein, about whom Bloch later wrote a fictionalized account, *The Shambles of Ed Gein*. Several people, including Noel Carter (wife of SF writer Lin Carter) and Chris Steinbrunner, and allegedly Bloch himself, have suggested that Bates was based on Calvin

---

[78] http://www.darkecho.com/darkecho/horroronline/bloch.html

Beck, publisher of *Castle of Frankenstein*.[79,80] Bloch's novel is one of the first examples of modern urban horror, relying on interior psychology rather than the supernatural. Hitchcock's film was based on the novel, but later films in the *Psycho* series bore no relation to Bloch's sequels. Indeed, his proposed script for the film *Psycho II* was rejected by the studio.

Bloch originally wrote for the Science Fiction magazine *Amazing Stories* (as did H. P. Lovecraft), and went on to contribute to various TV series including *Alfred Hitchcock Presents*, *Star Trek* and *Tales of the Unexpected*, as well as other movies such as the British portmanteau, *Asylum* (Roy Ward Baker 1972) and the book adaptation of the *Twilight Zone* movie. He is a writer well worth seeking out.

When seeing an adaptation of a novel or play, you should not expect a replica. 'It wasn't like the book' is a phrase often heard by moviegoers. It shouldn't be like the book. It should be different; sometimes this means the ending will change, or a character's narrative thrust will be highlighted or diminished. Entire story threads and subplots may disappear in the interest, not of linear plotting, but of clarity in the story spine. The integrity of the story must remain intact while at the same time being of a reasonable length. In 1924 Erich von Stroheim attempted a literal adaptation of the novel *McTeague* by Frank Norris, and made the film *Greed*, which was over 16 hours long. It was cut to eight hours and then four. Finally the studio cut the film to two hours and the result was incoherent and unwatchable. You have to murder your darlings.

Adaptation is a particular art form. To translate a novel, short story, play or real-life event into cinematic form is a complicated process. A translation is what it is – a different form with different rules, perceptions and audience expectations. In cinema the experience is passive, wherein the narrative presented is not one you can affect. You can react but you cannot, as in watching a DVD, pause or re-shuffle back to an earlier chapter. Some younger audiences do not appreciate this, being used to interactive games where they are asked to participate. A book, however, is participatory. You may approach it from any line or chapter, at any time that suits you. You can ruin the ending by reading it first. You can interpret the characters' inner emotions in your own way, and so too can you imagine the physicality of character and location as best suits you. Adapting it requires a tightrope walk as you transpose one form to another. The screenplay

---

[79] Bloch's basing the character of Norman Bates on Ed Gein is discussed in the documentary 'Ed Gein: The Ghoul of Plainfield', which can be found on Disc 2 of the DVD release of *The Texas Chainsaw Massacre* (2003).

[80] *Castle of Frankenstein* was an American horror, science fiction and fantasy film magazine, distributed by Kable News and published in New Jersey from 1962 to 1975 by Calvin Thomas Beck's Gothic Castle Publishing Company.

adaptation is in effect an original screenplay, neither a poor relation nor an easy option for the writer.

On occasion, an author allows his work to be adapted and then carps on about the result. Author Bret Easton Ellis believed that *American Psycho* should never have happened, reportedly stating that it was a book he did not think needed to be turned into a movie. It was conceived as a literary work, with an unreliable narrator at the centre; Ellis was unhappy because the medium of film demands answers and he wanted it left open. *American Psycho* (Harron 2000) deals with a nominal psychopath and his torture and killing of hookers and his co-workers. It both represents the conflict of desires of the *Id* and *Ego* and is a satire on 1980s/1990s corporate America, something absent from the book. Christian Bale, an actor who specializes in playing characters with a duality of purpose, took the lead role of Patrick Bateman, delivering a nuanced performance of a character who does not even believe in himself as 'real', as witnessed in his self destruction. It is of course our old friend(s) Jekyll and Hyde all over again, and screenwriters Mary Harron (who also directed) and Guinevere Turner produced a finely wrought script.

Bateman is emasculated by workmate Paul, who mistakes him for another worker, Marcus. Subsequently inviting Paul for dinner, Bateman later kills him with an axe. He breaks into Paul's apartment and makes out that Paul has gone to London. He proceeds to slash his way through hookers and homeless, and is barely concerned when a police detective (Willem Defoe) interviews him about Paul's whereabouts. Later, as his world begins to implode, he confesses all to co-workers, but is mistaken for another man, Davies. His friends do not even believe that he is Patrick Bateman and, as the construct tumbles, his Hyde and Jekyll finally come together. However, this madness passes. There is no retribution and no sign of the bodies. The apartment is as whitewashed as his sins. Bateman is utterly amoral. He gets away with it, regains his former status and laments that his confession meant nothing. It is a modern take on the old story of man's duality, placed in a corporate environment: an example of an adaptation that plays to all the strengths of the source material without losing the core values.

Interview with Jane Goldman, screenwriter, producer and author. Screenplay adaptation of *Woman in Black* (Watkins 2012)

How much did you know about writing horror when you first wrote the script? Was it simply from watching a lot or from a deeper analysis?

Having been a horror enthusiast since childhood, I'd read a fair few books on the milestones and conventions of horror cinema, as well as Stephen King's excellent 'Danse Macabre', which looks at the anatomy of horror and its place in storytelling generally, and is a really terrific read. But in terms of the practical business of writing horror, I'd also been to a couple of horror-specific writing seminars over the years – one given by Robert McKee and another one in London. Funnily enough, it was at the latter that I met the producer who ended up approaching me, years later, about adapting *The Woman in Black*, having recalled that I had an interest in writing horror.

How long did it take you to write the early draft(s)?

I can never recall exactly how long these things take, because one stage tends to organically roll into the next. In this case, as I usually do, I began by making a detailed outline, which took a couple of weeks, before getting started on a first draft, which usually takes four to six weeks to complete. Then I usually spend a couple of weeks editing and polishing before formally turning the draft over to the director/producers. In this case, it was the producers, as we didn't yet have a director on board.

I made a set of revisions for the producers, and then when James Watkins, the director, came on board, I did another set of revisions. I enjoyed that set very much, as James and I have a very similar approach, and we were able to pare things back that I had added at the behest of the producers; things that wouldn't necessarily have been my first choice creatively. Then I attended rehearsals and did another polish afterwards to reflect notes that James and I had made during that process. Polishing and revising tends to continue throughout pre-production, prompted by ideas and logistics (and sometimes budget!) and *The Woman in Black* was no exception.

Were there changes required due to logistics? How closely did you work with the director?

A few minor ones during pre-production – usually to do with the geography of a specific location – but none I can recall that were last-minute. The main changes I can think of, from script to screen, were some details of the action beats in the final scene, which were simplified during the shoot due to various logistical issues. But those were creative decisions made by James on the night that scene was shot, rather than being changes made preemptively to the script.

James and I worked together closely as soon as he came on board. We talked a lot about character and tone, and were always very much on the same page, which was great. Before James came along, there had been some interest from some of the producers in exploring the idea of a more fleshed-out backstory for Jennet (The Woman in Black), conveyed in a number of flashback scenes, as well as a slightly different motivation. I am always happy to explore different approaches, but wasn't wild about the idea. James felt the same way – he and I were both keen to keep the storytelling immediate and focused on Arthur and the intimacy and claustrophobia of staying on him, and his experiences, in the present.

How satisfied overall are you by your work?

I think there are always bits of my work that I'm satisfied with, and bits that I'm less satisfied with. But I think that films are such a collaborative venture that, as part of the team behind the camera, you'd have to be pretty egotistical to find it hard to watch! That's several hundred people's work up there!

When re-watching a film I've worked on, the things I love most and hate most are usually someone else's work, rather than my own. That said, my least favourite moments are usually things that I feel I could have improved upon if I'd had the chance – an actor's ad-lib that was too on-the-nose, or a bland, expository line of dialogue that got thrown in during an ADR[81] session. Whereas my favourite moments are always the things that I can't do – an actor's powerful performance, a director's beautiful shot, the moment that a wonderful bit of editing or score affects you viscerally, a stunningly choreographed action sequence, a cool stunt, a brilliantly executed effect.

---

[81] ADR = Additional Dialogue Recording.

When you write a new script, do you think about story first or visuals?

I think about story first. Story and character. Obviously visuals are an intrinsic part of that thought process, but in film they're very much the director's domain, so, as a writer, you'd be crazy to get too attached to your own visual ideas. You want to inspire the director and create an authentic world and sketch a picture as you're telling your story, but I think most directors really appreciate a writer who properly understands where his or her domain ends and the director's begins. It's all about the gaps you leave.

How has adapting someone else's work informed your own?

The act of taking something apart and putting it back together is always educational, in terms of learning how things work. (And why some things work more reliably and effectively than others.) Adapting other people's work has certainly fine-tuned my understanding of structure and pacing, not just in terms of the distinctions between a film and, say, a novel, but also the unique fluctuations in rhythm between a novel and a novella, or a short story, or a play, or a single issue of a comic book or a multiple-volume comic book story arc.

Who are your favourite horror movies writers/directors?

I always find it very hard to name favourite writers and directors because, by definition, you find yourself restricted to people who have a large and consistent body of work. There are all the obvious directors who most fans of the genre have love and respect for, not only for their body of work but for the way they changed the landscape. So the usual – Romero, Carpenter, Craven, Landis, Argento, Cronenberg. *The Shining* is in my top three favourite movies, so I guess I would have to add Kubrick. Takashi Miike and Hideo Nakata are another two obvious ones. Juan Antonio Bayona's work on *El Orfanato* was very beguiling and Sergio Sanchez's screenplay for it was incredible – the emotion, the pacing, the intricacy of the set-ups and pay-offs, that gut-punch reveal.

Although William Peter Blatty would more likely be found on someone's list of favourite writers rather than directors, I actually think that one of the most sublimely paced and directed little set-pieces in any horror film is the hospital nurse-station sequence in *The Exorcist Three*. It's just an incredibly effective bit of horror cinema, it delights me every time.

What advice would you give to the novice screenwriter?
Read as many scripts as you can. Read books on screenwriting. Read books on any kind of writing. Deconstruct scripts you think are brilliant, scene by scene, moment by moment, and figure out what makes them tick. Learn your craft. The artistry part is up to you, but don't underestimate the value of a strong technical foundation. And of course, write. A lot. And then write some more! Blog, write fan-fiction, keep a journal – whatever floats your boat and keeps you writing. You can obviously find people who are the exception to the 10,000 hours rule (the concept of the minimum amount of practice it takes to master any skill), but I think there's a great deal of truth to it, and hoping that you're the exception is likely to be a lot less productive than just putting the hours in.

Chapter 11
Cross-Genre

Genre blending has had varying results in horror, barring the successful vampire romance of the 'Twilight' series. The TV series *Buffy* and *Angel* were better suited to this, as their act and story arc structures are different to the 95-minute movie, in which all must be resolved.

Currently, the undead/vampire strain of horror is a deep vein. Anne Rice's *Interview with the Vampire*[82] was a short story and then a gothic novel. Once transposed by Neil Jordan (1994) it became, according to IMDB, a drama/ fantasy. Both story and film looked into the torment of being undead, and focused on the vampire's desire for eventual release. The idea of a child vampire expanded the mythology; an idea later explored further in Lundquist's *Let the Right One In* (Alfredson 2008). Since Bram Stoker's introduction, the vampire myth has proven highly flexible and seems able to suck up both comedy and drama in equal measure.

The general undead, in the form of zombies, has been the (un)friendly face of horror for nigh on a decade, and since every permutation has had the brains sucked from it, there is currently a reliance on comedy, with such paltry offerings as *Zombie Land* (Fleisher 2009), *Wasting Away* (Kohnen 2007), *Ozombie* (Lyde 2012) amongst others. As *Shaun Of The Dead* (Wright 2004) has proven, the lumbering aspect of the zombie has its funny side, and the genres of horror and comedy are quite compatible. They both rely on a suspension of disbelief and the need to provoke a visceral reaction – shock in horror and laughter in comedy: tension and release. Alfred Hitchcock once said that comedy and horror are Siamese twin genres, joined at the nervous laugh.

It is hard to get the balance right. If you set your stall out with too much comedy from the start (The Abbot and Costello way), it will undermine the foundations of story or sympathy. If the cast is continually spouting 'wisecracks' (cheap

---

[82] In Anne Rice, *The Vampire Chronicles*. New York: Alfred A. Knopf, 1976.

one-liners), this will only raise groans. If the monster is seen early and starts making 'jokes'. this veers off into camp. The feeling of dread and the sequence of events leading to the terror part of a horror movie must be constructed as in any other horror film, with any humour arising out of character and situation, as in a good sitcom. Use irony by all means, but one self-conscious wink-to-the-crowd breaks the fourth wall and becomes hammy. References to pop culture rarely help, as they will link your project to a specific time and place and will date your work. Comedy does not travel well outside of geographical and cultural boundaries, so be aware of the dichotomy between this and the more universal scope of the horror movie.

Parody can work, as in the first of the *Scary Movie* series (Kevin Williamson's original title for his *Scream* franchise). However, as in the *Airplane* series (1980), once you have used a ton of visual and verbal gags it again starts to rely on the law of diminishing returns, as with *Saturday the 14th* (Cohen 1981), *Repossessed* (Logan 1990) and *Dracula: Dead and Loving It* (Brooks 1995). Parody works when you are seeing for the first time the death of a particular format and are able to skewer its tired tropes. It is affectionate, because it is reliant on a love of that form, as with Mel Brooks's enduringly funny *Young Frankenstein* (1974) which spoofed the Universal 1931 original and its sequels.

Brooks shot in black and white, using the same sets and sound stages. He had a period score written and employed the filmic techniques of the era, such as iris outs, wipes and fades to black. The original idea came from its star, Gene Wilder, who, on the set of *Blazing Saddles* (Brooks 1974), suggested they made a Frankenstein movie. Brooks dismissed the idea as tired, but Wilder added, 'What if the grandson of Dr. Frankenstein wanted nothing to do with the family whatsoever. He was ashamed of these wackoes.'[83] What is so perfect about *Young Frankenstein* is that it is played straight, with the characters (aside from Marty Feldman's Igor) unaware that they are in a movie or comedic situation, no matter how farcical it gets. We laugh because they cannot see their predicament. The film is recognized as one of the great comedies and went on to inspire Aerosmith's 'Walk this Way', as well as a musical.

If parody is not enough, then try satire, which pokes fun at institutions, be they social, political, military, medical or academic. The zombie is a handy metaphor for the blindness of the masses being controlled by base desires or corrupt overlords. It has been claimed that *Hostel* (Roth 2005) is a critique of American foreign policy,[84] but perhaps Romero's sequels are better examples,

---

[83] Irene Lacher, 'The Sunday Conversation: Mel Brooks on his "Young Frankenstein" musical'. *Los Angeles Times*, August 1, 2010.
[84] In an interview, Roth claims it came out of stories he'd read about American businessmen paying

with *Dawn of the Dead*'s comments on consumerism (though Romero remains enigmatic) or *28 Days Later*'s (Boyle 2002) attack on the military. *Shaun of the Dead* (Wright 2004) spears our self-obsessed culture, where we are so bound up by our petty concerns that we do not notice the undead around us. Satire comes as a by-product of what you do, and if you have a big chip on your shoulder about an issue then remember Sam Goldwyn's maxim: 'If you want to send a message – use Western Union'.

Another way to go is gross-out or splatstick, which is the horror fans' term for slapstick involving blood, gore and intestines. Throw enough of these at the screen and we move beyond the stage of revulsion and disgust to laughter. It is Grand Guignol, the ballet of blood. David Cronenberg said, 'We all need periodic releases from the tyranny of good taste',[85] and if you don't believe him, watch his movies. This kind of comic horror deals with the abject. Because we do not believe our eyes, there is a cognitive failure at the sheer excess. If this were real life, we would be traumatized, but because it is fiction our laughter reflex cuts in to shut it down. Laughter is a form of social containment, an override, a steam release on a pressure cooker. As horror seeks to find the line on what is acceptable, so does comedy. They both, in their way, regulate and release our tensions.

If we can face the torrent of blood and guts and advancing chainsaws, then we are purged and recalibrated. Great examples of gore gone insane are Peter Jackson's *Braindead* (1992), *Slither* (Gunn 2006) with Michael Rooker's transformation and some great one-liners, and *Tokyo Gore Police* (Nishimuru 2008) with its crocodile vagina. These are played with a light touch, often focusing on the invasions to the body and its transformations, unlike the body horror of David Cronenberg, which is rarely played for laughs.

An American Werewolf in London (Landis 1981) is perhaps the perfect blend of comedy and horror, wherein a miserable hiking trip leads David Kessler and Jack Goodman to a Yorkshire pub. Duly warned of howling beasts, they fail to keep to the path, with the result that Jack is slaughtered and David is bitten. On his recovery, aided by saintly Nurse Price, David begins to have bizarre nightmares and undergoes nocturnal carnivorous wanderings as he starts to mutate.

Written as a cold synopsis, this is straight horror. The comedy comes in the use of music to lighten the mood (a non-verbal nod to the audience), and in the reappearance of his decomposing best friend, Jack. Griffin Dunne's sarcastic use of deadpan comedy lifts the whole ship. Even dead he remains jocular, and the mismatch creates the humour – that and the gallows humour of the victims. There is also some broad comedy when David awakens in London Zoo, naked

---

to shoot poor people in Thailand whose families needed the money. http://www.timeout.com/film/news/1007/hostel-eli-roth-q-a.html/

[85] Asma 2009.

(as he would be, in his post-lupine state), and tries to make his way back to nurse Alex's apartment, protecting his modesty with a red balloon and the theft of a woman's coat. Here, the comedy mind has thought deeply into the practical aspects of what happens if you were to become a werewolf. It is almost a stand-up routine played out as cinema.

For the writer using humour, it is important to see things afresh or from oblique angles: for example, think of the serial killer's den. There is nearly always a pit or a basement fitted out for torture. Are we assuming that all serial murderers are a dab hand at home construction? Certainly, Joseph Fritzl was (did his wife not suspect anything as he altered their house to accommodate all the new offspring?), but your average psychopath has lots to do: putting things in jars, keeping mad diaries and stalking fresh kills. He's going to have to get a builder in ... and they are going to ask questions.

Horror and comedy go way back (See *Bride of Frankenstein*: Whale 1935) to the EC Comics, founded in 1944 (by Max Gaines) in which the Crypt Keeper (*Tales from The Crypt* TV series, 1989–96) was always mocking with puns and deadly jokes. James Whale used a dollop of mordant wit in *The Old Dark House* (1932) and *The Invisible Man* (1933). The 1950s science fiction horror cross-overs were patently daft, especially in their titles, among them the *Attack of the Giant Leeches* (Kowalski 1959), *Attack of the Fifty Foot Woman* (Nathan Juran 1958), *Zombies of the Stratosphere* (Brannon 1952), and *I Married a Monster from Outer Space* (Fowler Jr. 1958).

Writer/director/producers Roger Corman (*Attack of the Crab Monsters*: 1957) and William Castle (*The Tingler*: 1959) had a field day. The unintentionally hilarious *Plan 9 from Outer Space* got made on a very low budget and the biopic (*Ed Wood*: Burton 1994) is hilarious. There are others too who have made a career crossing horror and comedy, including Joe Dante (*Gremlins*: 1984) and Sam Raimi with the 'Evil Dead' (1981) series.

After the comedy blend, there is always the horror musical, whose principal proponents are *The Little Shop of Horrors* (Corman 1960), remade by Frank Oz in 1986, and 'The Rocky Horror Show' (musical by Richard O'Brien 1973) remade as *The Rocky Horror Picture Show* (Sharman 1975). The latter has a huge fan base and film screenings are a cult event involving a lot of dressing up, transvestism and mess. Tim Burton's atmospheric *Sweeney Todd: The Demon Barber of Fleet Street* (2007), based on the Stephen Sondheim musical, fared less well as a movie, recouping only $9.3 million on a $50 million budget to date (Carolyn p. 155). It lacks the campness of the first two, despite stalwart comedy performances by Burton muse Helena Bonham Carter and Sacha Baron Cohen. Perhaps its time will come. The musical's natural home is perhaps the theatre, but from there it will often adapt and grow to become quite the monster.

Another crossover is that of psychological thriller and horror. Alfred's Hitchcock's career was based on dark psychology, starting with his early silent film *The Lodger* (1927), a story about Jack the Ripper. He went on to make *Rear Window* (1954) and *Vertigo* (1958), but it is only *Psycho* that tips over into pure horror. The key is the unknown, unfathomable actions of Norman Bates, the motiveless killing that weds us to the horror genre. The psychopath kills on compulsion. There is often rape, but this is not the prime motivator; there is no direct desire for revenge, or if there is it is insanely disproportionate. There is no need for fiscal gain (see how the money is discarded). It is not even a *crime passionel*, committed in the heat of the moment. It is cold, calculated slaughter, which in the real world accounts for a tiny proportion of murders.

If you are writing a movie in which there are multiple killings it is to motive you must look in order to define genre. Some are borderline, such as *Se7en* (Fincher 1995) described on IMDB as a 'thriller with horror and neo-noir elements'. Containing elements of *The Vanishing* (Sluizer 1988) and Michael Mann's *Manhunter* (1986), Fincher's bravura opening credits introduce much of what is now mandatory for the serial killer – the diaries with cut-out religious pictures and words, bits of stitching, defaced photographs, things in jars, deafening thrash metal and an antagonist who is barely there at all, a John Doe, a non-person.

Se7en focuses on Detectives Somerset and Mills as they try to piece together the killer's modus operandi, unaware that they too are part of the game. Horror tends not to focus on police procedure, and officers of the law or private eyes and the like are usually sidelined. Horror abhors the rational, the pedantic, the explainable. It deals in transgression, supernatural events: crimes against humanity not those of the statute book.

The final cross-genre link is with science fiction, a genre which began in 1516 with Thomas More's satirical novel *Utopia*, which set up the notion of utopian and dystopian futures. Francis Bacon's *New Atlantis* (1628) created the idea of the dangers of scientific experiment, hence the trope of bad science. These two, plus the idea of alien invasion, are what make up modern science fiction. The timeline goes from pre-nineteenth-century travel and fantasy literature (Jonathan Swift's *Gulliver's Travels*) to nineteenth-century reactions to the Industrial Revolution, then a view of scientific enlightenment and, finally, a late twentieth-century modernist view of the post-holocaust age, including feminist futures and cyberpunk/steampunk.

The Golden Age of science fiction pulp writing was in the 1930s, which is where Asimov and Lovecraft intersect. The pulp magazine *Amazing Stories*, launched in 1926, featured works by H. G. Wells and Jules Verne, and reprints of Edgar Allen Poe, and continued for a further 80 years. The second, or Silver Age, was in the 1950s (Ray Bradbury, Robert Heinlein, Arthur C. Clarke). It was

Forrest J. Ackerman who first coined the term Science Fiction, at UCLA in 1954. He later went on to produce the cult magazine *Famous Monsters of Filmland*, which became a bible for horror fans. Many, if not all, of the 1950s B movies were science fiction/horror blends, featuring malevolent aliens bent on our destruction, or communist infiltration metaphors, as in the *Invasion of the Body Snatchers* (Siegal 1956).[86] It was either this or giant irradiated monster insects, animals and women. All have been remade – *The Blob* by Chuck Russell in 1988, *The Fly* by David Cronenberg (1985) and *The Thing* by John Carpenter in 1982 – despite the shifts in our environmental and geo-political concerns.

Putting aside the bad science aspect of Baron Frankenstein, the most significant crossover in the SF/horror canon is Dan O'Bannon and Ridley Scott's *Alien* (1979), a haunted house/monster movie in space. The alien is a virus that takes no prisoners, a parasite that will be absorbed by, and then destroy, its host. The movie bears startling resemblances to early 1950s sci-fi movie *It! The Terror from beyond Space* (Cahn 1958) where a blood-drinking alien hides in the airshaft of a spaceship. O'Bannon has claimed inspiration from Christian Nyby's *The Thing from Another World* (1951), which concerns a blood-drinking vegetable alien.

Alien raises no scientific, technological or ontological argument, not does it seek to examine the condition of the human race, as does the 'pure' science of Stanley Kubrick and Arthur C. Clarke's *2001* (1968) or Tarkovsky's *Solaris* (1972). It is a killing machine, and the ride is one of pure terror. A *Starburst* magazine reviewer said that, 'as a science fiction film it's seriously flawed, but as a horror movie it works perfectly'. In classic stalk and slash mode Ripley, our Final Girl, tells everyone to stick together – and the first thing they do is separate. There is a rich sexual subject to the movie, which is full of birth imagery, wombs and amniotic fluid, also male–female gender issues, as the alien has both male and female genitals and invades the body regardless of sex. According to Ash, the ship's robot, it is 'a perfect organism, its structural perfection matched only by its hostility'. It is remorseless, with no conscience or morality – a trait that could also apply to Ash or to Ripley. The sequels explored the idea of motherhood in greater detail and the gender dysmorphia is evident in Scott's (2012) *Prometheus*, thus returning us once again to *Frankenstein*. *Alien* was followed by a rash of inferior imitations such as *Inseminiod* (Norman J. Warren 1981; *Horror Planet* in the US), *Possession* (Zulawski 1981), *Predator* (John McTiernan 1987) and *Species* (Donaldson 1995). However, as a monster-chases-girl story

---

[86]Subsequently remade by Philip Kaugman in1978, then again in 1993 as *Bodysnatchers* (Ferrara) and again as *Invasion* (Hirschbiegel 2007).

in space, it has yet to be bettered, and the face-hugger remains one of horror's most enduring images. I still think of it each time I eat breakfast.

For horror to have a science fiction element it will be either futuristic or involve evil alien life forms, germs or parasites. The current crop of contagion-based movies has science elements, but they tend to favour the horror route of stamp-it-out-and kill-it, rather than 'let's see what happens when things mutate'. David Cronenberg takes bad science to extremes, but it is worth looking out the work of Vincenzo Natali, whose *Cube* (1997) is a psychological horror–science fiction crossover and a serious cult classic. It was reportedly influenced by a 'Twilight Zone' episode, *Five Characters in Search of an Exit*, written by its creator Rod Serling. Vincenzo Natali's sophomore film, *Splice* (2009), is a superb genetically modified Frankenstein story. Neill Blomkamp's (2009) *District 9* was also influenced by *Alien* and its progeny. Although more SF than horror, it is a brilliant political metaphor for the former apartheid situation in South Africa.

What horror and science fiction share is a dystopian view of our future, as well as the ramifications of scientific experimentation. As man continues to play God there will be consequences and, when and if we do contact other life forms, the chances are it's going to be oogy.

Chapter 12
World Markets

For any writer of horror, it is important to have some idea of what has come before and what is current elsewhere in the globe. This and the following chapter are intended to inform the writer of significant past and present developments in the canon of notable movements and particular movies of note.

The horror movie is a worldwide phenomenon, not only for the audiences it attracts but also in the numerous countries that produce them. Whereas its origins are mostly German – *Der Golem* (Boese and Wegener 1920), *Nosferatu* (Murnau 1921), *The Cabinet of Dr. Caligari* (Weine 1920) – it was the USA's Universal Studios which popularized the genre in the 1930s with Todd Browning's *Dracula* and James Whale's *Frankenstein*.

The Hollywood system was by then firmly established; not only was it able to produce films and prints in greater numbers, but also it had access to worldwide distribution. Along with Universal, RKO Studios made *King Kong* (Cooper and Schoedsack 1933) and later Val Lewton's *Cat People* (1942) and *I Walked With a Zombie* (Tourneur 1943). World War Two halted most movie production, except in America, but eventually that too was curtailed, with many US stars, crew and film workers volunteering to go off to war.

After the war, British and Italian cinema managed to put themselves back on their feet, but the boom in science fiction/horror (the 'B' movie) was again American, and Hollywood has to date remained the central locus of most movie-making. Independent producers such as William Castle and Roger Corman worked outside the system, and this, for many of the horror auteurs, became the norm. Come the 1970s, Romero, Raimi and Hooper all launched their careers without studio funding.

In Britain, the hugely successful films of studios Hammer and Amicus ran from the late 1950s until the 1970s. The UK film industry suffered a collapse in the 1980s but was reborn in the 1990s with Film Council and Lottery funding, as well as that of BBC and Channel 4 films plus smaller production companies such Warp X, Ecosse, Hammer and co-productions with Ireland and Europe. Distribution was aided by the sadly now defunct Tartan Films.

Horror film production spread to Mexico with the 'Coffin Joe'[87] series, to Spain with Jess Franco and Italy with Mario Bava and Dario Argento's *Giallo*.

The last three decades of the twentieth century are an American story, from blockbusters such as *The Exorcist* (Friedkin 1973) or *The Omen* (Donner 1976) to the franchise boom of the 1980s, still in evidence with *Scream*, *Saw* and *Final Destination*. As the new millennium arrived, so did *The Blair Witch Project* (Myrick and Sanchez 1999) – the first 'found footage' film to be popularized by viral means, Ruggero Deodato's *Cannibal Holocaust* being its antecedent.

In the new century, Japanese supernatural horror flourished, led by *Ringu* (Nakata 1998), which created a tsunami of J- and K-Horror.[88] Increased funding has led to some startlingly original horror coming from France and Spain in recent years, as well as a growth in Scandinavia and the Low Countries. And let us never forget Canada, the home of David Cronenberg and a powerhouse of moviemaking. Theirs is a cinema that has produced many a sterling genre movie, such as *Pontypool* (McDonald 2009) and *Cube* (Natali 1997).

In today's digital world it is possible to write, direct and produce movies with no geographical boundaries. Budgetary issues are becoming less of a barrier to getting a film produced[89] and, as with music, a movie can be made and edited on a home computer. Guerrilla film-making is on the increase and we are moving towards a situation where anyone with the right tools can make a movie. Whether it is a good movie or not depends on your writing, directing and editing skills, as well as the crew and the actors, but we are at a new frontier. The stumbling block, as ever, is how to get it shown and distributed.

The lure of Hollywood is strong, and once a European writer/director has made his name in his home country, the temptation is to cross the pond. As Hitchcock and James Whale headed for the 'free world', so too did Brit directors Tony and Ridley Scott (*Alien*: 1979) and a slew of writing, acting and directing talent including French directors Pascal Laugier (*Martyrs*: 2008) and Alexandre Aja, whose *Haute tension* (2003) led to him remaking Wes Craven's *The Hills Have Eyes* (2006), then *Mirrors* (2008) and *Piranha 3D* (2010).

Directors such as Michael Hanake simply re-make their own work (*Funny Games*: 1997 and 2007) shot for shot; and others, such as Juane Balaguero

---

[87] Jose Mohica Marins (b. 1936) was a Brazilian exploitation film-maker who made soft-core porn and westerns before reinventing himself as Coffin Joe in 1963's *At Midnight I'll Take Your Soul*. He made many more of the same, and the character subsequently appeared in songs, music videos and comic books, and on TV.

[88] J-Horror: Japanese horror. K-Horror: South Korean horror (also Thailand and Hong Hong).

[89] See *Monsters* (Edwards 2010) and *District 9* (Blomkamp 2009) in Chapter 14, plus the interview with writer Andrew Phelps in Chapter 13 (p. 174).

and Paco Plaza *[REC]*, have seen it remade by Hollywood under new titles (*Quarantine*: John Erick Dowdle 2008, and John Pogue 2011) as have many of the Japanese and Korean horrors. A good idea is a good idea wherever it germinates, and that which attracts an audience in one country, given enough cultural symbiosis, is likely to work around the world.

An international success is as much of a sure thing for US producers as a sequel coming off the back of a home-grown hit. They clamour to imitate the original by relocating the setting to the US, where most cities are interchangeable, and changing the dialogue to (American) English. The majority of the American public is allergic to reading subtitles.

For a director to move to Hollywood, the advantages are myriad. Production values are multiplied, and with a higher budget you can get name actors as well as the opportunity to employ teams of dedicated CGI staff, prosthetics and stunt professionals. You'll have a second unit, possibly even a third, and the catering will be better. Hopefully, the end result of donating your soul to Hollywood is worldwide distribution of your movie and its concomitant increased publicity. This can be an albatross, as Hitchcock found when contracted to spend an entire year publicizing *Psycho*. He was unable to make *The Birds* until 1963.

As a writer, you will earn more, but you will be expendable. The Hollywood system takes no prisoners, relying, as it does, not on the auteur (a luxury afforded only in Europe and Asia) but on teamwork and its input of creative ideas. There are numerous analogies (none of them good or worth repeating) concerning writers, but the most apt is that of the workhorse. You come in, you do your job, and once you are tired you are replaced. This is also true of writing for television, until you can become a show runner or a brand name by launching your own show. If you are an American national, you should be in LA, as it is the home of the industry. If not, you may produce your films elsewhere, but you'll need an agent to get you into Hollywood.

Elsewhere, funding varies greatly, with the most common story being that of a small cabal of producers and funding bodies clubbing together for several years in order to get everything lined up for principal photography. It is a long drawn-out business and many a slip twixt cup and lip is commonplace. France and Spain fund horror, and more is starting to come out of Norway, Sweden and Australia/New Zealand. But there is one thing of which you can be certain: a great film begins with a great idea and a great script.

Watching some of the following international horror movies is, if not mandatory, then highly recommended for your awareness of the form. Many are unfettered by Christian ethics or by same sex or gender codes, as you might find in Hollywood. There are some beguiling takes on the unknown and what deeply frightens or disgusts us. We have chosen but a few personal favourites from each country, and boy was it hard to narrow it down. Be they by writers or writer/directors, they are created by those who add significantly to the canon.

The UK

Britain has a shared language and a special relationship with the US, and many of its actors, writers and directors have worked in both countries. The UK has boasted great horror writers, from Shelley to Stoker, R. L. Stevenson and latterly Clive Barker. It is an old country with plenty of rain, mist and aged properties, all fusing together to create the right conditions for tales of death, haunting and witchcraft. Hammer, Ealing and Amicus studios are discussed elsewhere, but their products were designed for an international market whether it wanted them or not. American censors went to work on Ken Russell's *The Devils* (1970) and Robin Hardy/Peter Schaffer's *The Wicker Man* (1973), which has a tortured history of lost footage (allegedly buried under a motorway), supposed curses and censorship. Despite this, it is a leading example of folk horror, a niche that has not been greatly explored unless one attempts a spurious connection to backwoods horror in its tale of an isolated community gone to ruin. *The Wicker Man* is far more pagan and potent. Hapless virgin Sergeant Howie is a victim of his trenchant beliefs, as much as Lord Summerisle is a villain in his eyes. To the villagers of this lonely Scottish island community, he is its saviour, and the movie is a meditation on belief structures and the nature of sacrifice.

The story concerns the murder of a child, Rowan Morrison, beginning as Howie arrives from the mainland in his seaplane. That he has to be rowed ashore by the locals immediately puts him at a disadvantage, a situation that intensifies as he finds himself adrift amongst villagers with more robust customs than he is used to, including coarse drinking songs, the worshipping of fertility gods in a phallic Maypole ceremony, and Britt Ekland's naked body double slapping her bottom to strange music. The conspiracy of silence is unravelled by the harassed Sergeant, leading to one of cinema's biggest reveals – the terrible secret of the Wicker Man. This unforgettable climax, pitting dogma against dogma, has a resonance rarely achieved in horror, showing mankind at its most deluded. Its most natural successor is Ben Wheatley's *Kill List* (2011), a hit man turned cult shocker that asks many more questions than it answers, and is essential viewing.

Clive Barker's *Hellraiser* (1987), based on his short story 'The Hellbound Heart', comes out of the twisted mind of one of England's great horror writers of recent decades. The story is Pandora's Box and the Monkey's Paw spliced inhumanly together, with more than a dash of fetishism and S&M zombies.

'The box' containing a portal to the world of Pinhead and the Cenobites is the literal expression of the saying 'be careful what you wish for'. On its release, Steven King provided the quote: 'I have seen the future of horror and his name is Clive Barker'. Although others of Barker's films (*Night Breed*: 1990; *Lord of Illusions*: 1995) and those based on his work, *Midnight Meat Train* (Kitamura 2008), *Rawhead Rex* (Pavlou 1986) and *Book of Blood* (Harrison 2009), have not achieved the same cult status, his place in the canon is assured. Barker's imagination equals that of Poe or Lovecraft, and his tales plumb the depths of the darkest of human souls. That he has no direct imitators speaks volumes.

Neil Marshall's *Dog Soldiers* (2002), a raw take on the werewolf myth, in which a squad of British Army recruits on manoeuvres in the Scottish highlands is attacked and outfoxed by carnivorous wolves, revitalized the British horror industry. Its dark humour, combined with blood, gore and senseless violence, soon became a firm favourite among horror fans. Marshall's follow-up, *The Descent* (2005), featuring a female cast trapped underground, was both claustrophobic and drenched in gore. His work helped writer/director Chris Smith[90] to obtain funds for *Creep* (2004) and *Severance* (2006), and since then British horror has been on the up and up.

James Watkins's *Eden Lake* (2007) was the first of the so-called Hoodie horrors (the 'hoodie', a sportwear jacket with a hood, was adopted by criminal youths in the mid-2000s as a way of maintaining anonymity). It identified a new horror among England's urbanites, a fear of children, further explored in *The Children* (Shankland 2008) where a virus from the woods turns little middle-class darlings into savage killers reminiscent of those in the *Village of the Damned* (Rilla 1960). There is also Johannes Robert's *F* (2010), in which a teacher and his pupil/daughter are menaced after hours by faceless hooded youths, and *Community* (Ford 2012). In *Eden Lake* a young couple, Jenny, a primary school teacher, and her boyfriend Steve, leave London for a camping trip during which he intends to propose marriage to her. When they are interrupted by local youths, Steve remonstrates with them. The alpha male order is questioned, and the feral youth begin a persecution that has the audience squealing and grimacing as things go from bad to much, much worse, with an ending that leaves one gasping in impotent rage. The film bites deep into a growing social problem in Britain, the *Daily Mail* culture of a fatherless underclass on benefits with no morals, responsibility or fear of reprisal. A pack of youths with a sense of entitlement to 'respect' and instant gratification may be a narrow view, but it became all too real in the England-wide riots in the summer of 2011. There

---

[90]See Appendix 2: Interviews (p. 209).

have also been a number of home invasion thrillers in the spirit of *Straw Dogs* (Peckinpah 1971), such as *Cherry Tree Lane* (Williams 2010).

The Irish film board helped co-produce Billy O'Brien's *Isolation* (2005), a Frankenstein tale of genetic mutations on a cow farm; also Paddy Breathnach's *Shrooms* (2007). Breathnach went on to make *Freakdog* (2008, aka *Red Mist*) but neither is particularly Irish in its locale or subject. Shot in Northern Ireland was *W delta Z* (in the US *The Killing Gene*: Shankland 2007), a tale of victims found with bizarre symbols tattooed on their skin.

Scotland has been more of a location than a film production base. Grave robbers *Burke and Hare* (Landis 2010) originated in Edinburgh, but otherwise we have seen few horror movies exploring the country itself bar the excellent *Outcast* (McCarthy 2010), the Highlands in *A Lonely Place to Die* (Gilbey 2011) and the village of Newton Stewart in the Galloway Hills for *The Wicker Man* (Hardy 1973). A good movie has yet to be made about the Loch Ness Monster.

Europe

Italy was a popular home for film-making in the 1970s, but the most significant films of recent times have come from France and Spain. Alan Jones, in the *Rough Guide to Horror Movies*, offers an opinion as to why this is: 'The boring answer is because local governments invest in film production, the funds are relatively easy to come by and horror is still the most bankable genre for a return on such an investment. This has gone hand in hand with quality digital cameras now being so low-cost, technology changing everything and making it so much easier. Look at any country and when financing was made easier, horror production increased, even in the UK when Hammer gained thanks to the Eady Levy. [91][92]

France

The first French horror to capture international interest was Henri-Georges Clouzot's *(Les) Diaboliques* (1954), after which he was dubbed the French Hitchcock. Set in a Parisian boarding school, it concerns a wife and mistress who murder their lover – a plan that goes awry when the corpse disappears.

---

[91] The Eady Levy (1957–85) was a tax on UK box office receipts intended to support the British Film Industry. To qualify, 85 per cent of the film had to be shot in the UK or the British Commonwealth.
[92] Jones 2005.

It was atmospheric and tense, and had a surprise ending, after which the end credits begged the audience not to spoil it for their friends – something of a precursor to the fuss made about *Psycho* (Hitchcock 1960).

Georges Franju's *Eyes without a Face* (1960) concerned a surgeon who tries to repair his daughter's face by grafting onto it the faces of other beautiful women. This mad scientist tale influenced both John Woo and John Carpenter, who used the faceless mask idea for Michael Myers. Another movie reminiscent of this is Pedro Almodóvar's *The Skin I Live In* (2011) which is, if possible, even more perverse.

The problem with French genre cinema, according to Alexandre Aja, director of *Haute tension* (aka *Switchblade Romance*: 2003), is that 'They [the French] don't trust their own language [when it comes to horror]. American horror movies do well, but in their own language the French just aren't interested.' This changed in 2000 when Lionel Delplanque made *Promenons nous dans les bois* (*Deep in the Woods*), which opened the gates to the funding of Christophe Gans's *Brotherhood of the Wolf* (2001) and Eric Valette's *Malefique* (2002) – a tale of four prisoners who discover an ancient book of black magic. However, it was *Haute tension* that gained Aja international attention. It is a survival thriller in the vein of Craven's *Last House on the Left* (1972), featuring two students, Marie and Alex, who go to Alex's country home to cram for exams only to be interrupted by a mysterious trucker who kidnaps Alex and slaughters her family. Marie, terrified, tries to alert the attendant at a gas station. This fails, leading to a bloody denouement in the woods. There is a huge reveal which, to Aja's credit, we do not suspect throughout the gore-soaked tableau. *Haute tension* has paved the way for psychosexual horrors such as Alexandra Bustillo's gruesome *L'Interior* (*Inside*: 2007) with Beatrice Dalle. Xavier Gens's *Frontier(s)* (2007) is a blend of *Hostel* and the Leatherface Family gone mad in the French countryside. The zombie invasion, too, has caught up with the Gallic in *La Horde* (Dahan and Rocher 2009).

If French cinema is a palette of grime, gore and ultra-violence in the extreme, then its crowning achievement must be Pascal Laugier's *Martyrs* (2008). In this, a young woman, Lucie, and her friend Anna seek revenge on those who kidnapped and tormented her as a child. The massacre of the family believed to be responsible leads to her death and Anna's capture, as she discovers an underground prison run by 'Mademoiselle', a member of a secret society seeking to discover the secrets of the afterlife through creating 'martyrs'. Anna is put through extreme deprivation and awful torture. Somehow managing to survive this – and being the only victim ever to have reached this point – she is flayed alive and subsequently reaches a religious visionary state. She whispers the secret of the afterlife to Mademoiselle, who summons the cult. However, before revealing the secret to them, Mademoiselle shoots herself in the mouth.

The film found no backers in French cinema and it was TV channel Canal Plus which funded it. It was given an '18+' rating. It is the marquee film of New French Extremity Cinema, a term quoted by Artforum critic James Quandt. The movement includes Xavier Gens (*Frontiers*) and Gaspar Noe, who made the sublime *Irreversible*, and has influenced Lars von Trier (*Antichrist*: 2009), Balaguero and Plaza (*[REC]*: 2007) and Ben Wheatley (*Kill List*: 2011).

Spain

Spanish horror is in a boom period, but it was never thus. Other than Cervantes, Spain lacks a literary or gothic tradition, which is surprising from the country that spawned the Spanish Inquisition. Having had no Industrial Revolution, there was no fear of technology that is so important to horror, and there was virtually no film industry until the early 1960s when Jess Franco (under a number of pseudonyms) made a version of *Eyes without a Face* called *The Awful Dr. Orloff* (1961). He then proceeded to make varying quality versions of works by Wilde, Le Fanu, Hugo and the Marquis de Sade. Amando de Ossorio created a series of zombie Knights Templar in a series that began with *La Noche del terror ciego* (*Tombs of the Blind Dead*: 1971), and Narciso Ebanez Serrador made *Island of the Damned* (1976) about a couple who travel to a fictitious Balearic island only to find feral children who have murdered the adults. Still in the Franco era, Jorge Grau made paella horror *The Living Dead at the Manchester Morgue* (1974) in Northern England because he had always wanted to go there. It was banned as a 'video nasty' for nearly 20 years and is not good.

Tras el Cristal (*In a Glass Cage*: 1987), written and directed by Agusti Villaronga, was based on the story of fifteenth-century French nobleman Gilles de Rais (a paedophile, sadist and Satanist) and explored the abuse fostered by a paedophile Nazi concentration camp guard later kept alive in an iron lung by his young home carer, Angelo. It was funded by the Ministry of Culture in Spain and the Catalan government, and was highly controversial for its subject matter.

Pedro Almodóvar's international success led to most horror being relegated to TV, but Alex De la Iglesia's *Day of the Beast* (1995) was a wonderful take on *The Omen* (Donner 1976) concerning a priest who deciphers ancient scrolls only to discover that the Antichrist will be born in Madrid on Christmas Day. Alejandro Amenábar made his debut with *Tesis* (*Thesis*: 1996) about a film student who finds her school being used for a snuff movie.

Amenábar followed this with *Open your Eyes* and the superb *Los Otros* (*The Others*: 2001) starring Nicole Kidman in a movie that echoes *The Innocents* (Clayton 1961) in that it too is based on Henry James's 'Turn of the Screw' (1898). 'I wanted to play with the supernatural in its simplest forms and craft a more classic adult horror than had been seen for a while,' he claimed.[93]

It was the first English-language film to win the best film award at the Goyas (the Spanish version of the Oscars) and has no Spanish in it – thus enabling it to travel worldwide with no alteration (it has been twice remade in Bollywood). Shot in Cantabria (green Spain) in an atmosphere of gothic gloom, it portrays a country house in German-occupied Jersey during World War Two. Grace Stewart lives with her two children who have an unusual condition, *xeroderma pigmentosa*, meaning they are allergic to sunlight. The arrival of three servants coincides with odd happenings, and Grace starts to believe they are not alone. It is a masterpiece of the supernatural with a number of heart-pounding scares and an awesome twist – one that is profoundly saddening.

Many of its ideas crop up in Juan Antonio Bayona's *El Orfanato* (*The Orphanage*: 2007) starring Belen Rueda, who had made her name as one of Spain's leading TV actresses. She plays Laura, who with her husband and adopted son Simon returns to the orphanage of her childhood, intending to turn it into a home for disabled children. Simon befriends a masked boy, Tomas, who is invisible to them. During a children's party, Simon argues with Laura and subsequently disappears. The resulting scares are beautifully handled by Sergio G. Sánchez, a writer who lists his influences as *Peter Pan*,[94] *Poltergeist* (Hooper 1982), *The Omen* (Donner 1976) and *Rosemary's Baby* (Polanski 1968). He wanted to direct but was repeatedly turned down. Bayona was given the script and was aided by Guillermo Del Toro, whom he met at Sitges[95] (Del Toro gets a producing credit). It premiered at Cannes where it received a 10-minute ovation, and went on to open at Sitges and close at FrightFest. It was the second highest grossing debut in Spain, beating *Pan's Labyrinth*. Rueda went on to star in *Julia's Eyes* (2011), another superb supernatural thriller directed by Guillem Morales and produced by Del Toro.

If the Spanish have proven themselves adept at the ghost story, they are also capable of time distortion mind-benders such as Nacho Vigalondo's *Time Crimes* (2007) in which a man named Hector invents a time machine that has thrown him back by an hour, creating a loop in which he sees himself again and again. However, the biggest Spanish franchise of late is '[REC]'. Co-written and directed by Jaume Balaguero and Paco Plaza in 2007, it is the story of news reporter Angela Vidal and cameraman Pablo who accompany the night shift

---

[93] In Jones 2005 (p. 246).
[94] The stage play of 'Peter Pan, or The Boy Who Wouldn't Grow Up', 27 December 1904. Written by J. M. Barrie, it was later adapted and expanded as a novel, published in 1911 as *Peter and Wendy*.
[95] Sitges hosts the foremost international horror and fantasy festival in Europe. Established in 1967, it takes place each October. Sitges is 34 kms from Barcelona.

of a local fire station on a call-out to a Barcelona block of flats, where an old woman has been 'taken ill'. What she has contracted is far more deadly, and we are thrown right into a 'rage epidemic', which turns people into bloodthirsty savages. After an hour of terrifying carnage, Angela and Pablo end up in a penthouse apartment where they find evidence of an envoy from the Vatican, who was researching a virus believed to have caused demonic possession.

It is a fresh take and a genre blend shot entirely with handheld cameras in the found footage style. What they find in the attic with their night vision camera is alive and deadly. On the Rotten Tomatoes aggregator it scores an unprecedented 96 per cent positive from critics. *[REC]2* appeared two years later, and begins as the previous film finishes, following Dr Owen, an official from the Ministry of Health who goes in after Angela and Pablo. As with *Psycho* (Hitchcock 1960) and *Martyrs* (Laugier 2008), the film severs the first narrative by killing the protagonist. It also contrives to end by going back to the start, with a demonically possessed girl passing something very horrible onto Angela. It is bravura film-making at its very best. *[REC]3 Re-genesis* premiered at FrightFest in 2012 and, although it is comic, the laughs are good ones and the ending is a nod to Romero. In all, Spanish horror cinema is in a healthy state, with high production values and a wealth of talented ideas, writers and directors.

Italy

Italian horror combines the visual and camp with plenty of gore, brutal violence, bad acting and dubbing. In 1956, Riccardo Freda made *I Vampiri* (aka *The Devil's Commandment*), about a kidnapped young women whose blood was drained. He left the film two days before its finish, being replaced by cameraman Mario Bava, who made *Black Sunday* (aka *Mask of Satan*: 1960), considered an all-time great. *Black Sunday* tells the tale of a witch who returns from the grave to seek revenge on the descendants of her killers, and it not only launched his career but also served as a star vehicle for actress Barbara Steele, who went on to appear in a further nine Italian horror movies. Bava followed up his success with *The Evil Eye* (1961) and *The Girl Who Knew Too Much* (1962), considered to be the first Giallo film. He later made *Black Sabbath* (1963), *Blood and Black Lace* (1964), and *Kill, Baby, Kill* (1968).

'Giallo' means 'yellow' in Italian. It refers to cheap paperback mystery novels with yellow covers. It also means a lot of stylized sex and lurid violence in its filmed counterparts, as well as musical scores by Ennio Morriconi and Prog Rock group Goblin. The masters of the form are Lucio Fulci, Umberto Lenzi, Dario Argento, Mario Bava, Sergio Martino and Aldo Lado. Bava went on to make many more Giallo films, but of all the Italian horror directors, best known to international audiences is Dario Argento, who popularized Giallo in the Italian mainstream and brought it to global attention.

His debut, *Bird with the Crystal Plumage* (1970), inspired many Italian horror movies with the names of animals – such as *Cat O' Nine Tails* and *Four Flies on Grey Velvet* (1971). He next made *Deep Red* (*Profondo Rosso*: 1976), taking a mystery narrative structure and adding his signature system of visual symbols. He developed operatic colour schemes for *Suspiria* (1976) as well as his follow up, *Inferno* (1980), and continued to make horror in the 1980s with *Tenebrae* (1982), *Phenomenon* (1985) and *Opera* (1987), the latter containing the sight of a girl forced to keep her eyes open because of needles taped under her eyelids – shades of *Clockwork Orange*.

Inspired by *Dawn of the Dead* (Romero 1978) and *The Exorcist* (Friedkin 1973), many Italian horror films turned to themes of zombies and demonic possession. Lucio Fulci's *Zombi II* (1979) (aka *Zombie Flesh Eaters*) pits zombie against shark. *City of the Living Dead* (1980, aka *Gates of Hell*) features a scene in which a character vomits up her own intestines. Fulci's *The Beyond* (1981) is about the lynch mob killing of an artist in a hotel, which opens the gates of hell thus allowing the dead access to the living. Several years later a woman from New York inherits the hotel and, in her haste to redecorate, opens up the portal.

A number of cannibal-themed films were made, the most notorious being Ruggero Deodato's *Cannibal Holocaust* (1979), in which a documentary crew heads into the Amazon jungle to search for a mythical tribe. In order to get more interesting footage they take to raping, torturing and killing the natives. Besides extreme simulated violence, it is known for showing the real-life deaths of a number of animals and the butchery of a live turtle. The last parts of the film contain found footage of the crew being hunted, mutilated and eaten. This is shown to New York Studio executives who predict massive ratings were it ever shown.

Cannibal Holocaust wasn't the first to use these tropes, as animal torture had been a mainstay of Italian exploitation movies since the Oscar nominated *Mondo Cane* (Paolo Cavara and Gualtiero Jacopetti) in 1962. Preceding it were Umberto Lenzi's *Deep River Savages* (1972) and Deodato's *Lost Cannibal World* (1977). It was banned, however, in 33 countries.

Bava's son Lamberto made his mark with *Demons* (1985) and *Demons II* (1987), combining themes of zombies and demonic possession into one film. By the 1990s Dario Argento had tried his hand in America and failed. *Cemetery Man* (aka *Dellamorte Dellamore*) was directed by Michele Soavi and starred Rupert Everett as a caretaker who finds that the corpses will not stay in the ground. It's worth catching for its campness, nudity and black comedy. Argento has of late returned to Gialli, making *Sleepless* (2001), *The Card Player* (2003) and TV movie *Do you like Hitchcock* (2005). Devotees still await the third of his trilogy that begun with *Suspiria*; otherwise it seems Italian horror cinema is in abeyance.

Belgium

Belgium is a small country, often at war with itself but also able to create great art in that of Rubens, Magritte and Hergé.[96] It has produced two horror movies of note. *Man Bites Dog* (Belvaux and Bonzel 1992) uses documentary realism, black humour and shocking violence to make pertinent points about how the media is culpable in its desire for graphic imagery. It stars Benoit Poelvoorde (who also co-directed with Belvaux and Bonzel) who plays a hit man going about his daily business with a fly-on-the-wall documentary crew – an idea employed later in *Behind the Mask*, the rise of Leslie Vernon (Glosserman 2006). Benoit jokes as he slaughters, and we are complicit in the fun until the crew is invited to join in, leading to a gang rape scene, by which time the irony has expired.

Fabrice Du Welz's *Calvaire* (2004) is backwoods horror – *Psycho* meets *Deliverance*. It's Christmas, and when cabaret singer Marc Stevens breaks down and is forced to stay in a ramshackle remote guesthouse, its owner Mr Bartel, a former stand-up comic is delighted to have the company (his wife having long ago abandoned him). So happy is he that he kidnaps Marc, shaves his head, semi-crucifies him and makes him wear his ex-wife's sundress. The local village men, when not having sex with livestock or dancing to the discordant noise of piano keys, lay siege to Bartel's property, believing him to have stolen their beloved calf/sex toy. Then it turns nasty. It is psychological terror with a bitter redemptive ending.

Germany

Despite Germany being the birthplace of the horror film, it was the novels, stories and plays of British crime writer Edgar Wallace that dominated German horror in the 1950s. They were nicknamed Krimis, from 'taschenkrimi', or pocket crime novel (like the Italian 'Giallo'). Christopher Lee appeared in many of them, such as *Die Schlangengrube und das Pendel* (aka *Blood Demon*: Reini 1967), based on an Edgar Allen Poe story, where Lee played Count Regula. There was not much after this until Stefan Ruzowitzky's *Anatomie* (2000). It stars Franka Potente as medical student Paula Henning who wins a place at the prestigious University of Heidelberg. During a course on anatomy, she finds the corpse is that of a student whom she met on the way. Her professor forces her to dissect his heart and she later finds strange marks on his ankles and discovers the Anti-Hippocratic Society, a coven which works without the restraint of medical

---

[96] The pseudonym of Georges Remi, who created Tin Tin.

ethics, making gruesome experiments on living patients, especially those whom they consider 'useless'. There are echoes of Nazi experimentation, and indeed the Society is connected to the Nazis from when the state began the Aktion T4 programme ('life unworthy of life') disposing of homosexuals and the disabled, and which led to Joseph Mengele's experiments in the concentration camps. Germany was for a long time unable to deal with its history, and it is only now that the past is being faced: in movie terms there has-been quite an interest of late in the mechanics of group control[97] in such films as *Das Experiment* (Hirschbiegel 2001) and *The Wave* (Gansel 2008).

Anatomie was a huge box office success, producing a sequel in 2003. For more autopsy fun, see the real-life exhibitions of plastinator Gunther von Hagens. A mention must also go to German writer, producer and director Uwe Boll, who came into horror with his English-language 2002 feature *Blackwoods*, in which a man is haunted by the death of a girl from an accident he caused. Years later he goes away for weekend with his new girlfriend Dawn. After lovemaking, Dawn goes for a walk and a strange man with an axe attacks boyfriend Matt. He goes looking for her and in the woods he meets Dawn's family, who tie him down and put him on trial for the murder of the girl. Found guilty, he is sent back to the forest to be hunted down. The deeper he runs into the forest the more his mind is lost to the Blackwood. Boll later moved on to adapting video games for the screen, including *House of the Dead*, *Alone in the Dark*, *Postal* and *Rampage*. These films have not been well received by critics, many naming them as the poorest examples of film-making ever. In 2007 Boll made *Seed*, for which he used footage of animal abuse obtained from PETA, the UK-based charity People for the Ethical Treatment of Animals, and donated 2.5 per cent of all profits to that organization.

Another unique German-language director is Austrian Michael Hanake, whose *Funny Games* (1997) is a test of endurance. Hanake did not intend to make a horror film, and stated that he wanted to make a message about violence in the media by making a violent but otherwise pointless movie. It deserves inclusion for its home invasion scenario and cold-blooded psychopathic violence. A loving family, Georg, wife Anna and son Schorschi arrive at their Austrian lake house (overhead shots mimic Kubrick's *The Shining*) Their next door neighbour is seen with two young men, Peter and Paul, who seem to be friends or relatives. The two young men come over to borrow eggs. Anna is in the kitchen and their friendly overtures soon take a bullying tone. When Georg tries to force the men to leave, Peter breaks Georg's leg with a golf club and they

---

[97]Echoing Philip Zimbardo's Stanford Prison Experiment of 1971, in which a group of students were divided into 'guards' and prisoners'. It was abandoned after two days when the guards started to physically harm the prisoners.

take the family hostage. Anna goes to call for help on the family's cellphone, but finds it unusable, having been earlier dropped in the sink by Peter. The family is forced to participate in a number of sadistic games in order to stay alive. Paul asks if the family wants to bet that they will be alive by 9 o'clock in the morning, though he doubts they will be. Schorschi escapes but is shot by Peter. Georg and Anna fight to survive but are mercilessly slaughtered. At one point, Anna succeeds in shooting Paul, but he grabs the TV remote and rewinds the scene, telling her she isn't allowed to break the rules. They kill Georg and take Anna, bound and gagged, out on the family's boat and nonchalantly throw her into the water to drown. They then dock at the neighbours' house and request some eggs, thus starting the cycle once more.

The character of Paul breaks the fourth wall, asking questions of the audience and winking at us, the viewer. This dark meditation plays with our expectations of genre and cinema itself. It is hard to carry off, as Joss Whedon discovered in *The Cabin in the Woods* (Goddard 2011), the film he co-wrote with director Drew Goddard. Hanake re-made *Funny Games* in the US in 2008, starring Tim Roth and Naomi Watts as the couple.

The Netherlands

In George Sluizer's *Spoorloos* or *The Vanishing* (1988), Rex's girlfriend vanishes in a service station. Three years later he meets up with her abductor, Raymond, who offers him the chance to find out what happened. It is a slow build of rising dread with a terrible twist. The director's US remake (1993) has a tacked-on Hollywood ending.

Director Dick Maas's *De Lift* (1983) was a tale about a killer elevator, which he remade for the US as *Down* in 2001, starring Naomi Watts. His next horror/thriller film, *Amsterdamned* (Maas 1988) has a Dutch serial killer using the canals of Amsterdam as his hunting ground and is effectively gruesome. *Sint* (Maas 2010) is a comedy horror about Sinterklaas, a figure based on Santa Claus. Unlike the jolly present giver, Maas's Sint is a ghostly madman who arrives on 5th December (when the Dutch celebrate Christmas) with his henchmen on a full moon for the slaughter of hundreds. More outrageous still is maverick writer/director Tom Six's *The Human Centipede* (first sequence 2009). Set in Germany, this film features Dr Heiter, who dreams of making a human centipede. To this end he captures a Japanese male and two unlucky American female tourists, sows them together mouth to anus, and breaks their kneecaps. It was influenced by the body horror of David Cronenberg and, according to the director, was inspired by a joke he made about punishing a child molester by stitching his mouth to the anus of a fat truck driver. Mengele and his experiments at

Auschwitz influenced him too. Six famously did not tell his investors the whole story and the financiers did not discover the mouth-to-anus sequences until the film was completed. It struggled with censorship (even at FrightFest) and claims that 100 per cent medically accurate are unsubstantiated. What is undeniable is that it is an exploration of revulsion and disgust, has many plot holes, and underneath it is a conventional mad scientist movie. It produced a sequel, *The Human Centipede 2* (final sequence 2011), which Six states is more graphic and disturbing, the original being like *My Little Pony* in comparison. It is.

Scandinavia

Scandinavian film history begins with Ingmar Bergman, whose *Jungfrukallan* (*The Virgin Spring*: 1960) is a revenge story of a father reverting to paganism in order to slaughter brothers who raped and killed his daughter. It heavily influenced Wes Craven's *Last House On The Left* (1972). In *The Seventh Seal* (Bergman 1957) a man plays chess with the grim reaper during the time of the plague, Black Death. In *The Devil's Eye* (1960) the Devil summons Don Juan from Hell in order to seduce a virgin. *Lake of the Dead* (Bergstrom 1958) was little known outside of its native land, but was a huge hit there. A group of upper-class Oslo residents head to a cabin deep in the woods of Osterdal. The cabin's occupant is missing but his dog is found dead on the bank of a nearby pond. Deciding to solve the mystery, the group falls prey to a legend that says anyone who stays in the cabin will drown themselves. This cabin in the woods theme reappears in *Villmark* (*Dark Woods*) (Øie 2003). A TV producer making a reality show about people forced to survive in the wilderness takes his crew to an isolated cabin where he used to spend his summers. A dead body is discovered and the killer begins to pick off people, rather bizarrely throwing dead bunnies at them.

Since *Villmark* there has been a renaissance in Norwegian horror with *Cold Prey* (Uthaug 2006) and its sequels, *Manhunt* (Syversen 2008), *Dead Snow* (Tommy Wirkola 2009) and *Troll Hunter* (Øvredal 2010). Both *Manhunt* and *Cold Prey* are strictly slice and dice, with *Manhunt* set in 1974 with all the feel of *TCM*. Hillbillies, it seems, are the same the world over. *Cold Prey* takes us snowboarding in the mountains, but an injury to one of the group requires them to seek shelter in an abandoned ski lodge, which is not as empty as they think and involves plenty of sharp objects. It developed a strong following in Norway and neighbouring countries, spawning a sequel in the morgue. *Hidden* (Oie 2009) concerns a young man who returns home to settle his dead mother's affairs. Horrible memories flood back, and a chilling series of flashbacks lends a psychologically thrilling atmosphere. *Dead Snow* is one of the most energetic zombie movies of the current crop. A group of medical students are on vacation high in the mountains when they come across a stash of stolen Nazi gold. *Evil Dead* meets *28 Days Later* as the zombie stormtroopers rise from the snow to track and kill and feast. It's gory, fun and funny, with a great tagline, Ein, Zwei, Die!

Last, but by no means least, is *Troll Hunter* (Øvredal 2010), which uses found footage. A group of college students set out to make a documentary about a bear poacher, Hans. Failing to be warned off by local villagers, they enter a dark wood, only to find Hans is a Troll Hunter working for the government. The CGI trolls range in size from small and ugly up to Cloverfield.

By far the biggest success is Sweden is *Let the Right One In* (2008), based on a novel and screenplay by John Ajvide Lindqvist (see Chapter 10). It was a huge hit, garnering many awards internationally, and was remade for the US as *Let Me In* with Matt Reeves directing.

Finally, Danish director Lars von Trier's *Antichrist* (2009), starring Willem Dafoe and Charlotte Gainsbourg as a grieving couple who retire to a country-cabin 'Eden' to get over the death of their child. Hugely stylized, it involves genital mutilation and torture, and was a cause célèbre for the radical film-maker when it premiered at Cannes in 2009. Von Trier chose the horror genre because of the freedom to make imagery, and this he does in spades (the film is dedicated to Russian film-maker Andrei Tarkovski). He drew inspiration from Japanese horrors *Ringu* and *Dark Water* and a documentary about the forests of Europe, which were seen as places of great pain and suffering as different species tried to kill and eat one another. It is a tour de force, with many jarring images as well as extremes of sex and mutilation.

European horror is in a healthy state, with co-productions expanding and many movies being shot in Prague, Germany and Bulgaria. New ideas are appearing and new versions of old stories turn up with regularity and quality. The novice writer is well advised to keep a watchful eye on 'the old countries'.

Asia

The most significant wave of foreign horror in the last decade has been from Asia. Japan underwent a huge economic recession in 1990s, but one event changed everything. On 20 March 1995 there was a terrorist attack in which 5000 commuters were exposed to the nerve gas Sarin. This was a nation that had been virtually crime free, and here was a paradigm shift which, as with America on 9/11, brought home the realization that death could be a part of everyday life.

Japan has always had a strong folklore of ghost stories. Much of their horror was based around local legends such as the *Guinea Pigs* TV series, which ran from 1985 to 1992. Many manga stories were based on supposed real-life encounters with ghosts, and the film *Scary True Stories* went straight to video in 1991. This influenced director Hideo Nakata who made *Ringu* in 1998, which launched the J-Horror boom. *Ringu*, based on a novel by Koji Suzuki, made back its investment 15 times over. A Korean remake followed (*The Ring Virus*: Kim 1999) and subsequently there were three Japanese sequels and several manga adaptations. Nakata's film toured the international festivals to unanimous praise, and bootleg tapes circulated everywhere. Gore Verbinski's US remake, *The Ring* (2002), was hugely successful, taking $128 million at the US box office. A sequel was made in 2005 and there followed a slew of re-tooled Asian products, including *The Grudge* (Shimizu 2004), *The Grudge 2* (Shimizu 2006), *Dark Water* (Salles 2005), *One Missed Call* (Valette 2008), *The Eye* (Moureau 2008) and *The Uninvited* (Guard 2009) – a remake of Korean hit *A Tale of Two Sisters* (Kim 2003).

The main trope of Japanese horror is a long-haired female ghost seeking to avenge her violent death. There is most often a curse, which cannot be ended or contained. Its pace is leisurely, something American audiences find hard to take. There is violent death but an almost total absence of gore, except in the subgenre of cartoon splatstick films, such as *Ichi the Killer* (Miike 2001) or *Tokyo Gore Police* (Nishimura 2008).

The waterlogged spirit girl reflects the conflicted role of women in Japanese society. There are fractured or dysfunctional families. There is child abuse. The problems of the Japanese tend to be internalized – they are an introverted race – and their ghosts appear in everyday settings in bleached-out surroundings. It all has a very masochistic feel; for example, see *Odition* (*Audition*) (Miike 1999). Finally there is always a female hero, something which has fed back into American horror.

It was Korean/American producer Roy Lee who saw the original *Ringu* (Nakata 2008) at the Korean Puchon festival and brought it to Vertigo films in the US, later launching the J-Horror craze. The sight of Samara crawling out of the well was a powerful iconic image after the minimal scares of *The Blair Witch Project* (Myrick 1999). The originals were not released in the United States, as American audiences were unused to subtitles, hated dubbed films and found the pace too slow. They were also unaware of the culture and its rules. In short, it was as confusing as opera. However, M. Night Shyamalan's *The Sixth Sense* (1999) had whetted appetites for the supernatural and opened up a new market for mainstream horror, which was by then being exploited in movies like *What Lies Beneath* (Zemeckis 2000).

J-Horror was extremely popular with Japanese teenage girls, and so too were its American counterparts. US teen girls were drawn into theatres in huge numbers for horror movies that were traditionally seen as date-movie territory, and this impact helped to popularize them. The US remake fed back to Japan and made more money there in two weeks than Nakata's original *Ringu* had done in its whole run. This encouraged local producers to start making more in the hope of getting a distribution or remake deal with the US. Hideo Nakata even got the privilege of directing his own remake of *Dark Water* (Nakata 2002), which concerned a single mother and her daughter who moved into a leaky haunted apartment. The original *Dark Water* was a character-driven piece of social drama about a 'Yurei' (spirit girl), Mitsuko, who had been the victim of negligence by her parents. The reason that ghosts are always female in Japan is that oppressed women are considered to be more powerful in death and more likely to take revenge. These Yurei are found in legends and folk tales and are often connected with water. In *Ringu*, Sadako died in a well: in *Dark Water* (2002) Mitsuko drowns in a water tank. Seeping or stagnant water is associated with sickness and decay in Japan, and 'wet' can also mean emotional, something to be avoided.

What is pertinent for the writer is the idea of image systems. The damp patches, the drips and the still water used in *Dark Water* are extremely unsettling, without any need for false scares. To create fear out of the mundane is a great achievement for any writer or director, and Japanese movies manage this with great mastery.

Ju-on (*The Grudge*: Shimizu 2004), too, was extremely effective in its scares, and its director Takashi Shimizu was offered the chance to direct both the remake and a sequel. The US remake was set in Japan, as it was decided that a long-haired American woman would not be as scary as a Japanese Yurei. The principal cast featured *Buffy* actress Sarah Michelle Geller, setting a precedent for star casting. *Ring Two* featured Naomi Watts and the *Dark Water* remake had Tim Roth and Jennifer Connolly. Sadly the latter failed to recoup its investment, heralding the end of the J-Horror craze (Roth and Watts went on to star in Haneke's *Funny Games* shot-for-shot remake).

Takashi Miike is a prolific writer and director, who had made several 'Yakuza' movies and straight-to-video titles before making *Odishon* (*Audition*) in 1999 (based on a novel of the same title). This stunning example of Asian extreme cinema was all about loneliness: 'the whole of Japan is lonely', noted the protagonist, widower Shigeharu, who after seven years of being alone is urged by his teenage son to seek out a new partner. His friend Yasuhia, a casting director in the movie industry, suggests they stage a mock casting audition in order for him to find someone to whom he is attracted. He is later drawn to elfin submissive Asami, a former ballerina. That her resumé is proven to be sketchy does not bother him, and once we see her waiting in her apartment (empty save for a sack and a telephone) for his call for four days, the words bunny and boiler spring to mind. This being a Japanese film, it goes way, way beyond any boundaries, and once viewed would make anyone think twice before considering acupuncture or, indeed, dating ever again. With the line 'Words create lies, pain can be trusted', the deeply damaged Asami saws off his left foot and in so doing enters the tiny canon of female horror icons. That she is young and attractive compounds this, and turns the idea of the submissive Japanese girl-woman on its head.

So too does *Tokyo Gore Police* (Nishimura 2008), in which a mad scientist engineers a virus which mutates humans into genetic mutations called 'Engineers' who sprout weapons from any injury. Protagonist Ruka's left arm mutates into an alien head with razor-sharp claws, and she goes about slicing and dicing with her katana sword, creating a perversely beautiful deluge of blood.

More widely known and hugely influential (not least on Tarantino's *Kill Bill* and *The Hunger Games*) is Kinji Fukasaku's *Battle Royale* (Fukasaku 2000), again based on a successful novel of the same name. It is extremely violent and directly criticizes Japanese society. It was given a severe 'R15' rating, the equivalent to the 'NC-17'. In fact the Japanese parliament was so shocked by this movie that they questioned the existence of the film censorship board. The official protests gave it more publicity and it never received a distribution deal in the US, although frequent rumours of a remake abound. Its violence was claimed to be responsible for a wave of youth crimes. Fukasaku died in 2003 but spoke of its meaning originating from distrust between the old, post-war, generation, who had lied to the population about World War Two, and the new.

In Korea, Japanese pop culture had been banned since 1945. There was also a quota system to restrict film imports. This censorship was abolished in the late 1980s and K-Horror, such as *Whispering Corridors* (Park 1998) and *The Ring Virus* (Kim 1999) remake appeared. Many of the Korean horrors are about the fast evolution of technology and the fact that we are ill-equipped to fully understand it. Kiyoshi Kurosawa's *Pulse* (Kurosawa 2001) demonstrated a distrust of technology in a country whose main export is computer electronics; see also *Phone* (Ahn 2002).

Vicious and overwhelming revenge is another big theme of K-Horror, and two of its finest exponents feature the same actor in roles of perpetrator and victim. Asian cinema legend Choi-Min Sik plays a man imprisoned for 15 years for no reason, in Chanwook Park's masterpiece *Oldboy* (Park 2003), as well as a psychotic serial killer in Kim Jee-woon's *I Saw the Devil* (Kim 2010). If Craven's *Last House on the Left* (Craven 1972), Peckinpah's *Straw Dogs* (Peckinpah 1971) or writer Mair Zarchi's *I Spit on your Grave* (Monroe 2010) are to your taste, then these two are highly recommended. *Oldboy* is perhaps the finest movie of the last decade (of any country).[98]

---

[98]*Oldboy* was voted Best Film at the Sitges International Film Festival in 2004. It was remade by Spike Lee (Lee 2013).

In Hong Kong, the Pang brothers' *Gin Gwai* (*The Eye*: 2002) is significant. Born in Hong Kong in 1965, Danny and Oxide Pang made police thriller *Bangkok Dangerous* (Chun and Pang 2008) and then shot *The Eye* (Chun and Pang 2002), which is steeped in Thai and Chinese beliefs, such as the calligraphy room and a black figure who carries away dead souls. It grossed $13 million in Hong Kong and was given a release in many countries. It has been remade twice: in India in 2005, and in the US in 2008 starring Jessica Alba. There have been two follow-ups, *The Eye 2* (Chun and Pang 2004) and *The Eye 10* (Chun and Pang 2005). 'The Eye' concerns the resting of spirits aided by the living (as a result of a cornea transplant) and evokes terrifying thoughts of a world that remains ever in our peripheral vision.

From supernatural wet dead girls to ultra-violence, the Asian continent is filled with useful stories and new storytelling modes. They do not always follow the three-act structure (as with *The Grudge*), and can be episodic, with large chunks of flashback or parallel narratives. Absorbing some of this may inspire the astute writer.

Australia and New Zealand

New Zealand has become a film-making base almost entirely due to the work of one man, Peter Jackson, whose WETA studios are responsible for the 'Lord of the Rings' Trilogy and much more. Jackson started out as a genre director, liberally applying gore, grunge splatter and comedy in equal measures in early works *Bad Taste* and *Brain Dead*.

In Australia, it was not until the introduction of government subsidy in the 1970s that the industry was able to take off. Director Peter Weir was the first to emerge, with *Picnic at Hanging Rock* (Weir 1975), based on the disappearance of some schoolgirls on Valentine's Day, 1900. There is brooding sexuality and menace in equal measure, as an ancient supernatural presence is evoked via stopped clocks and disturbances in nature. Psychic thriller *Patrick* (Franklin 1978) was written by Everett de Roche, an ex-pat American who continued to turn out excellent scripts for *Long Weekend* (Eggleston 1978), a precursor to many of the backwoods horrors of today, *Snapshot* (Wincer 1979), *Roadgames* (Franklin 1981) featuring Jamie Lee Curtis, and *Razorback* (Mulcahy 1984).

A theme that runs through Australian horror is man's alienation from nature. This is a vast country with a population living on its crust, the interior a vast inhospitable untamed wilderness – the Unknown. Insects and birds plague the bickering husband and wife in *Long Weekend*. In *Razorback* it is a giant boar, and in *Rogue* (McLean 2007) a giant crocodile. The external was then internalized into an awful psychopathology when *Rogue* director Greg McLean created the antipodean answer to the *Texas Chain Saw Massacre* in *Wolf Creek* (McLean 2005). As with *Picnic at Hanging Rock*, this too was based on a true story, this time of missing backpackers in Wolfe Creek National Park in the north-western Australian outback. The survivor of this terrible ordeal was still on trial for suspected murder as the film was due to be released, and the DPP asked for screenings to be postponed until the trial ended. Its monster, Mick Taylor, has a normal name for an abnormal person. He offers to help stranded tourists with their broken-down vehicle (there is an odd magnetic effect in the area that stops things working) by towing them to his breaker's yard. However, when he tells tales over the campfire and the smug gap year kids mock his lonely rural redneck ways, things take a wrong turn. Four words. Head on a stick.

As we have seen, horror around the world is often re-made and re-versioned, so for the non-Hollywood based writer there is the possibility of adaptation. Technology has freed us to research, to experiment and to make what was impossible before. Good story-telling is universal and there are echoes every-where of the same memes and tropes. Horror is idea-driven, and the cultural sensibilities of writers and directors on the other side of the world can amaze, thrill and inspire us; different ways – not just of killing one another, but differing fears, monsters, story structures and mythologies.

Chapter 13
Low Budget Horror

Writing and directing the low budget horror movie has traditionally been seen as the entry level to moviemaking. This has a creditable provenance. George Romero's *Night of the Living Dead* (Romero 1968) was shot on a shoestring, and so too were the efforts of 1970s movie brats, Wes Craven with *The Last House on the Left* (Craven 1972), John Carpenter with his science fiction debut *Dark Star* (Carpenter 1974), co-written with Alien writer Dan O'Bannon, Tobe Hooper with the broiling summer shoot that was the *Texas Chain Saw Massacre* (1974) and Sam Raimi with his *Evil Dead* (Raimi 1981). More recently we have Daniel Myrick and Eduardo Sanchez with *The Blair Witch Project* (Myrick and Sanchez 1999) and Oren Peli's *Paranormal Activity* (Peli 2006) – all allegedly done on a micro budget.

The first truly independent movie is cult classic Herk Harvey's 1962 *Carnival of Souls*, written by Harvey with John Clifford and made for an estimated $30,000. Harvey, a producer of industrial and educational films in Kansas, was inspired whilst on vacation in Salt Lake City when driving past the abandoned Saltair Pavilion. He hired unknown actress Candace Hilligloss, used local talent, and shot the film in three weeks. In it, Mary Henry is riding in a car with friends when they are challenged to a drag race, resulting in their being forced off a bridge. Miraculously she survives and, stumbling into town, accepts a job as a church organist. She is, however, pursued by a phantom apparition (played by Harvey) who lives in a run-down dark pavilion. She fends off another resident in her boarding house but is plagued by the apparition until drawn to the carnival where the souls come out and she discovers the darkest secret of all. It is the precursor to those big reveals in *The Sixth Sense* and *The Others*, both of which owe Harvey a huge debt.

Sadly, *Carnival of Souls* did not gain widespread approval when released and, similar to Romero's *Night of the Living Dead* (1968), the US release failed to include a copyright on the print, which placed it in the public domain so it could be shown for free by any TV station as and when they liked (this plagued Romero for years afterwards). As regards *Carnival of Souls*, John Clifford only managed to wrest back the rights in entirety as late as 1996, so there is a lesson to be learnt here.

If a truly independent movie becomes a breakout hit, what is good for publicity is to make interesting claims about how little it cost, the *reductio ad absurdum* being Marc Price's UK film *Colin* (Price 2008), which tells a zombie tale from the point of view of a man who has been infected and becomes one of the undead. Claimed to have cost just £45 (less than $80) it was shot on a 10-year-old Panasonic mini-dv camera with actors sourced from Facebook and MySpace, and edited with Adobe Premiere 6 on a home computer. It is not the only zombie picture to be told from the undead point of view (Brian Yuzna's *Return of the Living Dead 3*: 1993), but it was a high concept idea that achieved distribution.

In a similar vein, Chris Daly and Joey Evans's *Bubba's Chili Parlor* (Evans 2005) is supposed to have cost $13,000 and featured Bubba serving chili infected with mad cow disease, leading to a zombie outbreak. Sadly, the cheap zombie movie has become as epidemic as the undead themselves in recent years.

Another movie that traded on its low budget origins is writer/director Gareth Edwards's *Monsters* (Edwards 2010), publicized on release as costing $15,000 and produced on a home computer (using ZBrush and Autodesk 3d Max). It was shot on dv with a prosumer camera, and tells the story of an unspecified post-alien invasion in which a US journalist in Mexico agrees to help an American tourist through the infected zone back to the US border. More a tentative love story/road movie than a horror, the glimpses of the monstrous are as judiciously edited as anything in *Mist* (Darabont 2007) or *Cloverfield* (Reeves 2008). It is guerrilla film-making at its most raw, as they had no permission for location shooting and the extras consisted of people who happened to be there at the time. It was set in Mexico, Belize, Guatemala, Costa Rica and Texas, with two leads and a crew of seven people in a van; having no dolly, they shot out of the van window. When it came to the extras, Edwards states, 'The idea of scripting the film went out of the window. Instead I had a loose paragraph describing the scene with the main points that had to be hit.'[99] By the end they had a hundred hours of ad-libbed footage, which had to be edited to 94 minutes. This took eight months and, once locked, Edwards took a further five months to create 250 digital effects. It has grossed over $4 million to date.

The daddy of all DIY film successes is Daniel Myrick and Eduardo Sanchez's *The Blair Witch Project* (Myrick and Sanchez 1999). Shot on a shoestring in

---

[99]Gareth Edwards, 'Adventures in the Infected Zone', *Empire*, November 2010, 100–6.

eight days in both black and white on a hand held 16mm camera and colour on dv, it has grossed over £248 million worldwide to date and is considered to be a horror landmark. It was developed as far back as 1994, beginning with a 68-page outline of the script with dialogue to be improvised. Myrick and Sánchez advertised for actors in *Back Stage* magazine, narrowing down the field from 2000 hopefuls to the three leads, plus various experts and villagers who mixed with genuine people on location. For potential investors they created an eight-minute documentary, *The Blair Witch Project: The Story of Black Hills Disappearances*, along with newspaper articles and news 'footage'. Nineteen hours of usable footage was shot and edited down to 90 minutes, as they hoped for a cable release. Sanchez has claimed that the cost after principal photography wrapped was $20,000–$25,000. It was first shown at Sundance, where it was acquired by Artisan Films for $1 million, who then spent $25 million marketing it using an Internet campaign before release. The website not only claimed the events to be true but provided evidence of the *Myth of the Blair Witch* and the film-makers' disappearance. IMDB even listed their status as 'missing, presumed dead'.

Aside from shooting around Burkittsville, Maryland, and a brief stop in a motel room, it is all shot in the woods except for the final scene in a deserted house. The ramping-up of the tension is slow, intense and ultimately knife-edge as they lose their way, their possessions and their sanity.

Blair Witch aptly demonstrates the two most important considerations for creating an independent horror, those of location and characterization. Any kind of monster is going to look hokey on a low budget, which explains why the more successful are based on the supernatural. The maxim holds: it is what we don't see that is ultimately more dreadful than what we do, so it is prudent to fill as much of your screenplay with anything other than the pure terror of the reveal. This means getting the right location and the right characters.

Location

First consider your setting. Right now, the 'cabin in the woods' scenario has been done to death, and unless you can come up with some amazing new twist then it is best avoided. However, the woods themselves are always fruitful, as Sam Raimi illustrated with his tree rape in *Evil Dead* (Rami 1981). The reason the forest is so often used is that it represents infinity.

Once you lose your bearings, you are potentially lost for good. One tree looks just like another and the woods – as we know from our viewing experiences – can hide sprites, wolves, cannibal hillbillies and teddy bears. Also it represents vulnerability. Anything can come at you from any angle. You are unprotected. It is primal, feral, basic survival.

Remember too that shooting in the woods at night is costly, as there is no natural light (moonlight is not enough), so it has to be lit by big expensive lighting rigs. All that blue light and dry ice in 1980s horror cost a lot of money. A more generic rural setting is still a good one because one cornfield looks just like another until messed up by evil children or Mel Gibson (*Signs*: Shyamalan 2002).

You don't however want to pick somewhere that is easily spoiled. This is why few movies are made in the snow. Before explaining the reasons, here are the exceptions: *Let the Right One In* (Alfredson 2008), *30 Days of Night* (Slade 2007), *Misery* (Reiner 1990), *The Shining* (Kubrick 1980), *Dream Catcher* (Kasdan 2003), *Dead Snow* (Wirkola 2009), *Cold Prey* (Uthaug 2006), *White Out* (Sena 2009), *Frozen* (Green 2010), and *The Thing* (Carpenter 1982). These are all studio productions.

I [author MB] set my first horror script (*Sticks and Stones*) in a snowbound school and, despite selling it to three different production companies over the years, it has not yet been made. There is a UK company called Snow Business, which makes artificial snow for the movies, and which has the following to say.

Big expensive feature films have a 'running cost' of around $100,000 per hour, so if a team of people laying snow hold up camera for an hour, Production can see that as $100,000 wasted. Also on big features, the need to be prepared for anything reigns, so often we have to dress large areas with high quality snow just in case there is action or close camera work at any spot on the area. We have to go in with more kit, more people and more stock so we are ready for anything, and able to do everything with no 'down time'. That of course costs money, so on films such as *Day After Tomorrow* (Emmerich 2004) the budgets are big at $500,000 to $1,000,000. Also, being aware of money limitations the director will make it clear where the camera position is, so high quality snow is only used in foreground and under action areas, with cheaper infill everywhere else. As a result these productions complete 'big snow scenes' with budgets of $50,000 to $100,000.[100]

Once you mess with snow it becomes slush. Blood on snow looks great, but virgin snow does not stay like that for long with cast and crew tramping over it and we can't all be like Hansel and Gretel or Danny Torrance in *The Shining* and retrace our steps.

Bringing it inside, the apartment is an excellent single location so long as you can get a camera crew in there. Many movies have been shot almost entirely

---

[100] Personal communication.

in apartments, from *Repulsion* (Polanski 1965) and *Rosemary's Baby* (Polanski 1968) to Hammer's recent *The Resident* (Jokenen 2011). An apartment block is good too, such as in *The Toolbox Murders* (Hooper 2004); or an abandoned hotel, as in *See no Evil* (Dark 2006), *Mirrors* (Aja 2008) or the daddy of them all, *The Shining* (Kubrick 1980). Constructed at Borehamwood in Hertfordshire, UK, *The Shining* was the largest set ever made, including a full scale set of the exterior of the Overlook Hotel.

This might be overreaching. Try instead a simple motel room – *Psycho* (Hitchcock 1960) is our template here, providing enough chills for 90 minutes and successfully used again in *Vacancy* (Antal 2007), *Bug* (Friedkin 2006), *Identity* (Mangold 2003) and *Reeker* (Payne 2005). A single room is all you need if the idea is right, as in the Spanish film *Fermat's Room* (Piedrahita and Sopena 2007), based on a mathematical puzzle, and *Pontypool* (Burgess 2009), adapted from his novel *Pontypool Changes Everything*, which was mostly set in a radio station studio in Ontario. This is a low budget product worthy of note concerning a virus that affects language in three stages: first you repeat words, terms of endearments that 'get stuck'. Second, your words are scrambled; and third, you become infected and try to chew your way out of the mouth of another person. Inspired by Orson Welles's infamous 'War of the Worlds' broadcast (Welles 1938), the movie was simultaneously released as a radio play.

If you can imagine your movie being set on stage, then you might be halfway there, although the danger is that it becomes too stagey, as in *The Devil's Business* (Hogan 2011). *Fermat's Room* too suffers from this, but one example that works is *Cube* (Natali 1997), centred on a single white room in which six participants find themselves. In the centre of each wall is a hatch leading to another identical room – some of which are booby-trapped. Each character has amnesia but slowly discovers that each has something to contribute to their predicament, be it mathematical nous, medical or practical skills. As they begin to move from room to room, or are diced and spliced in the process, they discover a more mystifying conundrum. The rooms themselves are moving, creating an almost impossible number of probabilities, as if trapped in a Rubik's Cube or something from the mind of M. C. Escher. Each trap is different. The conceit is perfectly elegant in its limitation and the tension never drops for an instant.[101] *Cube* has produced two sequels, both equally intriguing.

What is so attractive here to producers is that you only need build one set, which you can control with lighting, and in the studio you can remove walls or ceiling as you wish for ease of filming. *Exam* (Hazeldine 2009) used a similar notion, this time in an alternate reality where most have succumbed to an

---

[101] *Cube* was voted Best Film at Sitges in 1998.

unnamed virus. In the windowless room, eight candidates vie for a position as PA to the CEO of a biotech company which may or may not have a cure.

If not a room, a simple hole in the ground will suffice, as in UK thriller *The Hole* (Hamm 2001), filmed in an abandoned bomb shelter (the second half of *Martyrs* never leaves that hell of the underground prison). Perhaps a World War Two German bunker, as in *Bunker* (Green 2001); or *Deathwatch* (Bassett 2002), set in a World War One trench.

All manner of places have been used as prime locations for horror. Deserted ship? *Ghost Ship* (Beck 2002) or *Triangle* (Smith 2009). Sanatorium? *Session 9* (Anderson 2001). Prison cell? *Malefique* (Valette 2002). You can even make a parking garage seriously scary, as in *P2* (Khalfoun 2007), or a shuttle bus as in *Shuttle* (Anderson 2008). You can abandon the earth altogether, and we're in *Alien* territory, the haunted house in space.

Why not set it all at sea? *Open Water* (Kentis 2003) is a story based on true events about a couple who get left behind on a scuba diving trip in the Caribbean. Shot in its entirety with handheld cameras, it was promoted as *Jaws* meets *Blair Witch* and its production costs were recouped when bought by Lionsgate for £2.5 million, eventually raking in over £30 million.

Can you come up with somewhere entirely new – or at least a fresh take on the haunted house/forest or building?

Relationships

Crucial to the low budget horror is the relationship between protagonists, even more so than that between them and the Unknown, as witnessed in *The Blair Witch Project* (Myrick and Sanchez 1999), a fine character study. The visuals are irrelevant to this tale, barring the stones, wooden icons and discovery of the teeth, which come later on in the movie. The characters provide a running commentary throughout their ordeal, one that could easily be produced as a radio play.

What marked out *Blair Witch* as new to the horror genre was its integrity. It was 'real', a trope that soon became prescriptive for every TV show over the next decade and spawned several inferior movies about reality TV shows. They appeared to be genuine young people on a camping trip with a difference.

From the moment that Heather encounters Michael there is tension – the characters share the same names as their actor counterparts. He barely acknowledges her as he leaves his home on day one, yelling goodbye to his 'mom', an ironic joke as we hear deafening music. Is it really his home or is it a student house? Heather and Josh are already giggling about him like teenage bullies. The soundman's relationship to Heather is not warm. He tolerates her, later protesting that the mission has not been scouted properly and losing patience with her strident attitude and egotistic behaviour. Heather and Josh (the cameraman) are not close either. She quarrels in the car over the metric readings on the 16mm camera, a coded emasculation of his prowess. Heather, the self-appointed leader, has placed herself in a complex maternal–paternal dichotomy, one that forces the men into roles as sullen children. They are desexualized – a shot of Heather scrabbling up a riverbank is mocking rather than voyeuristic. Their clothing is practical and identical, so much so that, when they first return to their abandoned tent, they cannot identify whose pack is whose. The men grimly follow, expecting her to make a mistake but bereft of any plan when she does. Neither man takes charge, nor do they defend one another.

These are people with only their professions to link them. Tradesmen, knights of old whose only point of contact is to talk of lances or armour (the equipment). It is remarkably prescient, a comment on a generation obsessed with technology and with recording events rather than living them, something which became more apparent in the following decade as passive video games took their toll, along with obesity and the desire for celebrity without the concomitant work involved. It is Michael who, as the bearings are lost and they become truly scared, insists that viewing life through a lens is not real. He demands they 'stop the game', but Heather, despite being repeatedly told to desist, doggedly continues to film. Only when threatened by physical violence does she reveal that her talisman, the camera, is the only thing protecting her from her fears and to remove it would take away her power over those fears.

It is as if the cameras are leading them. Not only can they record events, but they can also actively expose the Blair Witch and thus solve the riddle. This is technology developing beyond itself, a return to the fear of the machine, as in *Metropolis* (Lang 1930) or that of 'the computer', as in the post-war years.

The majority of the movie is about blame and responsibility, about finding their real and moral compasses. As exhaustion and hunger take over, they snap and fight. Michael remains truculent as Heather is self-serving. Both are cut from the same cloth and frequently come to blows, leaving laid-back Josh to assume the female placatory role with these two Alphas. In doing this he has adopted the traditional 'weaker sex' role, and for that he is punished. He is taken. It is as if the dominant female presence, the Blair Witch herself, is attacking the weakest first, as a male serial killer would do in a slasher.

His loss is crucial to the reading of the film, as there is now no sympathetic character for us to root for. It is only in the final scene, at night in the tent, that Heather finally admits to her culpability and immaturity. She apologizes on camera to the boys' mothers and in so doing both rescues her femininity and achieves maturity. It is, however, too late, because the die is cast and the Blair Witch takes no prisoners.

The point here is that you can create unsympathetic characters, so long as there is a degree of resolution at the end. There must be a story arc and *Blair Witch* conforms to this as any other. In horror there will always be unsympathetic characters among the protagonists. It is in the remit of every slasher that there be a bully or a practical joker. He is the one we love to hate, and he will draw the fire. A character like this behaves so moronically that we adjust our moral compasses to reach an agreement as to what is 'right' and 'wrong' behaviour. It is a bloodletting, and there is no cheer like the one when the dumb ass gets it! The role of the practical joker is similar to that of the court jester, to bring down the pompous, to equalize society and to take the heat out of a potentially difficult political or social situation. For this, as in a medieval court, he is often beheaded or otherwise purged from society once he has fulfilled his function. It doesn't matter, as practical jokers are closet psychopaths anyway.

Paranormal Activity (Peli 2007) concerns a young couple, Kate and Micah, who are haunted by supernatural goings-on in their tract home in San Diego. It was released in 2009 and has earned $194 million worldwide to date, producing two sequels and two more to come. Peli used his own house for the shoot, taking a year to prepare it and doing extensive research into the paranormal and demonology. It takes place largely at night because the vulnerability of being asleep taps into our primal fears. He states: 'If something is lurking in your home there's very little you can do about it.'[102] Peli also has said that the dialogue was natural because there was no real script, using the Blair Witch method of improvising and 'retro scripting.' Peli interviewed a hundred actors before choosing Katie and Micah, who use their own names in the movie. It was shot out of sequence on a seven-day run using a home video camera. It was shown at Screamfest, where Peli was signed by Creative Artists Agency CA and the film was sent out to as many industry people as possible. Miramax Senior Executive Jason Blum worked with him to re-edit the film and presented it to Sundance, but it was rejected. However, DreamWorks execs, including Steven Spielberg, cut a deal with Blum and Peli. They wanted to remake the film, keeping the original only as a DVD extra. Blum and Peli asked for a test screening first. People walked out, not because it was garbage, but because they were so scared. Paramount acquired the film and shot two endings, both of which are now on the DVD. The rest is history. And money.

What concerns us as writers is the prospect that dialogue seems to have gone out of fashion. Why spend months crafting perfectly honed lines when

---

[102] http://www.shocktillyoudrop.com/news/5123-exclusive-interview-oren-peli/

the two biggest hits of the last decade were 'non-scripted'? The answer to this is characterization and plot. *Paranormal Activity* – the movie in which 'so very little happens' – is meticulous in its storylining and its approach to character. Beginning on the day that Micah buys the camera (for 'half as much as he makes in a day as a trader'), we learn that they are trying to capture ghostly activity, which has followed Kate since her childhood. Again, as in *Blair Witch*, it is not real unless it is on camera, which supports the argument that the camera makes the news.

Micah plays with his new toy and sets it up in the bedroom. They have been together for three years. 'We're engaged to be engaged,' says Micah to friendly psychic Dr Mark Fredrichs, whom Kate has invited round. They are childless, indeed Micah talks to the camera as if it were his offspring and Kate is often seen knitting – an activity associated with preparing for birth. Perhaps she is broody or perhaps they are both scared to breed, as they are still children themselves. In middle-class Western society, the putting-off of having children until one's thirties is almost the norm. Generation Y is living in a state of arrested post-adolescence. They have the toys, the house, the pool, the car, the guitar and the gadgets, so why go spoil it all? Kate is, tellingly, still a student – one who may become a teacher, thus avoiding the real world altogether.

Fredrichs, the father/doctor figure, tries to determine her symptoms. This apparition has been following her since the age of eight, reminding us of a truism in supernatural thrillers, that it is people who are haunted and not places. He delivers the warning that this is a demon, not a haunting (seemingly on the basis of examining their furniture), and he is unwilling to deal with it. This is the betrayal by the parental figure. He nominates a colleague, Dr Johann Averies, who deals with demons, but this 'exorcist' never appears. A real paranormal investigator was cast but the footage was not used. They are on their own.

Katie wishes to contact the demonologist but Micah refuses, reverting to juvenile behaviour. He continues to drop hints about filming 'extra-curricular' activities, conforming to the cliché that, as soon as a man obtains new technology, he will use it for pornography. He tries to film her on the toilet. He belittles her fear of a spider in the bathroom. He does however become actively engaged in the investigation, reading up on demons ('they suck'), but his attitude is to provoke the demon. He is falling into the role of the fool.

On the fifteenth night, the footage shows Katie standing swaying over him in bed for some hours as he sleeps, before wandering out to the backyard swing. The audience is engrossed, so that when Micah then employs a Ouija board, we know he is signing his own death warrant.

The tension between this modern man and woman closely resembles that of the audience and not only a teenage demographic. She is troubled. He listens, because this is what modern man is expected to do. He tries to understand via rational means (technology). When this fails he reverts to childish tantrums, blame and provocation. He wants a fight because a man can understand the rules of a fight and its outcome. He craves simplicity over complexity, sex over love (which might lead to pregnancy, maturity and domesticity). Peli said that he chose the actors because they had 'chemistry' together. Indeed, they are a credible representation of a modern couple and all their problems of stagnation.

Another significant achievement of the *Paranormal Activity* movies relates not only to genre, but to modern cinema as a whole. Many detractors complain that 'nothing happens' or that the 'tricks' of the first movie were sophomoric, but what we are invited to do in those recorded night scenes is to watch, and to watch actively. Ninety-nine per cent of movie viewing is a passive experience in which the narrative is spoon-fed to us, but in *Paranormal Activity* there are great swathes of time when the CCTV camera, with four split-screen images, in *Paranormal Activity 2* (Williams 2010) or lashed to a fan motor in *Paranormal Activity 3* (Joost and Schulman 2011), is showing us nothing at all. What we are being forced to do is to look for the scare even when it is not there. The audience simultaneously shies away and cranes forward, eyes flickering to find the fear.

It is a truly interactive experience, the like of which we see in the films of Michael Hanake. *Hidden* (Haneke 2005) uses this gimmick as its central conceit and we have earlier discussed the breaking of the fourth wall and the complicity of the audience. The ideas of *Paranormal Activity* have been expanded on in *V/H/S*[103] which, although an uneasy watch (the handheld shaky camera and deafening music are akin to being violated at a SlipKnot gig), also asks a lot of its audience.

For the writer to create something that is fresh, cheap and attractive to producers, it is down to the quality of the idea and character writing, combined with what can be achieved with the predominant technology. The 2000s were a boom time for horror internationally, and the possibility of shooting and editing a movie is now within anyone's grasp. If 35mm is no longer the industry benchmark and if CGI effects are do-able at home (and non-cheesy), then we have to fall back on what made us writers in the first place and that is our ability to put credible characters into convincing scenarios with resonance and depth.

---

[103] This is a portmanteau movie directed by Adam Wingard, Glenn McQuaid, Radio Silence, David Bruckner, Joe Swanberg and Ti West (2012).

Interview with Jake Hawkins, writer/director of *Zombie Resurrection* (2012)

Did you first approach your script as a writer, a director, or both?

We'd initially started writing *Zombie Resurrection* with a view to selling it to a production company via a company called Ink Tip, but this quickly felt like a lost cause. We also approached several established film-makers in the latter parts of 2010/early 2011 with a view to have them produce. As we began getting sucked deeper into the writing we decided this was a project we could and should make ourselves.

How much did you know about writing horror when you first wrote your script?

I had learned the fundamentals of screen writing at university but had previously only produced short film scripts, the longest of which was 30 minutes. I had never written horror but was a fan of genre cinema, a regular FrightFest attendee and particularly interested (and often profoundly disturbed by) the French new wave which to me contained more thematic meat on the bones of an otherwise often tired genre (*Mutants* is a great example of this). I understood what I liked about horror films and what I didn't and these were mutual feelings Andy and I shared and wanted to carry over in our script.

Were you focusing on a particular USP or was it a long loved project?

Our USP was always our Zombie Messiah character; a zombie with the power to bring the undead back to life. It's a controversial and extremely powerful thematic core. It appears initially that this could be a cure; however, as the film reaches its horrific climax you begin to understand there is a much darker side to the resurrection process. The continuing cycle of being eaten, death, zombiism, then eventual resurrection is about as unnatural as it gets, and the human body and mind can only take so much. Suddenly the once divine is viewed in a very different light.

How long did it take you to write the early drafts?

We began working on characters and the backbone of the story in June 2010 as Andy began piecing the early screenplay together. We had a workable draft by September which we attempted to peddle to several film makers.

Are you aware of the various standard tropes of horror that exist in most horror movies?

Yes, and although we wanted to make something slightly different we are happy to say *Zombie Resurrection* is liberally peppered with classic horror tropes. We weren't trying to re-invent the wheel.

How many re-writes were required?

Our shooting script was Version 15 of the screenplay.

Did you ever feel you had to 'tone down' your vision for public consumption? Was there anything you think audiences could not handle?

In the early days when we were merely planning to write the script and sell it, we had initially planned an elaborate third act climax involving a crucified character hung by razor wire through a bell tower window as the weight of their body slowly sliced them to pieces alive, much like a human body going through a garlic press. In the script the sun was rising behind them before they passed through the wire in a grotesque wad of flesh and bloodied blubber, splattering messily on the ground below. When we came to produce the film, this was re-written to remove all elaborate and costly elements which ended up with the crucifixion happening against a wall indoors with DIY abortion instead of the razor wire – and no stunt hanging/razor wire/green screen/expensive grip gear required. And it still works in horrific fashion, in fact it's better than our initial vision, a case of innovation through limitation.

When it came to directing, how faithful were you to the script?

We were shooting a lot of pages a day and some days we had blood gags, non-actors, stunts, and blank-firing weaponry planned for a single day. When you are really up against it, the desire to get that precious line or single word quickly gets thwarted by the realism that if you don't act quickly and adapt to time and budgetary constraints you could jeopardize the entire shoot. Some key story elements obviously have to work, and if they don't on the day you need to make them happen on another day or in a way that works to your budgetary and time constraints.

How important were the actors' performances?
That's something we really did want to do differently with *Zombie Resurrection*. We didn't want to have cardboard characters you can't wait to see thrown to the slaughter. We wanted our audience to empathize and feel for our characters (most of them). Getting the right actors was absolutely critical to making our film stand out.

Do you think that the location and the input of DOP and actors improved your script/story?
Speaking as the DOP as well as co-writer/director I would say yes; if only in that knowing the logistics of how a key scene or action within a scene would be shot meant we could quickly write ideas off as too expensive or unachievable given the time scale. A good example of this is when we needed to re-write our opening scene because it didn't work on camera but sounded great or at least good on paper. We were able to come up with a clear idea both stylistically and thematically which could be shot on budget.

How satisfied overall are you by your work?
Given the film hasn't been released yet I cannot speak for how it will be received. But I can honestly stand by *Zombie Resurrection* as our first feature film. I've seen a lot of mediocre or just plain bad first films that only get released because they are genre and tick the required boobs and blood checklist. I am happy that this film isn't just about that.

Do you write as writer or director or both?
Coming from a production background I of course think about visual style a lot, but concept is absolutely the first thing. If you can't conceptualize in words it will never hold water.

Who are your favourite horror movies and writers/ directors? Why?
Not a horror film in the typical sense but Gareth Edwards's debut feature *Monsters* is a superb romantic road trip movie set against this backdrop

of huge monsters lurking in forests in Mexico. It also carries this amazing political statement about America and how it views the rest of the world, which is very smart. David Morlet's debut *Mutants* is a powerful film which again carries a strong theme of love and connection through it. Johannes Roberts had a breakthrough with *F* which both Andy and I saw at FrightFest and loved. David Schofield's aging protagonist was something we wanted to mirror in our character Sykes.

What advice would you give to the novice screenwriter?
Be tenacious, take criticism, and above all don't ever stop doing what you are doing. Talking as a producer who receives unsolicited materials and pitches, if we're not in a position to take on a third-party project we won't. It's nothing against the person writing – it's just how it is. But there may well be a producer out there who is, so keep looking ahead and move forwards.

Where do you think the horror genre is going?
I'd like to think with films like *Monsters*, *Mutants*, *Switchblade Romance*, *F* and even *Colin* to some extent (not for the marketing hype but the concept) that horror is getting a little more daring, a little smarter. I'd like to see more smart scripts and concepts in the future, rather than just a rinse and repeat of low budget schlock.

Interview with Andy Phelps, writer, *Zombie Resurrection* (2012)

Did you first approach your script as a writer, a director, or both?
The script was originally written as a work for sale – the master-plan being to come up with a unique horror concept, give it a thoroughly exploitative name and stick it up for sale on InkTip. By setting the budget at the lowest possible range, we figured that if InkTip had any merit at all for budding screenwriters we'd be sure to pick up some interest. And we got none – not a single script

download in six months. Maybe these thousands of producers were so overcome by the smorgasbord of filmic opportunity and writing talent on offer, that by the time they got to Z they were emotionally drained.

How much did you 'know' about writing horror when you first wrote your script?

I'm big into movie structure theory, and I'm a massive horror nerd. I've sat myself through an extraordinary array of really awful horror movies over the years, and it seems to me that 90 per cent of what makes them suck out loud could have been fixed in the screenplay. Once you realize this, you know where the attention needs to be paid when you're doing your own project. That said, I did do some specific narrative and character breakdowns on a couple of movies that we thought would be good templates – *Alien* and *Day of the Dead*.

Were you focusing on a particular USP?

We absolutely focused on the USP – we figured out the 25-word pitch before we started writing anything, and it was stuck on a yellow sticky above my monitor throughout the rest of the writing process. 'Fifteen months after the zombie apocalypse, and a group of survivors are forced to take refuge in an abandoned school, where they encounter a mysterious zombie with the power to bring the undead back to life.'

I have a few screenwriter pals who are still wrapped up in their pet projects, and I always think that it's a mistake to do this. Write lots, write to genre, and save the (probably unmarketable) life-long ambition project for the end of your career, when you have a reputation and a lifetime of favours to cash in.

How long did it take you to write the early drafts?

This isn't a particularly easy question to answer, as my particular process of writing is very modular. Jake (Hawkins, co-writer, co-director, co-producer) and I spent months chewing over the narrative twists, characters and the individual stories within the film, and for me this is the vast bulk of the writing. Only when we were totally happy with this did I put a finger on a keyboard. I wrote a beat sheet for the entire movie, expanded that into a long (30-page) treatment, and then further expanded that into a scene-by-scene map of the narrative and changing emotional states of the characters; only then did I open up Final Draft. From this point, it probably took about three weeks to get the first draft out, but from the beat-sheet onwards you're essentially editing.

I know a lot of writers like to start by throwing down a splash draft of all their ideas, with a view to completely rewriting it immediately afterwards, but the thought of allowing myself off on a wild flight of imagination with no structure to follow fills me with dread. Once something's down on paper it's much harder to be dispassionate about it, and I'm sure I'd end up keeping more than I should for the second draft if I wrote like that. I blame it on mild anal retentiveness.

Are you aware of the various standard tropes of horror?
Sure, and some of my favourite horror films follow this format (*Texas Chain Saw Massacre, Alien, A Nightmare on Elm Street*). It all seems a bit 1970s, though, and it doesn't tend to happen so much anymore. It's a much easier watch than the later teenage slasher model of having the jock, the stoner, the whore, the virgin, etc. in the terrorized party; from five minutes into the film you're made painfully aware that more imagination should have been brought to the table when they were writing the script. Hopefully *The Cabin in the Woods* has finally put paid to that for future audiences – it'll be interesting to see what horror short-cuts emerge over the next few years.

How many re-writes were required?
We ended up shooting the sixteenth draft of *Zombie Resurrection*. When it became clear that we'd have to make the film ourselves, we had to radically rethink some of the stuff we'd written; stuff that should have been someone else's problem. So, the two seven-year-old kids became one 16-year-old, the person getting diced into cubes falling through razor wire came out, the crucifixion was moved indoors, etc. There was another big re-write when we'd finally nailed down our locations, to match the screenplay to the space available, and along the way the script was under continual scrutiny for where it could be tightened up.

Because we were the producers, and the money to make the movie came from private investors, we weren't beholden to anyone to make changes we didn't want to make. That said, every time Jake and I found a problem in the script, once we'd figured out the root of the issue the solution was invariably better than anything we could have come up with separately. So, I wouldn't see getting studio and producer notes as an obstacle; my instinct is that as long as the producers understand what you're trying to do, the screenplay will be all the better for their input.

Did you ever feel you had to 'tone down' your vision for public consumption?

It's an 18-cert zombie movie that alludes to there being a zombie Messiah; the only people that are going to get overly grumpy about the content are hard-core Christians. Bring on the placards – it's all good publicity.

When it came to directing, how faithful were you to the script?

By the time the shoot started, we'd made sure that we'd blocked out all the narrative to match the location space available, so there was no running around at the eleventh hour. But of course things change on set – we didn't realize that blood gags and elaborate make-ups take so long to set up and film, so from about day three onwards we were re-thinking the gore as we went along. Because it was a really rapid shoot (24 nights), and we needed to get an average of four pages shot a day, everything tended to fall victim to the clock.

How important were the actors' performances?

It's a mistake to cast the zombies as the antagonist in a zombie movie; Romero never did, and who are we to argue? His premise has always been that the zombies are an unpleasant obstacle, but the real problems are the other survivors: in *Dawn of the Dead* the party have found a way to successfully survive the zombie hordes, until Savini's motorbike club turn up. The essence of drama is rooted in conflict and not peril, so you need to make sure you write your humans properly.

We spent a lot time planning who our characters were going to be – the kind of figures that you never normally find in zombie movies, or horror movies in general. The middle-class parent struggling to hold on to his pre-apocalyptic values, his bizarrely well-adjusted daughter, the cowardly zombie-rights activist, the pregnant religious zealot, etc. So, the performances were massively important. With an ensemble cast of characters that audiences can't immediately partition into standard archetypes, the actors have a lot of work to do. That said, there's still a number of gorgeous actors in the cast …

Do you think that the location and the input of DOP and actors improved your script/story?

It's difficult to see how the geography of the locations improved the story, as it was a case of making the script fit the constraints. The input of the DOP is taken as read – on set the breakdown of responsibilities was that Jake was the DOP and I was playing with the actors, and the directorial/authorial vision of the film up to that point has always been half his anyway.

The actors, though, were terrific, and absolutely improved the story as the shoot progressed. Because we were shooting so quickly, we needed to nail down a scene completely before filming it, and so this was usually pulled pretty closely from the script; on a more relaxed shoot it would have been great to give the actors a little space at the end of every shot to have a play and freestyle it a little more. But their instincts for changes to the script were always spot on, and universally made the movie better. In fact, the character of Asher (the repeat resurrectee) was almost completely changed on the shoot, as the ideas that the actor Georgia Winters brought to set were way better than the original script.

How satisfied overall are you by your work?

We're eighteen months in and still fighting through the last of the post-production morass, and the best I can say is that I don't hate it. And I'm pretty relaxed about that. As we were two people who had never directed a feature before, we decided to keep the shooting style pretty simple, and I'd certainly have more confidence next time round to try and move the camera about a bit more (and maybe hire some gripping gear). But nobody died, I'm still pals with most of the cast and crew, and we haven't run over-budget, so I'd take that as an away win for the first one.

When you write a new script, do you think about story first or visuals?

I'm very much the reluctant director; I'm much happier writing the screenplay than getting the bugger made. It was only when we realized that if we didn't do it ourselves, nobody was going to do it for us, and we had to step up our game. When our production designer asked us early on what colours we were reserving from the palette, and I didn't even know that this was something we should be thinking about, I realized that some people must get the whole directing thing in a way that I don't. But my assertion is that a well-written script in the hands of an inexperienced director is going to result in a much more entertaining watch than a well-directed turkey – go see *The Guard* if you don't believe me.

That said, my big bugbear is the writer/director horror auteur. A lot of people specifically study directing, and are presumably much more suited for doing it than we were; however, the number of directors that can also write well is a much smaller subset. The implied arrogance that anyone can write a proper screenplay does grate slightly. If that were true, there'd be a whole load more decent horror films out there than there are.

Who are your favourite horror movies and writers/ directors? Why?

Probably my favourite horror film is *The Thing*. John Carpenter is known for also being one of those writer/director types, and I think it's interesting that his best film is the one where he didn't pen the screenplay (Bill Lancaster). I have an early 1980s sensibility for my horror tastes, growing up through the whole video nasty era. The end of the in-camera special effects era was when the most interesting and creative horror was getting made – *A Nightmare on Elm Street, An American Werewolf in London, Re-animator.*

As for more recent horror, I thought *The Collector* was very well directed [Marcus Dunstan 2009]. *The Orphanage* is an almost perfect film in both writing and directing [Sergio G. Sánchez and Juan Antonio Bayona respectively], and I will watch anything that has been written by Joss Whedon. And there needs to be a special mention for the directors of *[REC]*, Jaume Balagueró and Paco Plaza, who managed to scare an audible squeal out of me in the cinema even though I knew the jump was about to happen.

What advice would you give to the novice screenwriter?

Make sure you enjoy the writing process. You'll need to turn out quite a few screenplays before you even begin to get any good at it, and that's never going to happen if you don't like sitting down in front of a computer. Chances are that most of your work will never get made, so the only tangible benefit you'll have at the end of a screenplay is the enjoyment of writing it. Other than that, don't be afraid to write within a genre, but make sure that you bring something new and innovative to the party. And then, when you're ready, go and make it yourself, safe in the knowledge that you're the most important cog in the machine. There is no career path for wannabe scriptwriters, and you have to take responsibility for your own development.

Where do you think the horror genre is going?

I think the most important development in the horror genre is going to come from the technology rather than any evolving trends. With the advent of DSLRs and £400 laptops that are powerful enough to edit a film, it is becoming easier and cheaper for anybody to get out and make their own good-looking feature, and I expect us to be swamped by low-budget DIY horror films over the next few years. There is inevitably going to be a lot more dross in there, and if you actually make an interesting movie the challenge is going to be getting heard above the noise.

Otherwise, zombies are hot at the moment, and we'll probably get another couple of years before vampires come back into vogue. And every so often we'll be given a really good cerebral horror movie (like *The Cabin in the Woods*, *Let the Right One In*, *F*, *Cube* and *The Signal*). However, there'll still be plenty of gorgeous young topless American girls getting slashed, bitten and tortured along the way.

Chapter 14

Forming the Idea:
Writing Exercises

Why be scared? Or rather, why induce the feeling when it is not necessary? Because fear keeps us alive. When we are in danger we go into fight or flight, which stimulates the hypothalamus, the region in the brain responsible for maintaining the balance between stress and relaxation, and this in turn sends out a chemical signal to your adrenal glands to release adrenaline into the bloodstream. The adrenaline rush is an intense feeling, making you feel stronger (people have been known to lift huge weights off a trapped child) and heightening your senses so you are hyperaware of smell, sound and perception. The adrenaline rush makes you feel powerful. Your energy is increased as the body releases glucose and sugar directly into the bloodstream. You value every moment. Once the danger has passed, the rush is over, your thumping heart returns to normal and the blood stops pumping in your ears. There is a great wash of relief. You are cleansed and ready to do battle once more.

The horror movie apes this, enabling you to experience vicariously the pains and pleasures of those characters with whom you identify. It stimulates the same adrenal functions – although we are not going to get into the specious 'movie-violence breeds copycat-slayings' argument here. Is this masochistic? Some would say so, but it is a useful way of purging unwanted feelings, as are our nightmares.

A horror film is an upgraded fairy tale. The Brothers Grimm's *Children and Household Tales* (1812) was a compendium of horrors, hardly suited to children. The first edition contained Snow White, Hansel and Gretel and Rapunzel, as well as many lesser-known tales with delightful titles such as The Story of The Youth Who Went Forth to Learn What Fear Was, The Devil With the Three Golden Hairs, The Death of the Little Hen, and of course, Cinderella.

'Sleep tight and don't let the bedbugs bite' was the advice given to us after a terrifying bedtime story – also to the Simpson children in the first Simpson's vignette on the Tracey Ullman Show (TV, 1987) and like them we probably ended up running to the safety of our parents' beds (maybe they didn't have bedbugs). And yet we listened to the tale with a fearful glee, squealing with delight, asking for the worst parts to be read again and again because, no matter how scared we might be of the monsters under the bed, we knew they weren't really there and that, when the story ended, the world would be righted again. Horror movies are bedtime stories for grown-ups.

Fear is the key. Only an infant lives without fear. Fear makes us alert: a natural and potent emotion, it is reasonable for protecting us from harm. It protects us from harm, prepares us for assault and it educates younger members of the tribe. As we grow, we begin to develop both rational and irrational fears. The rational ones are those such as the fear of abandonment by our parents. Remember the blind panic of losing your mother's grasp in a crowded place or straying just that little bit too far from home territory? Irrational fears are our phobias, which can develop from any number of perverse situations. There are myriad oddities, such as coulrophobia, the fear of clowns, which, although not existing in printed form, has been classified in DSM IV as Code 300.29.[104] It has only been in existence since the 1980s, coincidentally the time at which horror movies started portraying clowns as evil (Pennywise in *IT*).

Some phobias are partly reasonable, such as arachnophobia, the fear of spiders. Spiders are much smaller than you, nor do they own the bathroom, but some, as with Australia's funnel web spider, are potentially deadly (although antivenom has put paid to this).

As we become adolescents, we experiment with our fears and begin to enjoy the adrenaline rush some of those fears produce (we frighten our parents instead). Released from parental control, we believe we are superhuman and defy death and injury. We believe nothing can touch us. We experiment with drink and drugs, we go off on camping trips, gap years, bungee jump, sky dive, head off down the Amazon in a pair of flip flops with a rucksack on our back. It is also the time when we learn about sex, and with that comes commitment loss and danger – the adolescent cocktail of emotions is shaken and stirred. Here, the idea of the horror date movie is prominent as a courting ritual. The girl agrees to go along and is subsequently terrified, falling into the arms of her beau, who reassures her, as protector, and later, takes her home for some more 'protection and assurance'. It's as old as *The Hills Have Eyes*, but it works.

---

[104] The DSM IV-TR (the Diagnostic and Statistical Manual of Mental Disorders, Edition Four, text revision) is published by the American Psychiatric Association. It recognizes and lists all current mental health disorders. It's a compelling read and a great resource.

As we get older and more sophisticated, a different type of horror movie will appeal. Having despised or feared conformity, we lose this battle and new monsters appear. Bosses, co-workers – people who wish us ill. Will we find love and not just sex? If we do, will he or she be suddenly taken from us? Will our children die? And what about us, when will we die? Affluence and loss take their turn on life's treadmill and, as we age, we begin to fear the loss of our faculties, the descent into madness, loneliness, isolation, disease and death.

To summarize (omitting man's fear of God – for primitive religions only) our fears are as follows:

- Abandonment by the parent. Death of a parent. Phobias
- Fear of sex. Rites of passage. What is maturity and what are my gender roles?
- Death of a loved one or child. Loss of sanity or health
- Loneliness, isolation, abandonment and death.

Your writing will to some extent depend on what stage of life you are at. It is more than likely that if you are in your mid-twenties you will be addressing the fears of a young adult coming out of adolescence. If in your forties, more sombre events will concern you. Don't run from your area of interest or the stage of life you are at. Embrace it. Use your concerns. If it doesn't keep you up at night, it won't keep anyone else up either.

For basic screenwriting skills, we suggest you read Vikki King's *How To Write a Movie in 21 Days* (1988), *The Foundations of Screenwriting, A Step-by-Step Guide from Concept to Finished Script* (Field 2005), and *Story: Substance, Structure, Style and the Principles of Screenwriting* (McKee 1999).

As far as format goes, if you don't have Final Draft or CELTX, then there are several screenplay formatting templates and programs available to download for free or close to it. It is imperative you present your work in as professional a manner as possible, and that means it must look like a writer wrote it. It should be professionally laid out in an accepted format. You will also be expected to deliver a hard copy, unless asked otherwise. Log lines and synopses will be required too, so as part of your writing you must learn to express your movie pitch in five or 25 words, half a page or three pages. The InkTip website[105] has some excellent guidelines for this.

Finally, and our apologies if this seems patronizing, but correct use of syntax and grammar, proper punctuation and spelling are essential tools before you even build the edifice that is the screenplay. The odd typo will inevitably slip through,

---

[105] http://www.inktip.com/

but repeated mistakes are simply not tolerated. If you doubt your abilities, have your work assessed and corrected by a professional in this area.

A film is a STORY – a page-turning thrill ride that every actor in the DVD extras claims 'kept them up all night reading'. It has to look good on the page, and often the screenplay is sparse, with plenty of white around the words. That isn't for drawings, but the spaces between words are often where the sale is made. It is knowing your story and characters and choosing the right words so the powers of your imagination are unleashed and the producer or director is able to create his own imagery. It is allowing people to fill in the spaces, to join the dots. There is a reason why Stephen King has been at the top of this game for so long. He is first and foremost a storyteller.

His book, *On Writing* (King 2001), and his treatise on horror, *Danse Macabre* (King 1981) are both indispensable.

Setting the scene

It doesn't have to be a dark and stormy night, or a wilderness landscape, a cellar or even a dungeon. Yes, these places help, but horror can happen anywhere and keeping it to a specific location can be highly effective. Some of the best movies are located in some of the most mundane places. *P2* (Khalfoun 2007) was set in a parking garage on Christmas Eve. They can even be glamorous places – *Triangle* (Smith 2009) is set on a yacht, and most of the film is shot in daylight. It is the claustrophobia of the location that is so effective. The hotel in *The Shining* (Kubrick 1980) is first seen on a clear autumn day, and it is huge and sprawling. Kubrick creates a sense of intense claustrophobia with his use of single-camera perspective, all those endless corridors and empty rooms, the patterned carpets, the wooden floors, the empty gleaming kitchens. By the end, when we finally get out to the maze, we are transferring one sense of confinement and entrapment for another.

Exercise one

Think of a place you are familiar with, describe it in detail – it can be a room or a house or a school – keep it local and small, manageable. Take a look around. See what objects seem innocent but which could be lethal. Think of a room: in this case, your kitchen. Shut your eyes and visualize it. Write down everything you would see if you stood in the doorway. The coffee pot, the toaster, last night's plates, a box of cereal, the sink with a dirty white bowl in it.

Now look at the description and think what would happen if you walked in and one of those things was different. The toaster was a different make, or the bowl in the sink was grey instead of dirty white. Not a huge difference, just enough. No one has been in the kitchen since you left this morning but now the bowl has changed colour. At first you don't see it, it's just that something jars, that something isn't right. You look down. The bowl isn't just different, there's a pool of something in the middle. It's dark and viscous. As you look, a drip falls from above and joins the pool, which you now see is dark red. You look up, the ceiling is stained and another drip is forming. This exercise will engender unease and lead to dread.

Exercise two

It's around ten at night. The landline rings in the kitchen. What are your first thoughts? One, who is calling me at this time – because normal people do not call after nine pm. Second, it must be family, because my friends would use my cell. Therefore it must be important, and that means bad news. No one calls for a chat at that time unless they have a Jewish mother (believe you me, they always want *something*). Already you are caught offbeat. You reach for the phone and it stops. You press callback and there is no number listed. You go back through and it rings again, stopping once more before you can get to it. A third time it is your cell that rings. It is still untraceable. You are in a state of annoyance and fear. You are being targeted, but by whom? We can be trapped, rather than liberated, by technology.

Think of how you could extend or adapt this scenario this using the technology in your life. Could you now start receiving spam emails directed at you personally? Text messages? What if someone took over your Facebook entries or Twitter feed?

Use the everyday to unsettle us.

Exercise three

Location. Horror is a genre where we can work from the outside in, if we are clever enough. In this book we have referenced all manner of locations that have been used to varying degrees in horror, but let us now try to work around one that hasn't.

Let's say an oil rig.

It's isolated. It's deserted. It is only reachable by boat in good weather or by helicopter. Its radio mast and communications can easily be severed. It is a cramped environment with a galley kitchen, bunks, corridors and creaky rusty metal everywhere. Are we in the North Sea, or somewhere off Russia? Is it cold? Visualize it.

Who is going to go there? Has it been decommissioned and, if so, why? Is this story going to concern a team of rival professionals working for the oil industry? Perhaps the rig has been sold off (why?) and is due to change its purpose and be converted. Is it now a team-building course for business types? A training exercise? Maybe fresh supplies of oil have been located and drilling is to start again? We need a reason as to why the team is to be flown in.

Has something unknown been found under the water, or is the rig a cover for illegal activities? Could you bring rival groups together with differing agendas?

Or again, is this a Cthulhu story, an alien or supernatural one? Location here has defined a number of possible scenarios, but most important will be the characters that people this. Take the idea further, flesh out the characters and story into a brief synopsis. Get used to doing this.

On comedy horror

The use of comedy in horror, done well, is superb; done badly, it is embarrassing. It is hard to get comedy and horror right and, if it possible to legislate at all, the best method must be always to play it straight. The characters must never have the idea that they are in a horror movie or all is lost. Post-modern irony is over. Comedy works on surprise and incongruity. The comedy brain is one that is always thinking 'What if?'.

It is always asking questions and working the angles so that one perfectly honed idea can lead to endless riffing without forcing any subject. Many comedy horrors can be summarized in a strong idea, with a 'but' attached:

- Two hitchhikers are attacked by a werewolf; one dies, but keeps returning to tell the infected one to kill himself (*An American Werewolf in London*: Landis 1981)

- An experiment in genetic engineering turns harmless sheep into bloodthirsty killers on a New Zealand farm (*Black Sheep*: King 2006)

Often a one-line pitch will sell a movie (Ein, Zwei, Die: *Dead Snow*) but it will be the execution that makes a good one. In order to try to think up the former, here are some ideas for messing with the tropes.

- A serial killer is sewing up a dead woman's skin when his deadbeat brother comes to stay

- Ghosts are disturbed in their mansion when builders move in and refuse to recognize them
- A boy's invisible friend grows up to be a schizoid madman
- Area 52
- Gay demons
- Pet exorcism
- The Bride of Frankenstein survives and becomes a stripper to support herself.[106]

Some of these may provoke barely enough material for a sketch, but movies have been made on such one-note ideas (*Cockneys Vs. Zombies*: Hoene 2012). Try to come up with a new twist on some of the areas NOT being exploited currently (e.g. sexy Christian vampires and zombies)

On character

Madmen and monsters run riot in horror, and it is true that the antagonist is the most fun to write. You will have a fabulous time creating your monster, but remember that good horror holds back on the reveal, keeps the worst till last and allows the audience to use their overstimulated imagination to do the work. Hannibal Lecter had very little screen time in *Silence of the Lambs* (Demme 1990), but he walked away with every scene.

Before we get there, we have a whole cast of characters to deal with – especially your hero, the eyes and ears of the audience. If the audience can't relate to the protagonist it won't matter how scary your antagonist is: they won't care. It is to the credit of the writing of Wan and Whannell that we relate to the two men trapped in the cellar in *Saw* (Wan 2004), despite the fact that they clearly don't give a damn about anyone other than themselves.

Exercise four

Create a hero to whom you can relate – someone like you. Write down their inner and outer characteristics, what they want out of life and what is preventing them from getting it. Use a few well-chosen adjectives. Now create their opposite – their worst nightmare. This second character will be a crazy list of awful qualities

---

[106] Kind of done already in *FrankenHooker* (Henenlotter 1990).

such as those of a politician or a lawyer, but isn't there some stuff in there you can use and adapt to create a flaw for your hero? The protagonist in a horror movie needs to not be perfect (we have seen the drive to maturity as evidenced in the Final Girl), otherwise they will be unable to absorb the evil and make the jump from victim to hero. It is this shadowy area of characterization that makes the difference.

Another, deeper exercise is to look within yourself and face your worst aspects: those traits within yourself that you despise. Maybe picture an event you wish you could have changed. Why did you act in such a cowardly way? Why did you lie? Who did you hurt? Why didn't you apologize or try to right the wrong? Be honest about the drive that took you out of that situation and now either give it to the hero or base the monster around this trait. See where it takes you – but don't send us the therapy bills.

We need a hero who is flawed, just as we need a monster who isn't all bad. Buffalo Bill had his vanity. Frankenstein's Monster wanted a friend. We have to find something redeemable in even the worst monster because this is what makes the monstrous real – this is what creates the fear, this thought that, with just a small twist of fate, we are all capable of being monsters because, well, even Hitler had a mother.

To conclude, here is a final exercise that will take you through the stages of horror.

Exercise five

Write a scene about a man (or woman) brushing their teeth. Something we do every day, simple, routine, familiar. Slow right down, write the scene in painstaking detail, each fleck of spittle, each clump of paste, the tiny flecks of blood if you get too enthusiastic, the bits of pale gunk on the floss, the way the brushes feel, each one of hundreds, thousands of small spiked filaments rubbing against your teeth and gums. Keep going – use all the senses. Make it worse. As you continue to brush, things start to fall apart, teeth get loose, blood flows – take it as far as you like. What do you see in the mirror? Can you still talk? What has happened to your (now large and flapping) tongue? What comes out? Explore the abject as you go through unease and dread to terror. Take it to disgust. Go all the way, leaving all notions of good taste behind.

How does this make you feel?

This is how you must try to make the reader feel on the page.

Good luck, sicko.

Appendix 1: Horror Film Festivals Around the World

Submitting work to film festivals is considered to be the way in which an unknown film-maker breaks into the film industry (unless you sell a script direct to a studio). Whether you are a writer or a hyphenate director-producer, it is the stages after making your movie that are most important. Many films lie languishing, unproduced and unloved on the shelf, and unless you get them out there they will never get a distribution deal (tales of which litter this book). Even if you do not intend to become part of the publicity machine, it is important that you the writer attend at least one film festival, not only for the networking opportunities, but to see what your peers are doing. Listed here are some of the most prominent which are relevant to our genre (so Cannes doesn't really cut it).

A full list of film/horror festivals can be found online at http://www.biglistofhorrorfilmfestivals.com/

US

New York City Horror Film Festival

America's largest and most recognized genre film festival focusing solely on horror and science fiction. Each year the NYCHFF celebrates both the horror classics we grew up with and the new horror films and film-makers who created them. The NYCHFF fills the city with special screenings, parties, celebrity guests and free giveaways. This is the Halloween event not to be missed.

Texas

Texas Frightmare Weekend is presented by Warner Bros. and GameStop, in association with *Rue Morgue* magazine. Conceived by Lloyd and Sue Cryer in 2005 as a three-day horror convention, the event takes place annually in the Dallas/Fort Worth metroplex. True to its motto, 'The Southwest's Premier Horror Convention', their goal is to provide fans with an unrivalled experience by celebrating all aspects of genre films. Texas Frightmare Weekend hosts celebrity appearances, autograph signings, screenings, exclusive parties and horror memorabilia vendors from all over the US. The event is also extremely proud to have featured the rising talents of many Texas 'Frightmakers' in screenings, panel discussions and Q & A sessions.

South By South West

The South by South West® (SXSW®) Conferences & Festivals offer the unique convergence of original music, independent films and emerging technologies. Fostering creative and professional growth alike, SXSW® is the premier destination for discovery.

SXSW® began in 1987, and has continued to grow in size every year. In 2011, the conference lasted for 10 days, with SXSW Interactive lasting for five, Music for six, and Film running concurrently for nine days.

Canada

Fantasia International Film Festival

Running for over 15 years in Montreal for around four weeks. Fantasia International Film Festival (also known as Fantasia-fest, FanTasia, Fant-Asia) is a genre film festival that has been based mainly in Montreal since its founding in 1996. Regularly held in July and August of each year, it is valued both by hardcore genre film fans and by distributors, who take advantage of the eclectic line-up to select foreign and domestic films for release across North America. The history of the Fantasia Festival has roots in the Asian film scene in Montreal. Beginning with Asian films from Hong Kong and anime from Japan, the festival later expanded its international repertoire and screened genre films from all across the world. Since this time many world premieres have featured at Fantasia Fest, including Shaun of the Dead, Midnight Meat Train and Dread.

Europe

Sitges, Spain: Festival Internacional de Cinema Fantàstic de Catalunya

Beginning in 1968. Sitges has grown to become the most important European festival for fantasy and horror. Held just outside Barcelona each October, it is probably the most important film festival for horror fans and film-makers. There are numerous mentions in the book about its prizewinners.

FrightFest

Film4 FrightFest takes place at the Empire Cinema, Leicester Square, in the heart of London's West End cinema district, over five days during the August Bank holiday period. Each year over 40 films are premiered in Screen 1 (1,300-seat capacity) and Screen 4 (the 'Discovery' strand). Most are World, European or UK premieres and the majority will have directors, writers and cast in attendance for Q & A sessions. 2012 was its 13th year, with over 26,000 attendees. Director Guillermo Del Toro called FrightFest 'The Woodstock of Gore'.

The organizers of FrightFest also hold events in Glasgow in February and on Halloween.

Fantasporto: Oporto International Film Festival

Fantasporto takes place every February/March in Oporto, Portugal. Also known as Fantas, it is an international film festival, established in 1981. Giving screen space to fantasy, science fiction and horror-oriented commercial feature films, auteur films and experimental projects from all over the world, Fantasporto has created enthusiastic audiences, ranging from cinephiles to more popular spectators, with an annual average of 110,000 attendees. In spite of being organized by a private entity, the event is mostly state funded, with the Portuguese Ministry of Culture leading and the President of the Republic as head of the Honour Committee, along with several private sponsors.

Brussels International Festival of Fantastic Film

The Brussels International Fantastic Film Festival (BIFFF), previously named the Brussels International Festival of Fantastic Film (French: *Festival international du film fantastique de Bruxelles*; Dutch: *Internationaal Festival van de Fantastische Film van Brussel*) was created in 1983 as a venue for horror, thriller and science fiction films. It takes place every year in March. Initially organized by Annie Bozzo, Gigi Etienne, Freddy Bozzo, Georges Delmote and Guy Delmote (the Belgian PeyMey Directors group), it now has prizes in both feature length and short films.

Asia

Puchon International Fantastic Film Festival

The Puchon International Fantastic Film Festival (or PiFan) is an international film festival held annually in July in Bucheon, South Korea. Inaugurated in 1997, the festival focuses on South Korean and international horror, thriller, mystery and fantasy films, with particular attention to Asian cinema, mainly films from East Asia and Southeast Asia.

Appendix 2: Interviews with Writers, Directors and a Producer

Victor Miller

Victor Miller is the writer of *Friday the 13th*, thus the creator one of the foremost horror franchises. He is listed as creator of the characters for all the subsequent Jason spinoffs, but claims he has not seen any of them as he does not like the idea of Jason being the killer

What made you want to write Friday the 13th?
The success of the film *Halloween* gave me the impetus to write a screenplay in the same style, appealing to the same audience.

How much did you know about writing horror when you wrote the script? Was it simply from watching a lot, or deeper analysis?
I was in no way an aficionado of the horror genre. I had loved *Psycho*, but I simply studied the structure of *Halloween* in a single viewing and learned most of what I used in the structure of my screenplay. Carpenter and Hill had made it very clear.

Were you focusing on a particular commercial hook?
To tell you the truth, I had always thought I would make a success in the comedy genre, and *Friday* was a total fluke.

How long did it take you to write the early drafts?
I wrote the first draft in two weeks. I had worked with Sean Cunningham on several films prior to this one and our process was much more immediate. I would write scenes and we'd sit down and talk about them as I went along. We lived 20 minutes apart and we had established a method of work that made it well nigh impossible to count rewrites as such.

Did you ever feel you had to 'tone down' your vision for public consumption?
No. I had written a number of other scenes that were cut because of budgetary reasons but none for gruesomeness.

In your original vision the killer was Mrs Voorhees, a mother killing to avenge the death of her son. Do you think it's important to have a movie 'monster' that audiences can relate to?
I think that Mrs Voorhees was crucial to the success of my film. To quote a producer in Hollywood at the time, 'This kid took Mom and apple pie and turned them upside down.' A mother avenging the death of her challenged son is a meaningful mythic narrative even if her methods are wretchedly homicidal. I wish my own mother had been as strongly motivated.

How satisfied overall were you by your work on Friday the 13th?
I was amazed by the success of the film. In no way was I prepared for the fact that 30-plus years later I'd be autographing photos, going to horror conventions and answering questions about my work. I thought I had done a good job, but I hadn't even considered it becoming iconic.

Who are your favourite horror movies writers/ directors?
Hitchcock … followed by Carpenter and Hill. Hitchcock because he invented respectability in the horror genre. He gave it class. He elevated it in style and took genuine delight in constructing crazy Ferris wheels and awesome rollercoasters to take audiences on fantastic, stomach-dropping rides. And he had a lovely sense of humour even while creating paranoid universes where you couldn't trust anyone and nothing was what it seemed.

What advice would you give to the novice screenwriter?
Stop telling people you have a great idea for a horror screenplay, and write it.
Simply sit down and scribble the answers to the following question: 'And then
what happens?' 'And then what happens?' 'And then what happens?' When
you get to the end, go back and see if it makes any sense, and if it scares you.
Use your own childhood nightmares to guide you. Oh, and learn structure by
reading screenplays and going to movies and taking classes.

Steven Goldmann

Steve Goldman is a music video director with over 200 videos to his credit,
including work for Shania Twain, Bruce Springsteen, Faith Hill and Metallica.
He moved into the horror movie genre in 2007 with *Trailer Park of Terror*,
based on the titular *Imperium* comic book. He has always loved the genre and
the white trash shocker will never be the same.

What first attracted you to the script for Trailer Park of Terror?
For me it was the opportunity to develop a script from scratch. I was actually
handed the comic books and asked to come up with my own take. The comic
books are an anthology homage to *Tales from the Crypt*. I essentially pitched
an origins story – how did the Crypt Keeper become the Crypt Keeper? In this
case; how did Norma become Norma. Once the producer was sold on my take,
he introduced me to a writer who he wanted me to work with, and away we
went.

How many re-writes were required?
The writer and I only had to answer to the producer. I think we did four or five
drafts. Many of the changes had to do with budget and shooting schedule.
Now both the writer and the producer were not really horror fans, and neither
knew anything about Southern Redneck culture, so there was an awful lot of
explaining and selling to do on my part.

Were you already a horror fan?

I was already a fan, but I also wanted to play. I thought seriously about this kitschy grindhouse movie. There are homages everywhere to my favourite films and my heroes of the genre. It may be a little bit Seventies and Eighties, but from a story structure and character development point of view I think it is all Thirties and Forties! I looked to the Universal Monster model, where the monster was the lead and the audience loved them and hated what they did, but understood them because we knew their history.

Did you ever feel you had to 'tone down' your vision for public consumption?

I was told by Joe Leyton of Variety that he thought I went too far with the skinning scene. He felt it was just too real for a movie that was kitschy fun. Perhaps he was right.

During the rating phase, I had to pull back on the cutting off of an arm and the live skinning and deep frying of a young man. Just writing those words seems so wrong. By the way – the whole deep frying scene was inspired by a trip to Goliad, Texas, where I was taught to make deep fried turkey – so delicious.

In the end the issue of toning down was really one of marketing. The producer wanted two versions – so that there could be the 'Unrated' version and the one approved by the MPAA. The MPAA one took three or four tries to get the 'R'!! And I had no nudity! The difference between the two cuts is mere seconds, and a couple of shot substitutions.

When it came to directing, how faithful were you to the script?

I was surprisingly faithful to the script. The budgetary constraints did cause some real issues. Originally planned and budgeted at 20 days, two weeks into shooting my schedule was cut to 17 days. This had us cutting, rewriting and re-imaging anything that had not been shot already. I have always felt that it was kind of obvious where the big rewrite happened. We had a whole location created for a huge Smash-up Derby. We had cars with moving parts – like a rotating circular saw – that never got used. Now there are a couple of hits and boom! Norma sails through a trailer and crushes the boy in the cage. Though the story points are the same, all of that is different from the script – starting with the boy getting thrown into the cage.

Other changes occurred naturally as I discovered how good some of my real Southern actors were at improvising in their patois, but these were dialogue-related. I had to be careful about this, it could affect so many things. One was actually Nicole Hiltz – Norma. Not being Southern herself, improvising in character was harder for her, but in the end I'm so proud of her performance because she was fearless and true. Her performance has such spontaneity, like when she quotes from the bible, that people have asked me if she was improvising. Nope. That was written and she just went for it.

How important were the actors' performances?

Very. I would like to believe one of the most surprising things about *Trailer Park Of Terror* is how good all the performances are. Over and over again I've read and been told about how wonderful people/fans think Nicole/Norma is or how Myk Watford as Roach steals every scene he's in. I get a lot of 'for a low budget horror, the acting is above par'. All of the monsters had a backstory and all of the actors created monsters you would want see again … just not at night in the Trailer Park!

I feel that this is even true of the thankless cannon-fodder roles of the teens. Each actor was challenged to find ways to physically *be* fully realized characters, even while the script truly did not give them the pages to do it. They were a series of types. But I say above average types! It may have not been a surprise as to which of the teens survive in the end, but I would like to feel that the scene between Norma and the Goth girl – Jeanette Brox – is earned. Jeanette is a full character by that time.

Where I spent the most time clearly was with Norma and her crew. Norma is a killer, a monster, the villain, but also the hero of the movie just like the old Universal Monster movies: *Dracula, The Mummy, The Wolfman* … there is a backstory, a reason they are what they are, and the audience is both sympathetic and repulsed at the same time. I hope that Nicole and I pulled that off.

How satisfied overall were you by your work?

I'm proud of my work, but not satisfied. I think it's a bit of cliché, but it is what it is. I see all the seams, all the mistakes, all the problems. The interesting gauge for me has been my reaction to the negative reviews – they don't sting as much as I thought they would. There seems to be a divide, those who love it and those who hate it. There is something satisfying in those extreme positions. I guess I'm happy there were not too many bored take-it-or-leave-it reactions.

When you are sent a new script, what do you now look for?
If it is a horror script I look to be scared or horrified in the first 10 pages. If you don't get me there, there is nowhere to go. I want to feel the way I did reading *The Shining* for the first time. I want to feel like I have no control over my hands and they keep turning the pages because I have to know what happens next. I want to be so involved that I don't drift off or get distracted by formatting errors.

I also want a fresh new spin. I want to be surprised and excited about telling everyone I know about this really cool script I read. But if my eyes start to close, or nothing has happened and I have pushed on to page 20 … I stop.

Who are your favourite horror movie directors?
James Whale, Todd Browning, Terence Fisher – my childhood inspiration. We owned a 16mm projector when I was young. My dad would bring home three-reelers to watch in our basement. These three directors made my favourite films of my youth. They were entertaining, but there was always more. Subtext, passion and depth. Every film was so handsomely made. I made it a mission to try to see every Universal and Hammer Horror film made.

William Friedkin, David Cronenberg: *Exorcist* changed the way I thought about acting in a horror film, the way it was edited, it changed everything. Cronenberg, though completely different, continued to push the envelope. His fantasy could seem too real. He's also a Canadian: being one myself, that inspired me as well.

George Romero, Dario Argento: *Suspiria* and *Night of The Living Dead* and *Dawn of the Dead*. *Suspiria* may have actually influenced some of my music videos over the years! But seriously, like Cronenberg and Friedkin, they got me thinking. Their films were not just about scares. Again, there is a depth, something more going on beneath the horror veneer.

Sam Raimi, Wes Craven, John Carpenter: they simply made films that were so much fun! The best date movies *ever*! Guillermo Del Toro: I'm watching and waiting. He hasn't totally scared me yet, but he has amazed me visually. I want him to make the hairs stand up. He has certainly produced a few films that have.

What advice would you give to the novice horror screenwriter?

Scare yourself! Really!!! Don't write anything because you think it will sell. Don't write anything because it can get made cheap. Don't write anything because 'so and so' or 'it' is hot. Write because you have to tell this story, write because that nightmare needs to get out, because it makes you piss your pants!

When you sit in front of your screen and you can't stop typing no matter how late or early it is and it just keeps flowing and a sound from another room makes you jump because you are so in the zone ... you may be onto something.

Patrick Melton

Patrick Melton was the screenwriter of the 'Feast' trilogy, 'Saw' sequels 4, 5, 6 and 7, as well as *The Collector* (2009) and *Piranha 3DD* (2012). He wrote a draft on the mooted remake of Clive Barker's *Hellraiser*, which led to another collaboration on a TV project.

What made you want to write Feast?

Marcus (Dunstan, co-writer) and I were both new and struggling in Hollywood. We had bigger ideas, but we wanted to do something contained that could be made on a budget. So the idea of setting this monster movie within a bar was hatched. We were influenced by *Evil Dead 2* and *Dead Alive* so we tried to do something that was both scary and funny.

Were you working on a particular commercial hook or was it a project close to your heart?

Really, it was born out of frustration. Plus, horror was in a bit of a rut at the time (the years following the *Scream* phenomenon and its subsequent knockoffs). *Feast* was our response.

How long did it take you to write the early drafts?

We wrote the first draft pretty darn quickly. We were young, so we were still green in the process. I banged out a draft in a few days and then we honed. The first draft was done in 1999. But we didn't make the film until 2004. So, in between drafts, we learned a lot and often returned with a fresh perspective, making the script better.

How many re-writes were required?

We did a lot of rewriting. The purchased draft was budgeted at around $20 million. So our first job was to make it more affordable. That process can often take a long time. Every new draft hit with the 'budget guillotine' and we'd bemoan the latest set piece lost. In all, we probably did around 20 drafts.

How much emphasis did your script place on visual horror?

The director, John Gulager, was a first-time director, so the producers and studio were all over his ass. Everything had to be written and approved before it could be shot. However, once production got rolling, John was able to pick up a lot of stuff that wasn't in the script. Little inserts and things like that that made the scenes work better.

What attracted you to the 'Saw' franchise?

At the time, it was the new and hot thing. It came around when no one was doing anything like that. So, as a horror fan, I was naturally attracted to it. It was hardcore and completely adrenalized, which was different from everything else at the time. There isn't a lot the fans couldn't stomach. However, when you make seven films filled with different traps, your mind has to go into some pretty dark places to find something new. We had one trap in *Saw IV* that cut off the 'offending organ' of a rapist. However, it was cut because the producers and studio thought it was too much.

When writing a horror screenplay, how aware are you of the tropes of horror cinema?

With *Feast* we were very aware of horror tropes and constantly tried to flip them. For example, the people at the bar aren't very heroic at all. In fact, if anyone tries to be heroic, they die. The 'Saw' films have a certain amount of irony, but they're not funny in the least bit. So, we couldn't really play with the tropes in the same manner.

How much did you know about writing horror when you wrote your first script?

I watched a lot of horror films as a kid, so I was familiar what had been done in the past. We did analyze the genre in a way, attempting to do something different with *Feast*. As I've said, it makes fun of a lot of familiar horror moments we saw as kids. The problem with that, though, is that you can sometimes confuse the audience. Horror hounds get certain nods, but mass audiences often don't. When we tested *Feast*, the audience was totally split. As a result, the studio didn't know how to market it. The recent *The Cabin in the Woods* was marketed as a straight horror film but it isn't. It's as much a comedy as it is a horror film. However, trying to convey that in a trailer would likely confuse viewers not as savvy as most horror hounds.

How satisfied overall were you by your work on the 'Saw' franchise?

You can't revise history, you can only learn from it. We came onto the 'Saw' franchise three movies in, so the machine was already in motion. It was our job to continue that. And we did, for four more movies. It made a lot of money and reached a lot of people. We learned with *Saw VI* that it was most effective when Jigsaw was an active part of the narrative, but when he's been dead since the third film, it's hard to come up with new ways to keep him active. If everyone knew there were going to be seven films in total, I think Jigsaw wouldn't have been killed off in the third film.

Who are your favourite horror movie writers/directors?

I grew up in the 1980s, so I was influenced by a lot of the guys of the 1970s and 1980s who were suddenly available on VHS. It's the usual suspects: John Carpenter, George Romero, Wes Craven, Dario Argento, Stephen King, etc.

What advice would you give to the novice screenwriter?

Persistence is the key to success. Make a decision that writing movies is the *only* thing you can do, and then do it. Come to LA, learn your craft, and keep on moving. Your first screenplay probably sucks, same with your second. But just keep writing and keep working. Be aware of what a professional screenplay looks like. Be aware of what the town is looking for. Don't follow trends, analyze why they're successful and then do something different. People in Hollywood often talk of making 'elevated' horror films. That's executive talk for a person who doesn't like horror but sees that they make money, so they want to make them. It means don't write a story about teens in the woods being chased by an axe murderer. Joss Whedon and Drew Goddard have already ended that movie for good, so do something different.

Horror just means scary, so it doesn't have to be something that can be made in the woods for a million dollars. Place it in a different time or with heightened action, or with some re-imagined literary figure. But don't write some tired, dopey movie that's already been made a million times before. And don't get discouraged by failure. Failure is a way of life. Not everyone gets a trophy and pizza party in the real world. It's damn tough. So, you have to be tough and you have to have thick skin and you have to keep working. Eventually, everyone else will leave or die off and you'll be the last person standing.

Oh, also, being fast and easy to get along with are two very important traits. Meaning, write fast and be cool. That'll keep you around. If you're a slow asshole, you won't last long. But if people like you and know you can get the job done quickly, you'll work until you're six feet deep and your spoiled kids are fighting over your estate.

Marcus Dunstan

Marcus Dunstan is Patrick Melton's co-writer

What made you want to write Feast?
I wanted to see a movie like *Feast*. I worked at a Blockbuster. I went to the theatre every weekend … and there was no *Return of the Living Dead* … There was no *Evil Dead 2* … There was no *Dead Alive* … there had yet to be a *Shaun of the Dead*.

There was a total vacancy of wild card horror entertainment. I started working on a draft of *Feast* with Patrick on Halloween weekend 1999. I went to a Virgin record store and bought up every last AC/DC album I could find, lined them up by date of release and then plugged in. The dialogue and attitude flew out from there. People spoke like bumper stickers. People died like Vikings … and monsters humped like blind rabbits. That felt good. Hahaha

Were you working on a particular commercial hook?

It was a long loved reaction to what was missing in the present and what had been a grand surprise in the past. Patrick and I and anyone reading this article can download, rent, buy an entire genre's milestone films and digest them at the speed of playback. For any other film-maker or storyteller before the concept of home video, cable, they had to endure the slog of time as the milestone films were released with a sap's trickle over 25 … 50 years …

Video and download made film history instantly available.

That is pure film school. You digest what you want.

You find what you like, and you realize what you love.

Wild card horror was the most satisfying type of film for me. They were rare … divisive … complex … and gave birth to some of the most imaginative moments of media which still inspire action figures today ('Farewell to Arms Ash') … Ya don't see NECA announcing a new line of some kind of wonderful action figures ('Wavy Hair Andrew McCarthy or Extra Wavy Hair Andrew McCarthy').

Those wild card films usually didn't make much bucks … but everyone knows them … everyone sees them … and they withstand.

How many re-writes were required on Feast?

The producers at NEO were ready to roll with the first/second draft. The problem was that film would have cost 25 million bucks and we had 1 million …which then became 4 million courtesy of the Maloof brothers. In the six weeks leading up to production, Patrick and I executed 22 drafts. We worked in 12-hour shifts. Patrick wrote from 7am to 7pm and I woke up at 7pm and wrote until 7am. We weren't going to let that script suck. No matter what. If we only had a dollar to make it … we would have figured it out.

You only get *one* first time.

How much emphasis did your script place on visual horror?

That is where being an aspiring director and a new writer tripped over itself for me. I wrote too much detail into the action, complete with sound fx cues, song cues, blocking, set décor … it left zero to the imagination. It was also 126 pages long. The shooting draft was 96 … I think?

Self-editing was the big challenge. Learned a ton.

Director John Gulager had a vision for the violence and the action that was just stunning. He knew so much film history that he was the perfect mad scientist for the script. He kept the humour working by keeping the performances straight. He kept the monsters scary by keeping them mean. He kept the low budget hiding because he knew where to put the camera so the film stayed on story and moved like a rocket.

Watching the man in action is an education.

What attracted you to the 'Saw' franchise?

With *Feast* we had an exorcism of all of the wild card horror passion and had yet to tap into the reality version of horror. We had an immense reservoir of ideas to donate to the world of terror without the salve of dark humour. *Saw* made smart, plot-driven, adult cast, and detective-horror relevant again. *SE7EN* was firmly marketed as a thriller. But *Saw* cranked up the horror. It was smart, scary and landed a knockout punch of an ending.

I loved it.

So, to be a part of that storytelling was tremendous. It was a peek behind the curtain. We were very lucky to be a part of that world.

Did you have to tone down your vision?

Every time! Yes! There were traps and/or plot twists that were always put into a dark closet and locked away for fear of pushing an audience too far.

Every

Single

Time.

How aware are you of the standard tropes of horror cinema?

Feast was dependent upon clichés. We needed clichés to exist in order to make it work:

White tank top? Check.

Little kid who's gonna live? Check.

Mom kicks ass? Check.

A guy named 'Hero' surely is the star … Check.

The foul-mouthed dickhead has got to be the first to go. Check.

The bombshell is going to get naked and die bad. Check.

Then … we lined up all of those moments and flipped every damn one of them:

Asshole lives.

Bombshell is the smartest one.

Kid dies bad.

Mom dies too but Hero dies first.

That helped stick the landing.

With *Saw*, the real flattery is when *Scream 4* references *Saw IV* as a new cliché. Wow … in five years we went from making fun of them to being made fun of. Each is a compliment.

You don't get ribbed if nobody knows the film exists. The 'Saw' series is a loud burst in horror history.

How much did you know about writing horror when you wrote your first script?

Reading critiques of horror (by people who love it, made it, lived for it) helped a great deal. It was as if those scholars of horror shared a vocabulary.

It helped a great deal to read them.

How satisfied overall were you by your work on the 'Saw' franchise?

For four years, I was able to sit next to Patrick, our families and our friends in a dark theatre and watch horror films we had something to do with.

That made every single experience special.

Were there things we wished we had done differently? Absolutely.

Are there things we're glad we got right? Absolutely.

Someone out there is staying up too late watching all seven of those films back-to-back right now and making a list of ways to react to that media. That person will write until her/his fingers go numb and maybe … just maybe … we'll all reap the reward of being blown away by the imagination of someone we never saw coming.

That would be wonderful.

When horror wins, we all win.

You directed The Collector from a script you co-wrote with Patrick Melton. When it came to directing, how faithful were you to the script?

If watching films constitutes as school, and writing films constitutes university … then directing a first film is boot camp, triage, birth and hospice all wrapped into one.

I loved it.

Faithful to the script? Yes.

Editing on the fly? Yes.

Having to shoot a 30-day film in 19 days … ROUGH.

But, ya get it done.

Ya bleed for it.

It becomes a shared kid and you can only raise it with a great team.

With *The Collector*, when a scene wasn't budgeted with enough time, I began shooting what I couldn't afford to do on my own, knowing I could afford to shoot the close-ups, the details, or the moments of more artistic purpose (a slow drift into a glowing Holiday ornament, a fishhook slowly running down skin, the iris of an eyeball reacting to light, etc.). They were shots the 19-day shoot could not employ a full crew to get. It would have been a waste of resources to use 50 people and two hours of a shooting day to grab an extreme close up of a doorknob. I can do that in my garage with a borrowed light kit and a short end.

I was very fortunate to have the resources from writing the 'Saw' sequels to fund my own shoots to deliver the film I promised to the writers and to the people who have a choice to spend time in the dark with us or the next film.

We had to earn it by any means necessary. I wrote projects on the side to get fx favours, begged, bled … and that is my *real* hand in a *real* Zippo lighter's very *real* flame, so I literally burned for that film. Hahahaha … but man … what a shot!

Who are your favourite horror movie writers/directors?

Dario Argento: *Suspiria* taught us that horror could be beautiful. *Deep Red* taught us that horror could be brilliant. *Tenebrae* taught us that daylight could be savage. *Inferno* taught us that sequels don't have to suck.

John Carpenter: Far more eloquent writers have complimented this man. His horror was elegant. His science fiction had a middle finger. His female characters were smart, real and never from the world of movies – the women characters in a John Carpenter film are created in admiration.

For *The Collection* (2012 sequel to *The Collector*) I researched Argento's fetish for beautiful violence, Carpenter's anamorphic 35mm gliding camera, and – Bob Fosse.

Bob Fosse: I wanted the style of *All That Jazz* and the energized cruelty of *Star 80* to find a moment or two with our story. Both *Star 80* and *All That Jazz* feature characters racing towards their demise … one doesn't know it, the other sees it coming and smiles.

What advice would you give to the novice screenwriter?
I revelled in being told to quit. Not try. Give up. Go home.

If that helps, then 'Quit! Give up, you novice!'

But, if it is encouragement you seek, if you need to write – if you *need* to write – then nothing can stop you.

There is never a surplus of great stories. *Major League 2* is lasting proof of this. There is nothing that can stop you but *you*.

The first screenplay is a great relationship. It is a place to hide, a place to create. Any story, any direction … it is an epic download of everything all at once.

My ultimate advice?
DON'T LOOK BACK.
DON'T EVER STOP.
IT IS YOU VERSUS PAPER … A PRETTY FAIR FIGHT.
THAT'S IT.
NOW, STOP READING THIS AND GET TO WORK!!

Joe (JS) Cardone

Joe Cardone was the director of *The Scare Hole* (2004) and *Wicked Little Things* (2006) among many others, and was the writer of *The Covenant* (2004) and the *Prom Night* remake (2008). He was a major in political science, was in a rock band for four years, and wrote for three years for Universal Television.

What first attracted you to the script for Wicked Little Things?

The original script didn't attract me at all. It was a straight zombie movie. But no one had made a film in a long time where children were the antagonists. What I wanted to make and ultimately did was a *very* dark fairy tale.

How many re-writes were required?

One. It was a page one re-write that I worked with the writer on. I had the story in my head once I saw the Bulgarian location potential. The producers and studio were not really involved. I had made films for them before and they trusted my instincts on the changes.

Were you always a horror fan?

I was a horror film fan from childhood. Fear is a great dramatic motivator for narrative and plotting. But I don't consider myself just a horror film-maker. Many of my films have been thrillers, more in the Fifties film noir area.

Did you ever feel you had to 'tone down' your vision for public consumption?

Yes. It was most evident on *The Forsaken*. We had to cut down on the violence because the Columbine shootings had just taken place and the studio got pressure not to glorify youth killing youth. Now *Hunger Games* comes along and everyone embraces the concept. Ironic! Having said that, I do think there is limit to what a film-maker can and should do. But the censorship should rest in his or her hands, not the studio's ... or public opinion. That's why I have never ventured into 'torture horror'. Just doesn't interest me.

When it came to directing, how faithful were you to the script?

Ultimately, all the scripts I have personally directed have been my own or I have made them my own. It's hard for me to visualize the story unless I have a personal connection to the events that design the plot and characters. Even though that may be the case, changes are made at every level when on location and related to budget. On *Wicked* we were limited to less than $2 million to make the film and that in itself caused us to keep things simple.

Christopher Smith

Chris Smith is the UK writer and director of *Creep* (2004) and *Triangle* (2009) and director of *Severance* (2006) and *Black Death* (2010).

What led you into making horror?

I wanted to go to film school and wanted to write films, but I had no particular objective about working in a specific genre. I'm a big horror fan, I love comedy, I love drama, I love cinema full stop. I did an MA at Bristol University in film, which was a theoretical and practical degree. I made a couple of short films, neither of which were horror. At that time Neil Marshall had just made *Dog Soldiers* (2002), which revitalized the whole horror genre in the UK. I had already started to write *Creep* and suddenly everyone was interested in developing horror.

Horror is a good stepping-stone for first time film-makers, as it is much easier for a financier to feel safe investing in a proven genre. A film like *Rat Catcher* (Ramsey 1999) (which I love) can be extremely hard to attract funding, whereas, because it has to work for a specific audience, horror is visceral and is something that can be easily seen as commercial.

What were your horror influences?

I grew up watching horror films and slasher films of the Eighties, the whole 'Box of the Banned' thing (those films denied distribution by the 1982 Video Recordings Act). Also *Curse of the Werewolf* and the canon of Romero and Carpenter, especially *The Thing*, which I would watch repeatedly, and of course, *Exorcist* and *Texas Chainsaw Massacre*.

As I developed, my influences became wider. Something like *Triangle* was inspired by *La jetée* (Chris Marker 1962), another film that loops in on itself, as well as *Dead of Night* (Ealing's first portmanteau horror in 1945). For *Black Death* it was *Aguirre, Wrath of God* (Herzog 1972).

What are your top three horror films of the last decade?

Martyrs (Laugier 2008), *Switchblade Romance* (*Haute tension*: Aja, 2003) and *Wolf Creek* (McLean 2005).

What was the process in developing Creep?

If you've got a commercial idea you're more likely to get the money. Also the most successful horror films are location based; that's a simple locked-in, known, environment such as a house or room. There needs to be something familiar about it; even *Alien*, set on a space ship, was grubby and had the feel of a lorry depot or industrial space, it didn't look like *2001 A Space Odyssey*. As for my influences for *Creep*, it was very much *An American Werewolf in London* and the climactic tube station scene at Piccadilly. I thought: what about a whole film set down there? I hadn't even seen *Death Line* (1972) at that point.

The first draft of *Creep* took about three months. I didn't have a third act and managed to get development money with this core idea. I only had about 60 pages, which I developed with the producers over a further six months to a year of writing. By contrast, *Triangle* took three years to write all told, a much longer process. Being a writer/director is a huge asset to producers, plus doing 'genre' is easier and it is much more commercial to have an idea with an obvious hook to it.

What was the German connection? (Smith's leading actress was German-born Franka Potente)

I was a big fan of Franka Potente, who was already an established actor having been in *Run Lola Run* (Tom Tykwer 1998). It helped so much to have an established actor to get co-production money – in short, to come with a 'package' and of course German co-production money made things happen much quicker. We shot all the sewer scenes there and some of the underground ones too. Later, *Black Death* was mainly shot in Germany as well.

Were you pleased with the way Creep turned out?

I think with every film you do there are things you'd do differently, but I couldn't be happier with the way it turned out because it certainly got me on to my second and third films. There were some negative reviews, but at film festivals I still find 50 kids lining up with DVDs to sign for *Creep*, 25 for *Severance* and 5 for *Triangle*. Something about that film really clicked with people.

Was Severance your idea, or writer James Moran's?

Severance was James's characters and script, very much his baby; he came up with the concept. Once I put the actors in place, I just manipulated the scenes a bit with him and came up with ideas like putting the escort girls

Olga and Nadia in the pit. It wasn't a horror comedy in the traditional sense because we wanted to be scary, so we had to play it straight. You have to really care about these guys.

How was it, turning to comedy for the first time?

I'm an enormous Woody Allen fan, as well as of Nora Ephron's *When Harry Met Sally*. I love characters that are just funny people in real scenarios. That's when mad stuff happens. I was trying to create that and James already had good characters. It's so important not to have characters just doing silly things, they have to be credible. The comedy comes from the way they would behave anyway – it has to be real. My reference for horror comedy was *American Werewolf*. It's funny all the way through but you are also just as scared. It's a horror film that made you laugh, which is what I aspired to.

Did the casting help a lot?

Definitely. I was huge fan of 'Black Adder' in the first place, so Tim McInnerny got the part immediately. Andy Nyman was a discovery. When he auditioned for the role, he was funny but real. Gordon (Nyman's character) could have been a camp pantomime performance but it wasn't – Andy made it real, even when his foot was severed and put in a fridge. And Danny Dyer is naturally a very funny guy, so it all clicked.

What was the process with writing Triangle?

That film drove me mental. I had spent a year writing a first draft in 2004 and then *Severance* came along. I wouldn't have been able to do *Triangle* if I'd not followed *Creep* with *Severance*. The idea of a girl who was being chased by herself was written in at the start. Because of shooting *Severance* I stopped writing for a year, and then in 2006 I wrote solidly for another year and half. I was working on the script for three years.

But with your next film, Black Death, the material was already there.

This was the job you always look for. I came in late and was able to jump in, as all the pre-production had been done. I read the first five pages of the script and saw 1348, Black Death, plague, and revenge: what's not to like? Another director had developed it, but I had a different spin on how I wanted it to develop. Dario Poloni (the writer) was great and so was the team. Ecosse (the film production company) wanted it to have the feel of *The Name Of The*

Rose, which was unusual as producers usually want more gore and jump moments, but they encouraged this more interesting, darker side.

All my films are quite dark, they all go into their own weird places, I don't like roller coaster films where everything is safe and clean, I prefer this kind of dirty emotional feel. There's always empathy in my films but there isn't black and white, there's a lot of grey. I interviewed Ray Winstone once, who said that even with the most reprehensible character you have to find something you can connect to. I took this and used it, so that even with *Creep* or *Severance* you have to find something in these characters.

You are never sure if Kate's worse or better than the creep. So there's greyness in the film. In *Creep* the creep is this weird, abused, damaged man.

Like in *Wicker Man*, you know he's being titillated by what he sees but he doesn't want to acknowledge it.

What advice would you give to the novice screenwriter/film-maker?

Scorsese says that he considers himself a film student, in that film is bigger than everyone. When you are trying to get your first film made you must find what excites you, what interests you and what kind of film would you like to see made, but also ask yourself is it something you can sell to a financier?

If you are trying to get an art-house movie made like *Martyrs*, it will be a struggle. If your film is $300,000 dollars fine, but if it's going to cost $3 million then you will need to get a star in it, make it into a product that financiers feel safe putting money into. Star power has its benefits. It is best to write a stepping stone movie – don't write *Triangle* until you've written *Creep*.

Do you see any new trends in horror?

It's almost impossible to tell. You cannot cynically plan a found footage film, for example. There are many poor rip-offs that never get seen, but *The Blair Witch Project* and *Paranormal Activity* were made by good film-makers. All the planets lined up at the right time for these to be successes. To merely ape this strand as a spoof documentary is not easy, as these films are much harder to make than they seem. Better to go away and create a new Freddie Krueger. I love imaginative horror – what I find most interesting is not so much *The Cabin in the Woods* style of invention (although I really liked that film); what I like are emotionally devastating films like *Martyrs*. Something that reinvents through simple emotional clarity.

Jason Ford

Jason Ford is the UK-based writer/director of *Community* (2012). This is New Town Films' first feature, which premiered at FrightFest and Sitges in 2012.

Did you first approach your script as a writer, a director, or both?
I naturally approach each project as a director, as initial ideas tend to fire up images and set-ups that interest and excite me. Then I have to become a writer in order to make sense of those images and how they can be equally as effective and emotionally involving for the viewer. That's where the fun, trouble, horror begins. The horror ... oh the horror!

How much did you know about writing horror when you wrote your first script?
I knew nothing about writing horror. In fact, I hadn't written horror before because I didn't feel confident enough to do it justice. It was only through working on a thriller script with another writer that he remarked I was pushing it into the realms of horror, which became a debate it itself. When does thriller become horror? When it deals with the supernatural? The nature of the victim's death? The amount of blood spilled? I believe it's very much a grey area (even more so today, as horror has so many subgenres).

I guess watching a lot made me realize that. *The Wicker Man* is a very different horror film to *Halloween*, as *Blair Witch* is to *Hostel*. But in some senses it freed me up. My main influence was that if it felt real and frightening and you see pain and suffering, then it's horror. Very much like the lone crazed gunman: to me, that is the ultimate horror, as it's social horror. My approach always tends to come through reflecting and expanding on the current climate, socially, economically and environmentally.

Were you focusing on a particular USP – a hook to sell your spec script?
I'd had the idea of a sinister housing estate for some time but I thought it was a TV series. Maybe it still could be. Our original USP was 'Blair Witch on a council estate', and naturally the idea was to shoot it cheap with video cameras etc. But as we developed the idea, it began to gain interest, then of course the budgetary goalposts change and you find yourself in the midst of a conventional feature again.

How long did it take you to write the early drafts?

Everything I've written thus far has been done in between working at day job(s). It took me approximately three to four months to write an exploratory draft (a pre-first draft where I bulldoze through any obvious problems). It then took a further two to three months to have a draft we (my producer and I) were happy to send out. But this came after eight months of developing the idea from synopsis to 10-page treatment, fleshing out the entire story.

We send this out early on to some readers, to get some feedback on ideas, structure etc. It's worth noting that one such reader, Marc Blake, was a great source of encouragement.

Ultimately it was the first draft that caught the attention of our sales agent. I did a second draft over another couple of months, and that's ultimately what we shot. But don't be fooled: if there was more time and development money it would have had another draft. But you can go on forever, no script is perfect, and you never stop rewriting, even when filming, because of all the elements and creative talent involved. Then, after all that, the film changes in the edit because it becomes it's own beast.

How hard was it get funding?

After we released our first feature in 2005, the saying was that the funding would become easier to obtain. Well, in 2008 the recession began and the game changed. From the beginning this project had been a 'reaction' project to a lack of funding becoming available. We had several sit-downs with possible investors and co-productions, but they all fell by the wayside. Maybe the fact that we started to get angry and 'Hulk' with frustration before their eyes didn't help. (My producer is Hulk. I'm more Teenwolf!) The final budget was made up of some private investment and clearing out everything our company had earned from corporate videos. So, for a large part, we have funded this project again.

Ian Rattray (who we knew as being the glamorous, charming side of FrightFest) got a copy of the film from our sales agent whilst in Cannes.

When it came to directing, how faithful were you to the script?

About 25 per cent of the dialogue was cut due to time and budget. As far as directing, a good 50 per cent of the creative and artistic angles were dropped. The reality is that our premise was ambitious from the beginning, as we had to show a number of exterior set-ups due to the fact we had to 'see' a community setting (as opposed to the interior of one controlled location that is usually associated with low budget horrors). So it was always going to be tough. A perfect example was that we were shooting probably our most climactic scene which involved a gunshot to one head and a decapitation to another, and the set was being taken down around us as we had to be out of the studio. In many ways it is the hardest type of film-making, as it calls for the most creativity, temperament and talent, across all departments.

How important were the actors' performances?

Acting in horror is very underrated. Good horror demands very good, strong actors, especially if you want the unknown to be believable. One of our actors screamed so much he threw up his lunch. (That could be a tag line!) As for characterization, I guess it depends on the subgenre you're dealing with. Ours is very much psycho and social so we were dependent on a fair amount of character and exposition so we needed good, strong, believable performances.

How satisfied overall were you by your work?

I've only ever had micro budgets so the optimistic side of me reminds me I did the best I could within the constraints. You have to put it all into perspective, which, ironically, is what this industry is famous for *not* doing, as we all get wrapped up in the illusion of it all. It's a mammoth task, a beast with a hundred different limbs and orifices that can strangle and drag you under at any given moment.

The fact that you can begin and complete a project (to final edit and sound mix stage) is a feat of Olympian proportions, and none more so than when you're on a micro budget, as the chances are you have taken on several departments yourself as well as your own, and then you go back to your day job during the edit.

Yes, you are forever gutted that you couldn't get that shot or develop that character or sequence, and the occasional shot makes you wince, but you have to learn to pat yourself on the back that you achieved anything at all. So I try to improve at *not* being so hard on myself. And you comfort yourself in the knowledge that those prospective financiers and co-producers who deliberated about getting involved are still there, talking about it.

When you write a new script, do you think about story first or visuals?

I'm learning to start as a writer, as ultimately it's the story that is the backbone. Yes of course you can have a great effective visual idea, especially with horror, a child, deformity etc. … but if it has no real story or believable reason behind it, it will feel flat and empty once it is revealed. It's the suspense that is key and that has to be written to begin with, not visualized.

Who are your favourite horror movies writers/ directors?

My favourite film is *Jaws*, and it still remains the ultimate monster movie and it's pretty much influenced everything I've done. If I had to choose I would say Hammer, especially, the TV series 'Hammer House Of Horrors', very British, sinister characters, dated now and cheesy but that somehow that makes them more unnerving.

Carpenter is a big influence. He was king for me as far as his versatility, scale and execution. *The Thing, Halloween*. He even composed the music, which are benchmarks themselves. My weakness is that I'm influenced by lots of different styles, picking the bones and parts of the best and trying to sew them together. In that case I should say *Frankenstein*, which is ultimately what *Community* is, a monster that society has created.

What advice would you give to the novice screenwriter or anyone trying to make an independent horror film?

First I would say, begin with the simplest set-ups. *Blair Witch* was the simplest of ideas. Then *Paranormal Activity* came along and simplified it even further. When you begin writing, treat it all as an experiment. That way, it will help with the criticism. Show it to people that have done it, whose work you respect. Don't start out by saying 'I'm going to write the best script'; say, 'I'm going to learn to make my script better'. That's all you can do. Make it as good as you can within the allotted time you have.

Making any film is ultimately about trust and partnerships and working as a team. For the majority of the time it will demand you put your hand in your own pocket to help get it made. It is the ultimate leap of sacrifice to make it yourself, but if you don't at least attempt to confront the beast, it will haunt and eat away at you for evermore.

Stephen Woolley

Stephen Woolley was instrumental in bringing cult films to London audiences at the Screen on the Green in Islington and programming the legendary all-nighters at the Scala Cinema. He premiered and championed Sam Raimi's *Evil Dead*.

He is the producer of over 50 movies including *Interview with a the Vampire, Company of Wolves* and *Byzantium.*

What do you consider is the role of the producer?
Each film/producer is so different, it's difficult to qualify. All of them go in different ways – no one film is the same. Genre films, even though they have great directors and/or auteurs, they are traditionally driven by producers (I'm thinking William Castle, Herschell Gordon Lewis – the drive-in style movies). The material is in the producer's realm, much more so than for dramas.

Horror films are put together as something that will appeal to the audience – it is a manipulated genre. Bob Shea was very influential in the making of *Nightmare on Elm Street* and worked with Wes Craven. It wasn't an exceptional film, but aligning it with New Line and Bob Shea is the reason that film worked – they knew what they were going for in terms of audience. That kind of combination is much stronger in horror and genre movies than in drama. It feels to me, as a film-maker, that there is a closer collaboration with the producer in the horror genre. Each producer takes a different role in each film though, so this is just my experience. With *The Company of Wolves,* I leapt on that as a producer and released it as distributor as well, always with the audience in mind.

Why do you enjoy producing horror movies?

I'm a huge fan of the horror genre, as you can see from the films I get involved with, right from the Screen on the Green days. Horror is so maligned that, once a film is known as a horror movie, it has a very narrow bar of critical response. For example, *Peeping Tom*[107] was dismissed critically, either slated or ignored by film critics, but it's now seen as a classic of the genre. I looked through archives from when the film came out and couldn't find a good review anywhere. Horror is traditionally a maligned genre; the producers, marketers, publicists and distributors have always had a much stronger say on what the audience wants and there is also the issue that it is directed towards a younger audience, who are by nature capricious.

Would you consider films like Twilight to be horror?

'Twilight' and 'Harry Potter' are stories with strong elements of horror in them, but not technically within the horror genre. 'Twilight' is more a teenage melodrama/love story, but demand for these films is high. These films need a strong producer/studio in charge because the audience is so manipulated by the material. The guiding hand, therefore, has to be the source material as well as the producers. 'Twilight', although it has vampires in it, is not really horror, no more than is 'Harry Potter', which is not to say they are not admirable films, or that I don't like them. Those franchises are built on strong elements of the horror and use horror expectations – i.e. vampires, ghosts etc. – but they are no more horror than *Nightmare on Elm Street* is melodrama, but there is enough of a sense of horror to attract the young audience.

This is also true of *Hunger Games* (there is an argument that it is reminiscent of Seventies dystopian societal films such *Soylent Green* or *I am Legend*[108]); this again is not really a horror film, but it is similar to 'Twilight' and 'Harry Potter' in that it deals with teenage angst in a contemporary nature.[109]

Your new film, Byzantium, deals with vampires. Is it a horror film?

Byzantium includes some elements that you'd expect from a horror film. There is a sense of foreboding and it feels subversive. It deals with amoral/

---

[107] Michael Powell 1960.

[108] Richard Matheson's story, 'I am Legend', has been adapted three times for the screen to date.

[109] It also pays tribute to *Battle Royale*.

immoral characters, which is where horror begins and ends, outside of reality and in the realm of dreams, the irrational. People who love horror love the unexplainable and the irrational. People go back to *Dracula* and *Frankenstein* because of this, because the films deal with things that can't be explained. That's what I perceive as horror; movies by Polanski or Dario Argento that subvert your expectations of the genre, that deal with fear, disturbance and psychological issues; the things that you don't identify with any other genre.

Why do you think more major actors (such as Gemma Arterton) are drawn to horror these days?

It started with *Silence of the Lambs* or before that with *The Exorcist*, when actors began to be drawn to material that is difficult. Generally the protagonist is a male who meets a bad ending or saves the heroine, so it is a bit stereotypical. This type of film does not appeal to big names looking for interesting material, but in horror it is difficult for a big star to play someone who goes around killing people. I think that for Gemma it is about finding an interesting role. Lead roles for women are few, so horror appeals to female actors like Gemma. Horror also appeals to women more as viewers now. The rise during the 1980s and 1990s of video and DVD has made horror more accessible to women as viewers. Women are more interested in the genre. There is less of a male/female divide in horror. I think there is a big gap in market for films like *Kick Ass* for young women protagonists and strong action characters. Other young women identify with this as roles in society are blurred. The reality is there are so few roles for women anyway. Actresses are drawn to horror as it enables them to stretch themselves, but in horror, as in most films, the director, producer and distributors are all still male.

What do you look for in a script?

Originality and respect for what's gone before. Skill and expertise in the way it is put together – not writing words backwards or just switching roles, but knowing that although everything has been done before there is an original way to speak to an audience and be contemporary (even in a period piece) and subversive.

Finally – your personal top five horror movies are?

Psycho (Hitchcock 1960) has to be in there – the use of imagery, music and lighting all make an incredible film. *Eyes without a Face* (Franju 1960) – hard not to put it in, just a really interesting film. *Deep Red (Profundo Rosso*: Argento 1975) – watch it, the film *Deep Red* was horribly butchered and cut, but *Profundo Rosso* is incredible, it will change your mind about Argento. *Peeping Tom* (Powell 1960) – Michael Powell had balls to take the risks he did with this film. Last but not least, *The Evil Dead* (Raimi 1981), because it transferred the video company I had into a force, it was a revolutionary film for me on many levels and still stands up today. And one more, if I'm allowed: *Vampyr* (Dreyer 1932).

Appendix 3: Our Top 20

What follows are 20 of the authors' personal favourites. We have kept away from the classic canon, as enough has been written about them and we would hope that our readers would have seen them or will be making urgent plans to do so. The list attempts to cover a range of subgenres and periods. These are oddball films that we love, and there are many others we fought over and would love to have included in the book. All are well worth catching as exemplars of the continued strength of the horror genre.

MB

Exorcist III
Invaders from Mars
Oldboy
Martyrs
Night of the Demon
Hell Raiser 2
Theatre of Blood
Feast
Village of the Dammed
Brain Dead

SB

Dr Terror's House of Horrors
Splice
The Woman
Trick 'r Treat
Bride of Chucky
Tokyo Gore Police
Ginger Snaps 2
Let the Right One In
Wolf
Bride of Frankenstein

Filmography

13 Ghosts. DVD. Directed and produced by William Castle. 1960. USA: William Castle Productions.

28 Days Later. DVD. Directed by Danny Boyle; produced by Andrew Macdonald. 2002. UK: DNA Films; British Film Council.

A Nightmare on Elm Street. DVD. Directed by Wes Craven; produced by John Burrows. 1984. USA: Smart Egg Pictures; New Line Cinema; Media Home Entertainment.

A Nightmare On Elm Street. DVD. Directed by Samuel Bayer; produced by Michael Bay. 2010. USA: New Line Cinema; Platinum Dunes.

A Nightmare on Elm Street Part 2: Freddy's Revenge. DVD. Directed by Jack Sholder; produced by Stephen Diener. 1985. USA: Smart Egg Pictures; Second Elm Street Venture; New Line Cinema.

A Nightmare on Elm Street 3: Dream Warriors. DVD. Directed by Chuck Russell; produced by Wes Craven. 1987. USA: Smart Egg Productions; New Line Cinema; Heron Communications.

A Nightmare on Elm Street 4: The Dream Master. DVD. Directed by Renny Harlin; produced by Stephen Diener. 1988. USA: Smart Egg Pictures; New Line Cinema; Heron Communications.

A Nightmare on Elm Street 5: The Dream Child. DVD. Directed by Stephen Hopkins; produced by Rupert Harvey. 1989. USA: Smart Egg Pictures; New Line Cinema; Heron Communications.

A Nightmare on Elm Street 6: Freddy's Dead – The Final Nightmare. DVD. Directed by Rachael Talaley; produced by Michael de Luca. 1991. USA: Nicolas Entertainment; New Line Cinema.

A Serbian Film [*Srpski film*]. DVD. Directed by Srdjan Spasojevic; produced by Nikola Pantelic. 2010. Serbia: Contra Film.

Alien. DVD. Directed by Ridley Scott; produced by Gordon Carroll. 1979. USA: Twentieth Century Fox; Brandywine Productions.

All the Boys Love Mandy Lane. DVD. Directed by Jonathan Levine; produced by Keith Calder. 2006. USA: Occupant Films.

Alone in the Dark. DVD. Directed and produced by Uwe Boll. 2005. Canada/Germany/USA: AITD Productions; Boll Kino Beteiligungs GmbH & Co. KG; Herold Productions.

Alone in the Dark II. DVD. Directed by Michael Roesch; produced by Hans Baer. 2008. USA/Germany: HJB Filmproduktion; Boll Kino Beteiligungs GmbH & Co. KG; Brooklyn Independent Studios.

Amsterdamned. DVD. Directed by Dick Maas; produced by Laurens Geels. 1988. Netherlands: First Floor Features.

An American Werewolf in London. DVD. Directed by John Landis; produced by George Folsey Jr. 1981. UK: Lyncanthrope Films, PolyGram Filmed Entertainment.

Anatomy [Anatomie]. DVD. Directed by Stefan Ruzowitsky; produced by Jakob Claussen. 2000. Germany: Claussen & Woebke Filmproduktion; Deutsche TriStar Filmproduktion.

Angel Heart. DVD. Directed by Alan Parker; produced by Elliott Kaster. 1987. USA: Carolco International N.V.; Union; Winkast Film Productions.

Antichrist [Antychryst]. DVD. Directed by Lars von Trier; produced by Bettina Brokemper. 2009. Denmark: Film i Väst; Lucky Red; Canal+.

Attack of the 50 Foot Woman. DVD. Directed by Nathan Juran; produced by Jacques Marquette. 1958. USA: Woolner Brothers Pictures Inc.

Attack of the Giant Leeches. DVD. Directed by Bernard L. Kowalski; produced by Gene Corman. 1959. USA: American International Pictures.

Attack of the Killer Tomatoes! DVD. Directed and produced by John de Bello. 1978. USA: Four Square Productions.

Attack the Block. DVD. Directed by Joe Cornish; produced by Jenny Borgars. 2011. UK: Studio Canal; UK Film Council; Big Talk Productions.

Asylum. DVD. Directed by Roy Ward Baker; produced by Gustave M. Berne. 1972. UK: Amicus Productions; Harbour Productions Limited.

Audition [Ôdishon]. DVD. Directed by Takashi Miike; produced by Satoshi Fukushima. 1999. Japan: Omega Project; AFDF; Creators Company Connections.

Autopsy. DVD. Directed by Adam Gierasch; produced by Michael Arata. 2008. USA: Lion Share Productions; A-Mark Entertainment; FlipZide Pictures.

Bad Taste. DVD. Directed and produced by Peter Jackson. 1987. New Zealand: Wingnut Films; New Zealand Film Commission.

Baise-moi [Fuck Me]. DVD. Directed by Virginie Despentes and Coralie; produced by Philippe Godeau. 2000. France: Toute Premiere Fois; Canal +; Pan Européenne Production.

Basket Case. DVD. Directed by Frank Henenlotter; produced by Arnold H. Bruck. 1982. USA: Basket Case Productions.

Batman Begins. DVD. Directed by Christopher Nolan; produced by Larry Franco. 2005. USA: Warner Bros. Pictures; DC Comics; Syncopy.

Behind the Mask: The Rise of Leslie Vernon. DVD. Directed by Scott Glosserman; produced by Al Corley. 2006. USA: Glen Echo Entertainment; Code Entertainment.

Black Christmas. DVD. Directed by Bob Clark; produced by Gerry Arbeid. 1974. Canada: Vision IV; August Films; Film Funding Ltd. of Canada.

Black Sheep. DVD. Directed by Jonathan King; produced by Philippa Campbell. 2006. New Zealand: New Zealand On Air; New Zealand Film Commission; Live Stock Films.

Blackwoods. DVD. Directed and produced by Uwe Boll. 2001. Canada/Germany: Boll Kino Beteiligungs GmbH & Co. KG; Cinemedia; Shavick Entertainment.

Blood Demon / The Torture Chamber of Dr. Sadism. *[Die Schlangengrube und das Pendel / The Snake Pit and the Pendulum]*. DVD. Directed by Harald Reinl; produced by Erwin Gitt. 1967. West Germany: Constantin Film Produktion.

Blood Feast. DVD. Directed by Herschell Gordon Lewis; produced by David F. Friedman. 1963. USA: Friedman–Lewis Productions.

Boo. DVD. Directed by Anthony Ferrante; produced by David E. Allen. 2005. USA: Kismet Entertainment Group; Graveyard Filmworks.

Book of Blood. DVD. Directed by John Harrison; produced by Clive Barker. 2009. UK: Scottish Screen; Matador Pictures; Midnight Picture Show.

Braindead. DVD. Directed by Peter Jackson; produced by Jim Booth. 1992. New Zealand: Wingnut Films; New Zealand Film Commission; Avalon/NFU Studios.

Bride of Frankenstein. DVD. Directed by James Whale; produced by Carl Laemmle Jr. 1935. USA: Universal Pictures.

Bride of Re-Animator. DVD. Directed by Brian Yuzna; produced by Hidetaka Konno. 1990. USA: Wild Street.

Brotherhood of the Wolf [*Le pacte des loups*]. DVD. Directed by Christophe Gans; produced by Richard Grandpierre. 2001. France: Natexis Banques Populaires Images; Canal+; Eskwad.

Buffy the Vampire Slayer. TV Series. Directed and produced by Joss Whedon. 1997–2003. USA: Sandollar Television; Kuzui Enterprises; Mutant Enemy.

Burke and Hare. DVD. Directed by John Landis; produced by James Atherton. 2010. UK: Fragile Films; Ealing Studios; Quickfire Films.

Cabin Fever. DVD. Directed by Eli Roth; produced by Evan Astrowsky. 2002. USA: Tonic Films; Deer Path Films; Down Home Entertainment.

Calvaire [*The Ordeal*]. DVD. Directed by Fabrice du Welz; produced by Michael Gentile. 2004. Belgium: Teledistributeurs Wallons; Studio Canal.

Candyman. DVD. Directed by Bernard Rose; produced by Clive Barker. 1992. USA: Propaganda Films; PolyGram Filmed Entertainment.

Cannibal Holocaust. DVD. Directed by Ruggero Deodato; produced by Franco Di Nunzio. 1980. Italy: F. D. Cinematografica.

Cape Fear. DVD. Directed by Martin Scorsese; produced by Barbara de Fina. 1991. USA: Amblin Entertainment; Cappa Films; Tribeca Productions.

Captivity. DVD. Directed by Roland Joffe; produced by Valery Chumak. 2007. USA/Russia: Foresight Unlimited; Captivity Productions; RAMCO.

Carnival of Souls. Directed and produced by Herk Harvey. 1962. USA: Harcourt Productions.

Cat People. DVD. Directed by Jacques Tourneur; produced by Val Lewton. 1942. USA: RKO Radio Pictures.

Chernobyl Diaries. DVD. Directed by Bradley Parker; produced by Rob Cowan. 2012. USA: Alcon Entertainment; FilmNation Entertainment.

Chemical Wedding / Crowley. DVD. Directed by Julian Doyle; produced by Paul Astrom Andrews. 2008. UK: Bill and Ben Productions; Focus Films; E-Motion.

Cherry Tree Lane. DVD. Directed by Paul Andrew Williams; produced by Mark Foligno. 2010. UK: Steel Mill Pictures.

Children of the Corn. DVD. Directed by Fritz Kiersch; produced by Donald P. Borchers. 1984. USA: Gatlin; Hal Roach Studios; Cinema Group.

Children of the Damned. DVD. Directed by Anton Leader; produced by Lawrence P. Bachmann. 1963. UK: Metro-Goldwyn-Mayer British Studios.

Child's Play. DVD. Directed by Tom Holland; produced by David Kirschner. 1988. USA: United Artists.

Citizen Kane. DVD. Directed and produced by Orson Welles. 1941. USA: Mercury Productions; RKO Radio Productions.

Cloverfield. DVD. Directed by Matt Reeves; produced by J. J. Abrams. 2008. USA: Bad Robot; Paramount Pictures.

Colin: Love of the Dead. DVD. Directed by Marc Price; produced by Justin Hayles. 2008. UK: Nowhere Fast Productions.

Contagion. DVD. Directed by Steven Soderbergh; produced by Gregory Jacobs. 2011. USA/UAE: Regency Enterprises; Warner Bros. Pictures; Double Feature Films.

Crash. DVD. Directed and produced by David Cronenberg. 1996. Canada/UK: Recorded Picture Company; The Movie Network; Telefilm Network.

Creep. DVD. Directed by Christopher Smith; produced by Julie Baines. 2004. UK/ Germany: Dan Films; Zero Films GmbH; Filmstiftung Nordrhein-Westfalen.

Cry of the Werewolf. DVD. Directed by Henry Levin; produced by Wallace MacDonald. 1944. USA: Columbia Pictures Corporation.

Cube. DVD. Directed by Vincenzo Natali; produced by Colin Brunton. 1997. Canada: The Feature Film Project; Odeon Films; Viacom Canada.

Dagon. DVD. Directed by Stuart Gordon; produced by Carlos Fernández. 2001. Spain: Via Digital; Estudios Picasso; Fantastic Factory.

Dark Water [Honogurai mizu no soko kara / 'From the Depths of Dark Water']. DVD. Directed by Hideo Nakata; produced by Takashige Ichise. 2002. Japan: Toho Company; Oz Productions; Video Audio Project.

Dark Water. DVD. Directed by Walter Salles; produced by Doug Davison. 2005. USA: Pandemonium Productions; Touchstone Pictures; Vertigo Entertainment.

Das Experiment [The Experiment]. DVD. Directed by Oliver Hirschbiegal; produced by Marc Conrad. 2001. Germany: Fanes Film; Senator Film Produktion; Seven Pictures.

Dawn of the Dead. DVD. Directed by George A. Romero; produced by Richard P. Rubinstein. 1978. Italy/USA: Laurel Group.

Dawn of the Dead. DVD. Directed by Zack Snyder; produced by Marc Abraham. 2004. USA: New Amsterdam Entertainment; Metropolitan Filmexport; Toho-Towa.

Day of the Dead. DVD. Directed by George A. Romero; produced by Salah M. Hassanein. 1985. USA: Dead Films Inc.; Laurel Entertainment Inc.; Laurel-Day Inc.

De lift [The Lift]. DVD. Directed by Dick Maas; produced by Matthijs van Heijningen. 1983. Netherlands: First Floor Features; Sigma Film Productions.

Dead & Breakfast. DVD. Directed by Matthew Leutwyler; produced by Miranda Bailey. 2004. USA: Anchor Bay Entertainment; Goal Line Productions; Ambush Entertainment.

Dead Mary. DVD. Directed by Robert Wilson; produced by Patrick Cameron. 2007. Canada/USA: 235 Films; Archetype Films; 235 Horpic Eight.

Dead of Night. DVD. Directed by Alberto Cavalcanti, Charles Crichton, Basil Deardon and Robert Hamer; produced by Michael Balcon. 1945. UK: Ealing Studios.

Dead Meat. DVD. Directed by Conor McMahon; produced by Michael Griffin. 2004. Ireland: Three Way Productions.

Dead Ringers. DVD. Directed by David Cronenberg; produced by Carol Baum. 1988. Canada/USA: Mantle Clinic II; Morgan Creek Productions; Telefilm Canada.

Dead Snow [Død snø]. DVD. Directed by Tommy Wirkola; produced by Magne Ek. 2009. Norway: Barentsfilm AS; Zwart Arbeid; News on Request.

Deep Red [Profondo rosso]. DVD. Directed by Dario Argento; produced by Claudio Argento. 1975. Italy: Rizzoli Film; Seda Spettacoli.

Der Golem, wie er in die Welt kam [The Golem: How He Came Into the World]. DVD. Directed by Carl Boese and Paul Wegener; produced by Paul Davidson. 1920. Germany: Projektions-AG Union.

Devil. DVD. Directed by John Erick Dowdle; produced by Drew Dowdle. 2010. USA: Relativity Media; Media Rights Capital; Night Chronicles.

Devil Doll. DVD. Directed by Lindsay Shonteff; produced by Richard Gordon. 1964. UK: Gordon Films; Galaworldfilm Productions.

Devil's Advocate. DVD. Directed by Taylor Hackford; produced by Barry Bernadi. 1997. USA/Germany: New Regency Pictures; Warner Bros. Pictures; Taurus Films.

Diary of the Dead. DVD. Directed by George A. Romero; produced by Steve Barnett. 2007. USA: Romero-Grunwald Productions; Artfire Fims.

District 9. DVD. Directed by Neill Blomkamp; produced by Bill Block. 2009. USA/Canada/New Zealand/South Africa: TriStar Productions; CPTC; WingNut Films.

Doctor Blood's Coffin. DVD. Directed by Sidney Furie; produced by George Fowler. 1961. UK: Caralan Productions Ltd.

Dog Soldiers. DVD. Directed by Neil Marshall; produced by David E. Allen. 2002. UK/Luxembourg/USA: Luxembourg Film Fund; Kismet Entertainment Group.

Donkey Punch. DVD. Directed by Oliver Blackburn; produced by Peter Carlton. 2008. UK: EM Media; Screen Yorkshire; UK Film Council.

Don't Look Now. DVD. Directed by Nicholas Roeg; produced by Peter Katz. 1973. UK/Italy: Eldorado Films; Casey Productions; D. L. N. Ventures Partnership.

Down / The Shaft. DVD. Directed by Dick Maas; produced by Laurens Geels. 2001. USA/Netherlands: First Floor Features.

Dr. Jekyll and Mr. Hyde. DVD. Directed by Rouben Mamoulian; produced by Adolph Zukor. 1931. USA: Paramount Pictures.

Dr. Strangelove Or: How I Learned to Stop Worrying and Love the Bomb. DVD. Directed and produced by Stanley Kubrick. 1964. USA/UK: Columbia Pictures Corporation; Hawk Films.

Dr. Terror's House of Horrors. DVD. Directed by Freddie Francis; produced by Max J. Rosenberg. 1965. UK: Amicus Productions.

Dracula. DVD. Directed by Tod Browning; produced by E. M. Asher. 1931. USA: Universal Pictures.

Dracula. DVD. Directed by Terence Fisher; produced by Michael Carreras. 1958. UK: Hammer Film Productions.

Dracula. DVD. Directed by Francis Ford Coppola; produced by Michael Apted. 1992. USA: American Zoetrope; Columbia Pictures Corporation; Osiris Films.

Dracula: Dead and Loving It. DVD. Directed and produced by Mel Brooks. 1995. USA/France: Brooksfilms; Castle Rock Entertainment; Gaumont.

Drag Me to Hell. DVD. Directed by Sam Raimi; produced by Grant Curtis. 2009. USA: Universal Pictures; Ghost House Pictures; Mandate Pictures.

Dressed to Kill. DVD. Directed by Brian de Palma; produced by George Litto. 1980. USA: Cinema 77 Films; Filmways Pictures.

Eden Lake. DVD. Directed by James Watkins; produced by Christian Colson. 2008. UK: Aramid Entertainment Fund; Rollercoaster Films.

Eraserhead. DVD. Directed and produced by David Lynch. 1977. USA: American Film Institute; Libra Films.

Event Horizon. DVD. Directed by Paul W. S. Anderson; produced by Jeremy Bolt. 1997. UK/USA: Impact Pictures; Paramount Pictures; Golar Productions.

Eyes without a Face [*Les yeux sans visage*]. DVD. Directed by Georges Franju; produced by Jules Borkon. 1960. France/Italy: Lux Film; Champs-Élysées Productions.

F. DVD. Directed by Johannes Roberts; produced by Paul Blacknell. 2010. UK: Gatlin Pictures; Black Robe; Capital Markets Film Finance.

Fail-Safe. DVD. Directed by Sidney Lumet; produced by Max E. Youngstein. 1964. USA: Columbia Pictures Corporation.

Faust – Eine deutsche Volkssage [Faust: A German Folk Legend]. DVD. Directed by F. W. Murnau; produced by Erich Pommer. 1926. Germany: Universum Film (UFA).

Feast. DVD. Directed by John Gulager; produced by Ben Affleck. 2005. USA: Dimension Films; LivePlanet; Neo Art & Logic.

Feast. DVD. Directed and produced by Erick Adam. 2009. USA: Scared-E-Cat Pictures.

Feast II: Sloppy Seconds. DVD. Directed by John Gulager; produced by Michael Leahy. 2008. USA: Dimension Extreme; Neo Art & Logic; LivePlanet.

Feast III: The Happy Finish. DVD. Directed by John Gulager; produced by Michael Leahy. 2009. USA: Dimension Extreme; Neo Art & Logic; LivePlanet.

Fight Club. DVD. Directed by David Fincher; produced by Ross Greyson Bell. 1999. USA/Germany: Fox 2000 Pictures; Regency Enterprises; Linson Films.

Final Destination. DVD. Directed by James Wong; produced by Richard Brener. 2000. USA/Canada: Hard Eight Pictues; New Line Cinema; Zide-Perry Productions.

Final Destination 5. DVD. Directed by Steven Quale; produced by Richard Brener. 2011. USA/Canada: New Line Cinema; Parallel Zide; Practical Pictures.

Flesh For Frankenstein. DVD. Directed by Paul Morrissey and Antonio Margheriti; produced by Andrew Braunsberg. 1973. USA/Italy/France: Braunsberg Productions; Rassam Productions; Yanne et Rassam.

Frankenhooker. DVD. Directed by Frank Henenlotter; produced by James Glickenhaus. 1990. USA: Levins-Henenlotter; Shapiro-Glickenhaus Entertainment.

Frankenstein. DVD. Directed by James Whale; produced by E. M. Asher. 1931. USA: Universal Pictures.

Frankenstein Created Woman. DVD. Directed by Terence Fisher; produced by Anthony Nelson Keys. 1967. UK: Hammer Film Productions.

Frankenstein Meets the Wolfman. DVD. Directed by Ray William Neill; produced by George Waggner. 1943. USA: Universal Pictures.

Freakdog / Red Mist. DVD. Directed by Paddy Breathnach; produced by Simon Bosanquet. 2008. UK: Framestore CFC; Geronimo Films; Northern Ireland Screen.

Freddy vs. Jason. DVD. Directed by Ronny Yu; produced by Stokely Chaffin. 2003. Canada/USA/Italy: Yannix Technology Corporation; WTC Productions; Avery Pix.

Frenzy. DVD. Directed and produced by Alfred Hitchcock. 1972. UK: Universal Pictures.

Friday the 13th. DVD. Directed and produced by Sean S. Cunningham. 1980. USA: Paramount Pictures; Georgetown Productions Inc.; Sean S. Cunningham Films.

Friday the 13th. DVD. Directed by Marcus Nispel; produced by Sean S. Cunningham. 2009. USA: Paramount Pictures; New Line Cinema; Crystal Lake Entertainment.

Friday the 13th: A New Beginning. DVD. Directed by Danny Steinmann; produced by Frank Mancuso Jr. 1985. USA: Georgetown Productions Inc.; Paramount Pictures; Terror Inc.

Friday the 13th Part 2. DVD. Directed and produced by Steve Miner. 1981. USA: Georgetown Productions Inc.

Friday the 13th Part III. DVD. Directed by Steve Miner; produced by Lisa Barsamian. 1982. USA: Georgetown Productions Inc.; Paramount Pictures; Jason Films.

Friday the 13th Part VII: The New Blood. DVD. Directed by John Carl Buechler; produced by Iain Paterson. 1988. USA: Paramount Pictures; Friday Four Films Inc.

Friday the 13th Part VIII: Jason Takes Manhatten. DVD. Directed by Rob Hedden; produced by Randolph Cheveldave. 1989. USA: Paramount Pictures; Horror Inc.

Friday the 13th: The Final Chapter. DVD. Directed by Joseph Zito; produced by Lisa Barsamian. 1984. USA: Georgetown Productions Inc.; Paramount Pictures.

From Beyond the Grave. DVD. Directed by Kevin Connor; produced by Max Rosenburg. 1974. UK: Amicus Productions.

Frontier(s) [Frontière(s)]. DVD. Directed by Xavier Gens; produced by Hubert Brault. 2007. France/Switzerland: Europa Corp.; Pacific Films; Cartel Productions.

Frozen. DVD. Directed by Adam Green; produced by Peter Block. 2010. USA: ArieScope Pictures; A Bigger Boat.

Funny Games. DVD. Directed by Michael Haneke; produced by Veit Heiduschka. 1997. Austria: Filmfonds Wien; Öesterreichisches Filminstitut; ORF.

Funny Games U.S. DVD. Directed by Michael Haneke; produced by Philippe Aigle. 2007. USA: Lucky Red; Celluloid Dreams; Tartan Films.

Ghost of Frankenstein. DVD. Directed by Erle C. Kenton; produced by George Waggner. 1942. USA: Universal Pictures.

Ginger Snaps. DVD. Directed by John Fawcett; produced by Steve Hoban. 2000. Canada: Unapix Entertainment Productions; Space: The Imagination Station; Canadian Television Fund.

Gremlins. DVD. Directed by Joe Dante; produced by Michael Finnell. 1984. USA: Amblin Entertainment; Warner Bros. Pictures.

H6: Diario de un asesino [H6: Diary of a Serial Killer]. DVD. Directed by Martín Garrido Barón; produced by Mark Albela. 2005. Spain: Kanzaman.

Halloween. DVD. Directed by John Carpenter; produced by Debra Hill. 1978. USA: Falcon International Productions; Compass International Pictures.

Halloween. DVD. Directed by Rob Zombie; produced by Malek Akkad. 2007. USA: Trancas International Films; Dimension Films; Nightfall Productions.

Halloween II. DVD. Directed by Rick Rosenthal; produced by Barry Bernadi. 1981. USA: Universal Pictures; De Laurentiis.

Halloween III: Season of the Witch. DVD. Directed by Tommy Lee Wallace; produced by Barry Bernadi. 1982. USA: Universal Pictures; Dino De Laurentiis Company.

Hannibal. DVD. Directed by Ridley Scott; produced by Dino de Laurentiis. 2001. USA/UK: Universal Pictures; Dino De Laurentiis Company; Metro-Goldwyn-Mayer.

Hatchet. DVD. Directed by Adam Green; produced by Scott Altomare. 2006. USA: ArieScope Pictures; High Seas Entertainment; Radioaktive Films.

Haute tension [Switchblade Romance]. DVD. Directed by Alexandre Aja; produced by Alexandre Arcady. 2003. France: Europa Corp.; Alexandre Films.

Hellbound: Hellraiser II. DVD. Directed by Tony Randel; produced by Clive Barker. 1988. UK/USA: Film Futures; New World Pictures; Troopstar.

Hellraiser. DVD. Directed by Clive Barker; produced by Mark Armstrong. 1987. UK: Film Futures; Rivdel Films; Cinemarque Entertainment BV.

Henry: Portrait of a Serial Killer. DVD. Directed by John McNaughton; produced by Malik B. Ali. 1986. USA: Maljack Productions.

Hostel. DVD. Directed by Eli Roth; produced by Chris Briggs. 2005. USA: International Production Company; Next Entertainment; Raw Nerve.

Hostel: Part II. DVD. Directed by Eli Roth; produced by Chris Briggs. 2007. USA: Screen Gems; International Production Company; Next Entertainment.

House of 1000 Corpses. DVD. Directed by Rob Zombie; produced by Andy Given. 2003. USA: Universal Pictures; Spectacle Entertainment Group.

House of Frankenstein. DVD. Directed by Erle C. Kenton; produced by Paul Malvern. 1944. USA: Universal Pictures.

Human Centipede 2. Tom Six. Prod Tom and Ilona Six 2011 USA Six Entertainments.

I Know What You Did Last Summer. DVD. Directed by Jim Gillespie; produced by William S. Beasley. 1997. USA: Mandalay Entertainment; Columbia Pictures Corporation; Summer Knowledge LLC.

I Married a Monster from Outer Space. DVD. Directed and produced by Gene Fowler Jr. 1958. USA: Paramount Productions.

I Spit on Your Grave / Day of the Woman. DVD. Directed and produced by Meir Zarchi. 1978. USA: Cinemagic Pictures.

I Spit on Your Grave. DVD. Directed by Steven R. Monroe; produced by Lisa Hansen. 2010. USA: Cinetel Films; Anchor Bay Films; Family of the Year Productions.

I vampiri [*The Devil's Commandment*]. DVD. Directed by Riccardo Freda; produced by Luigi Carpentieri. 1956. Italy: Athena Cinematografica; Titanus.

I Walked With a Zombie. DVD. Directed by Jacques Tourneur; produced by Val Lewton. 1943. USA: RKO Radio Pictures.

Ichi the Killer [*Koroshiya I*]. DVD. Directed by Takashi Miike; produced by Akiko Funatsu. 2001. Japan: Omega Project; Alpha Group; Omega Micott Inc.

Identity. DVD. Directed by Michael Cooney; produced by Stuart M. Besser. 2003. USA: Konrad Pictures; Columbia Pictures Corporation.

Ils – them. DVD. Directed by David Moreau and Xavien Palud; produced by Frédéric Doniguian. 2006. France/Romania: Castel Film Romania; Canal+; CinéCinéma.

In a Glass Cage [*Tras el cristal*]. DVD. Directed by Agustí Villaronga; produced by Teresa Enrich. 1987. Spain: T.E.M Productores S.A.

Inseminoid / Horror Planet. DVD. Directed by Norman J. Warren; produced by Richard Gordon. 1981. UK: Jupiter Film Productions.

Inside [*À l'intérieur*]. DVD. Directed by Alexandre Bustillo and Julien Maury; produced by Priscilla Bertin. 2007. France: Canal+; CinéCinéma; La Fabrique de Films.

Insidious. DVD. Directed by James Wan; produced by Jason Blum. 2010. USA/Canada: IM Global; Stage 6 Films; Alliance Films.

Interview With the Vampire: The Vampire Chronicles. DVD. Directed by Neil Jordan; produced by David Geffen. 1994. USA: Geffen Pictures.

Invasion of the Body Snatchers. DVD. Directed by Don Siegel; produced by Walter Mirisch. 1956. USA: Allied Artists Pictures; Walter Wanger Productions.

Invasion of the Body Snatchers. DVD. Directed by Philip Kaufman; produced by Robert H. Solo. 1978. USA: Solofilm.

Isolation. DVD. Directed by Billy O'Brien; produced by Stephanie Denton. 2005. UK/Ireland/USA: Bórd Scannán na hÉireann; Element Films; Blue Orange Productions.

Jack the Ripper [*Die Dirnenmoerder von London*]. Directed by Jesus Franco; produced by Erwin C. Dietrich. 1976. Switzerland/West Germany: Ascot Film; Cinemec; Elite Film.

Jack the Ripper. DVD. Directed by David Wickes; produced by Al Burgess. 1988. UK/USA: Lorimar Television; Thames Television; Euston Films.

Jason Lives: Friday the 13th Part VI. DVD. Directed by Tom McLoughlin; produced by Don Behrns. 1986. USA: Paramount Pictures; Terror Films Inc.

Jaws. DVD. Directed by Steven Spielberg; produced by David Brown. 1975. USA: Universal Pictures; Zanuck/Brown Productions.

Jungfrukällen [The Virgin Spring]. DVD. Directed and produced by Ingmar Bergman. 1960. Sweden: Svensk Filmindustri.

Ju-on: The Grudge. DVD. Directed by Takashi Shimizu; produced by Takashige Ichise. 2002. Japan: Nikkatsu; Pioneer LDC; Xanadeux Company.

King Kong. DVD. Directed by Peter Jackson; produced by Jan Blenkin. 2005. New Zealand/USA/Germany: Universal Pictures; WingNut Films; Big Primate Pictures.

La horde [The Horde] DVD. Directed by Yannick Dahan and Benjamin Rocher; produced by Thomas Cappeau. 2009. France: Canal+; CinéCinéma; Coficup.

Lake of the Dead [De dødes tjern]. DVD. Directed by Kåre Bergstrøm; produced by Gunnar Sønstevold. 1958. Norway: Norsk Film.

Land of the Dead. DVD. Directed by George A. Romero; produced by Steve Barnett. 2005. Canada/France/USA: Universal Pictures; Atmosphere Entertainment MM; Romero-Grunwald Productions.

Last House on the Left. DVD. Directed by Wes Craven; produced by Sean S. Cunningham. 1972. USA: Lobster Enterprises; The Night Co.; Sean S. Cunningham Films.

Les sorcières de salem / The Crucible [The Witches of Salem]. DVD. Directed by Raymond Rouleau; translated by Marcel Aymè; produced by Raymond Borderie. 1957. France/East Germany: CICC; Pathé Consortium Cinema; Films Borderie.

Let Me In. DVD. Directed by Matt Reeves; produced by Tobin Armbrust. 2010. UK/USA: Hammer Film Productions; EFTI; Overture Films.

Let the Right One In [Låt den rätte komma in]. DVD. Directed by Tomas Alfredson; produced by Gunnar Carlsson. 2008. Sweden: Sandrew Metronome Distribution Sverige AB; Filmpool Nord; The Chimney Pot.

Little Shop of Horrors. DVD. Directed and produced by Roger Corman. 1960. USA: The Filmgroup; Santa Clara Productions.

Little Shop of Horrors. DVD. Directed by Frank Oz; produced by David Geffen. 1986. USA: The Geffen Company.

Long Time Dead. DVD. Directed by Marcus Adams; produced by Mairi Bett. 2000. UK/France: Canal+; Studio Canal; Working Title Films.

Long Weekend. DVD. Directed and produced by Colin Eggleston. 1978. Australia: Australian Film Commission; Dugong Films; Victorian Film.

Love at First Bite. DVD. Directed by Stan Dragoti; produced by Joel Freeman. 1979. USA: Melvin Simon Productions.

M. DVD. Directed by Fritz Lang; produced by Seymour Nebenzal. 1931. Germany: Nero-Film AG.

Magic. DVD. Directed by Richard Attenborough; produced by C. O. Erickson. 1978. USA: Twentieth Century Fox Film Corporation; Joseph E. Levine Produtions.

Maléfique. DVD. Directed by Eric Valette; produced by Olivier Delbosc. 2002. France: Mars Distribution; Canal+; Fidelite Productions.

Man Bites Dog [C'est arrivé près de chez vous]. DVD. Directed and produced by Rémy Belvaux, André Bonzel and Benoît Poelvoorde. 1992. Belgium: Les Artistes Anonymes.

Manhunt [Rovdyr]. DVD. Directed by Patrik Syverson; produced by Torleif Hauge. 2008. Norway: Euforia Film; Fender Film.

Manhunter. DVD. Directed by Michael Mann; produced by Richard Roth. 1986. USA: De Laurentiis Entertainment Group; Red Dragon Productions S.A.

Martyrs. DVD. Directed by Pascal Laugier; produced by Frédéric Doniguian. 2008. France/Canada: Wild Bunch; Canal+; CinéCinéma.

Midnight Meat Train. DVD. Directed by Ryuhei Kitamura; produced by Clive Barker. 2008. USA: Lakeshore Entertainment; GreeneStreet Films; Lions Gate Films.

Mirrors. DVD. Directed by Alexandre Aja; produced by Marc S. Fischer. 2008 USA/Romania/Germany: Luna Pictures; Castel Film Romania; Regency Enterprises.

Misery. DVD. Directed by Rob Reiner; produced by Steve Nicolaides. 1990. USA: Nelson Entertainment; Castle Rock Entertainment.

Monster. DVD. Directed by Patty Jenkins; produced by David Alvarado. 2003. USA/Germany: Media 8 Entertainment; DEJ Productions; MDP Worldwide.

Monster Man. DVD. Directed by Michael Davis; produced by Ehud Bleiburg. 2003. USA: Dream Entertainment; Road Brothers Inc.

Monsters. DVD. Directed by Gareth Edwards; produced by Nick Love. 2010. USA: Vertigo Films.

Mortuary. DVD. Directed by Tobe Hooper; produced by Andrew Cohen. 2005. USA: Echo Bridge Entertainment.

Mum & Dad. DVD. Directed by Steven Sheil; produced by Amanda Martin. 2008. UK: Film London; EM Media; 2am Films.

Naked Lunch. DVD. Directed by David Cronenberg; produced by Gabriella Martinelli. 1991. Canada/UK/Japan: Recorded Picture Company; Film Trustees Ltd.; Nippon Film Development and Finance.

New Nightmare. DVD. Directed and produced by Wes Craven. 1994. USA: New Line Cinema.

Night of the Demon. DVD. Directed by Jacques Tourneur; produced by Frank Bevis. 1957. UK: Columbia Pictures Corporation; Sabre Film Production.

Night of the Eagle. DVD. Directed by Sidney Hayers; produced by Samuel Z. Arkoff. 1962. UK: Independent Artists.

Night of the Living Dead. DVD. Directed by George A. Romero; produced by Karl Hardman. 1968. USA: Image Ten; Market Square Productions; Off Color Films.

Night of the Living Dorks [*Die Nacht der lebenden Loser*]. DVD. Directed by Mathias Dinter; produced by Marion Dany. 2004. Germany: Hofmann & Voges Entertainment GbmH; Constantin Film Produktion.

Nightbreed. DVD. Directed by Clive Barker; produced by David Barron. 1990. USA: Morgan Creek Productions.

Nosferatu, eine Symphonie de Grauens [*Nosferatu, a Symphony of Horror*]. DVD. Directed by F. W. Murnau; produced by Enrico Dieckmann. 1922. Germany: Jofa-Atelier Berlin-Johannisthal; Prana-Film GmbH.

Oldboy. Chan park Wook Dong Joo Films 2003. S. Korea. Egg Films Show East.

Open Water. DVD. Directed by Chris Kentis; produced by Estelle Lau. Vol. 2003. USA: Plunge Pictures LLC.

Orphan. DVD. Directed by Jaume Collet-Serra; produced by David Barrett. 2009. USA/Canada/Germany/France: Studio Canal; Dark Castle Entertainment; Appian Way.

Outcast. DVD. Directed by Colm McCarthy; produced by Eddie Dick. 2010. UK/Ireland: Fantastic Films; Head Gear Films; Makar Productions.

Ozombie. DVD. Directed by John Lyde; produced by Daniel W. Cardwell. 2012. USA: Arrowstorm Entertainment.

Panic Room. DVD. Directed by David Fincher; produced by Ceán Chaffin. 2002. USA: Hofflund/Polone; Indelible Pictures; Columbia Pictures Corporation.

Paranormal Activity. DVD. Directed by Oren Peli; produced by Jason Blum. 2007. USA: Blumhouse Productions.

Peeping Tom. DVD. Directed by Michael Powell; produced by Albert Fennell. 1960. UK: Michael Powell (theatre).

Piranha 3D. DVD. Directed and produced by Alexandre Aja. 2010. USA: Atmosphere Entertainment MM; Dimension Films; Chako Film Company.

Piranha Part Two: The Spawning. DVD. Directed by James and Ovidio G. Assonitis; produced by Ovidio G. Assonitis. 1981. USA/Italy/Netherlands: Chako Film Company; Brouwersgracht Investments.

Plan 9 from Outer Space. DVD. Directed by Edward Wood Jr.; produced by Charles Burg. 1959. USA: Reynolds Pictures.

Planet Terror. DVD. Directed by Robert Rodriguez; produced by Elizabeth Avellán. 2007. USA: Dimension Films; Troublemaker Studios; Weinstein Company.

Poltergeist. DVD. Directed by Tobe Hooper; produced by Kathleen Kennedy. 1982. USA: Metro-Goldwyn-Mayer; SLM Production Group.

Pontypool. DVD. Directed by Bruce McDonald; produced by Jeffrey Coghlan. 2009. Canada: Shadow Shows; Ponty Up Pictures.

Possession. DVD. Directed by Andrzej Zulawski; produced by Marie-Laure Reyre. 1981. France/West Germany: Marianne Productions; Oliane Production; Soma Film Produktion.

Postal. DVD. Directed and produced by Uwe Boll. 2007. USA/Canada/Germany: Boll Kino Beteiligungs GmbH & Co. KG; Running With Scissors; Pitchblack Pictures.

Predator. DVD. Directed by John McTiernan; produced by John Davis. 1987. USA: Twentieth Century Fox Film Corporation; Silver Pictures; Amercent Films.

Prom Night. DVD. Directed by Nelson McCormick; produced by Chris J. Ball. 2008. USA/Canada: Original Film; Newmarket Films; Alliance Films.

Prometheus. DVD. Directed by Ridley Scott; produced by Michael Costigan. 2012. USA/UK: Scott Free Productions; Brandywine Productions; Dune Entertainment.

Psycho. DVD. Directed and produced by Alfred Hitchcock. 1960. USA: Shamley Productions.

Psycho. DVD. Directed and produced by Gus van Sant. 1998. USA: Imagine Entertainment; Universal Pictures.

Quarantine. DVD. Directed by John Erick Dowdle; produced by Sergio Agüero. 2008. USA: Screen Gems; Vertigo Entertainment; Andale Pictures.

Quarantine 2: Terminal. DVD. Directed by John Pogue; produced by Sergio Aguero. 2011. USA: Third Street Pictures; RCR Media Group.

Rabid. DVD. Directed by David Cronenberg; produced by Don Carmody. 1977. Canada: Canadian Film Development Corporation; Cinema Entertainment Enterprises.

Rampage. DVD. Directed and produced by Uwe Boll. 2009. Canada/Germany: Event Film Distribution; Pitchblack Pictures; Amok Productions.

Rawhead Rex. DVD. Directed by George Pavlov; produced by Kevin Attew. 1986. UK/Ireland/USA: Green Man Productions; Alpine Productions; Paradise.

Re-Animator. DVD. Directed by Stuart Gordon; produced by Michael Avery. 1985. USA: Empire Pictures; Re-Animator Productions.

[Rec]. DVD. Directed by Jaume Balagueró and Paco Plaza; produced by Carlos Fernández. 2007. Spain: Castelao Producciones; Filmax; Televisión Españolas

[Rec] 2. DVD. Directed by Jaume Balagueró and Paco Plaza; produced by Carlos Fernández. 2009. Spain: Castelao Producciones; Filmax; Ministerio de Cultura.

[Rec] 3 Génesis. DVD. Directed by Paco Plaza; produced by Jaume Balagueró. 2012. Spain: Canal+ España; Filmax; Ono.

Repossessed. DVD. Directed by Bob Logan; produced by Jean Higgins. 1990. USA: Carolco Productions.

Repulsion. DVD. Directed by Roman Polanski; produced by Gene Gutowski. 1965. UK: Tekli British Productions; Compton Films.

Resident Evil. DVD. Directed and produced by Paul W. S. Anderson. 2002. UK/ Germany/France/USA: Constantin Film Produktion; Davis-Films; Impact Pictures.

Revenge of Frankenstein. DVD. Directed by Terence Fisher; produced by Michael Carreras. 1958. UK: Columbia Pictures; Hammer Film Productions.

Right at Your Door. DVD. Directed by Chris Gorak; produced by Julie M. Anderson. 2006. USA: Lionsgate; Thousand Words.

Ringu. DVD. Directed by Hideo Nakata; produced by Masato Hara. 1998. Japan: Toho Company; Imagica; Omega Project.

Rope. DVD. Directed by Alfred Hitchcock; produced by Sidney Bernstein. 1948. USA: Transatlantic Pictures; Warner Bros. Pictures.

Rosemary's Baby. DVD. Directed by Roman Polanski; produced by William Castle. 1968. USA: William Castle Productions.

Saturday the 14th. DVD. Directed by Howard Cohen; produced by Jeff Begun. 1981. USA: New World Pictures.

Saw. DVD. Directed by James Wan; produced by Lark Bernini. 2004. USA/Australia: Evolution Entertainment; Saw Productions Inc.; Twisted Pictures.

Saw II. DVD. Directed by Darren Lynn Bousman; produced by Peter Block. 2005. USA/ Canada: Twisted Pictures; Evolution Entertainment; Got Films.

Saw III. DVD. Directed by Darren Lynn Bousman; produced by Troy Begnaud. 2006. USA/Canada: Twisted Pictures; Evolution Entertainment; Saw 2 Productions.

Saw IV. DVD. Directed by Darren Lynn Bousman; produced by Troy Begnaud. 2007. USA/Canada: Twisted Pictures.

Saw V. DVD. Directed by David Hackl; produced by Troy Begnaud. 2008. USA/Canada: Twisted Pictures.

Saw VI. DVD. Directed by Kevin Greutert; produced by Troy Begnaud. 2009. Canada/ USA/UK/Australia: Twisted Pictures; A Bigger Boat; Saw VI Productions.

Saw 3D. DVD. Directed by Kevin Greutert; produced by Troy Begnaud. 2010. Canada/ USA: Twisted Pictures; A Bigger Boat; Serendipity Productions.

Scary Movie. DVD. Directed by Keenen Ivory Wayans; produced by Lisa Suzanne Blum. 2000. USA: Dimension Films; Wayans Bros. Entertainment; Gold/Miller Productions.

Scary Movie 2. DVD. Directed by Keenen Ivory Wayans; produced by Rick Alvarez. 2001. USA/Canada: Brillstein-Grey Entertainment; Dimension Films; Gold/Miller Productions.

Scary Movie 3. DVD. Directed by David Zucker; produced by Phil Dornfeld. 2003. USA/ Canada: Dimension Films; Brad Grey Pictures.

Scary Movie 4. DVD. Directed by David Zucker; produced by Phil Dornfeld. 2006. USA: Dimension Films; 415 Project; Brad Grey Pictures.

Scream. DVD. Directed by Wes Craven; produced by Stuart M. Besser. 1996. USA: Dimension Films; Wood Entertainment.

Se7en. DVD. Directed by David Fincher; produced by Stephen Brown. 1995. USA: Cecchi Gori Pictures; New Line Cinema.

Seed. DVD. Directed and produced by Uwe Boll. 2007. Canada: Pitchblack Pictures; Boll Kino Beteiligungs GmbH & Co. KG; Seed Productions.

Session 9. DVD. Directed by Brad Anderson; produced by Dorothy Aufiero. 2001. USA: USA Films; Scout Productions; October Films.

Severance. DVD. Directed by Christopher Smith; produced by Alexandra Arlango. 2006. UK/Germany: Owerty Films; Dan Films; HanWay Films.

Shaun of the Dead. DVD. Directed by Edgar Wright; produced by Tim Bevan. 2004. UK/France/USA: Universal Pictures; Studio Canal; Working Title Films.

Shivers. DVD. Directed by David Cronenberg; produced by Don Carmody. 1975. Canada: Cinepix; CFDC; DAL Productions.

Shrooms. DVD. Directed by Paddy Breathnach; produced by Simon Channing Williams. 2007. Ireland/UK/Denmark: Capitol Films; Ingenious Film Partners; Bórd Scannán na hÉireann.

Silence of the Lambs. DVD. Directed by Jonathan Demme; produced by Grace Blake. 1991. USA: Strong Heart/Demme Production; Orion Pictures Corporation.

Sint [*Saint*]. DVD. Directed by Dick Maas; produced by Tom de Mol. 2010. Netherlands: Parachute Pictures; TDMP.

Sleepaway Camp. DVD. Directed and produced by Robert Hiltzik. 1983. USA: American Eagle.

Slither. DVD. Directed by James Gunn; produced by Marc Abraham. 2006. Canada/USA: Gold Circle Films; Strike Entertainment; Brightlight Pictures.

Snow White and the Huntsman. DVD. Directed by Rupert Sanders; produced by Laurie Boccaccio. 2012. USA: Roth Films; Universal Pictures.

Society. DVD. Directed by Brian Yuzna; produced by Keizo Kabata. 1989. USA: Society Productions Inc.; Wild Street Pictures.

Son of Frankenstein. DVD. Directed and produced by Rowland V. Lee. 1939. USA: Universal Pictures.

Sorority Row. DVD. Directed by Stewart Hendler; produced by Bill Bannerman. 2009. USA: House Row Productions; Karz Entertainment; Summit Entertainment.

Species. DVD. Directed by Roger Donaldson; produced by Mark Egerton. 1995. USA: Metro-Goldwyn-Mayer.

Splice. DVD. Directed by Vincenzo Natali; produced by Joseph Boccia. 2009. Canada/France/USA: Gaumont; Copperhead Entertainment; Dark Castle Entertainment.

SS Experiment Love Camp. [*Lager SSadis Kastrat Kommandatur*]. DVD. Directed by Sergio Garrone. 1976. Italy: Società Europea Films Internazionali Cinematografica.

Stigmata. DVD. Directed by Rupert Wainwright; produced by Frank Mancuso Jr. 1999. USA: Metro-Goldwyn-Mayer; FGM Entertainment.

Straw Dogs. DVD. Directed by Sam Peckinpah; produced by Daniel Melnick. 1971. USA/UK: Talent Associates; ABC Pictures; Amerbroco.

Survival of the Dead. DVD. Directed by George A. Romero; produced by D. J. Carson. 2009. USA/Canada: Blank of the Dead Productions; Devonshire Productions; New Romero.

Sweeney Todd: The Demon Barber of Fleet Street. DVD. Directed by Tim Burton; produced by Brenda Berrisford. 2009. USA/UK: Warner Bros. Pictures; DreamWorks Pictures; Parkes/McDonald Productions.

Teeth. DVD. Directed and produced by Mitchell Lichetenstein. 2007. USA: Teeth.

Tetsuo: The Iron Man. DVD. Directed and produced by Shin'ya Tsukamoto. 1989. Japan: Japan Home Video; K2 Spirit; Kaijyu Theater.

Tetsuo II: Bodyhammer. DVD. Directed by Shin'ya Tsukamoto; produced by Hiromi
   Aihara. 1992. Japan: Kaijyu Theater; Toshiba EMI.
The Amityville Horror. DVD. Directed by Stuart Rosenberg; produced by Samuel Z.
   Arkoff. 1979. USA: American International Pictures; Professional Films; Cinema 77.
The Amityville Horror. DVD. Directed by Andrew Douglas; produced by Michael Bay.
   2005. USA: Metro-Goldwyn-Mayer; Dimension Films; Radar Pictures.
The Awakening. DVD. Directed by Nick Murphy; produced by Jenny Borgars. 2011.
   UK: Scottish Screen; Lipsync Productions; BBC Films.
The Bad Seed. DVD. Directed and produced by Mervyn LeRoy. 1956. USA: Warner
   Bros. Pictures.
The Black Cat. DVD. Directed by Edgar G. Ulmer; produced by E. M. Asher. 1934.
   USA: Universal Pictures.
The Blair Witch Project. DVD. Directed by Daniel Myrick and Eduardo Sánchez;
   produced by Robin Cowie. 1999. USA: Haxan Films.
The Boston Strangler. DVD. Directed by Richard Fleischer; produced Robert Fryer.
   1968. USA: Twentieth Century Fox.
The Brøken. DVD. Directed by Sean Ellis; produced by Lene Bausasger. 2008. France:
   Gaumont International; Ugly Duckling Films; Left Turn Films.
The Brood. DVD. Directed by David Cronenberg; produced by Pierre David. 1979.
   Canada: Mutual Productions Ltd.; Elgin International Films Ltd.
The Cabin in the Woods. DVD. Directed by Drew Goddard; produced by Jason Clark.
   2012. USA: Mutant Enemy; Metro-Goldwyn-Mayer; United Artists.
The Cabinet of Dr. Caligari [Das Cabinet des Dr. Caligari]. DVD. Directed by Robert
   Wiene; produced by Rudolf Meinert. 1920. Germany: Decla-Bioscop AG.
The Canterville Ghost. DVD. Directed by Jules Dassin and Norman Z. McLeod;
   produced by Arthur L. Field. 1944. USA: Metro-Goldwyn-Mayer; Loew's.
The Changeling. DVD. Directed by Peter Medak; produced by Garth H. Drabinsky.
   1980. Canada: Chessman Park Productions.
The Children. DVD. Directed by Tom Shankland; produced by Simon Fawcett. 2008.
   UK: BBC Films; Screen West Midlands; Vertigo Films.
The Collector. DVD. Directed by Marcus Dunstan; produced by Brett Forbes. 2009.
   USA: Imaginarium Entertainment Group; LD Entertainment; Fortress Features.
The Company of Wolves. DVD. Directed by Neil Jordan; produced by Chris Brown.
   1984. UK: Incorporated Television Company; Palace Pictures.
The Craft. DVD. Directed by Andrew Fleming; produced by Ginny Nugent. 1996. USA:
   Columbia Pictures Corporation.
The Crucible. DVD. Directed by Nicholas Hytner; produced by Robert A. Miller. 1996.
   USA: Twentieth Century Fox Film Corporation.
The Curse of Frankenstein. DVD. Directed by Terence Fisher; produced by Anthony
   Hinds. 1957. UK: Hammer Film Productions.
The Day the Earth Stood Still. DVD. Directed by Denis Johnson; produced by Julian
   Blaustein. 1951. USA: Twentieth Century Fox Film Corporation.
The Dentist. DVD. Directed by Brian Yuzna; produced by Mark Amin. 1996. USA:
   Trimark Pictures.
The Descent. DVD. Directed by Neil Marshall; produced by Christian Colson. 2005. UK:
   Pathé; Northmen Productions; Celador Films.
The Devil Rides Out. DVD. Directed by Terence Fisher; produced by Anthony Nelson Keys.
   1968. UK: Hammer Film Productions; Associated British-Pathé; Seven Arts Productions.

The Devils. DVD. Directed and produced by Ken Russell. 1970. UK: Russo Productions.

The Devil's Eye [Djävulens öga]. DVD. Directed by Ingmar Bergman; produced by Allan Ekelund. 1960. Sweden: Svensk Filmindustri.

The Devil's Rejects. DVD. Directed by Rob Zombie; produced by Peter Block. 2005. USA/Germany: Cinerenta Medienbeteiligungs KG; Lions Gate Films; Firm Films.

The Driller Killer. DVD. Directed by Abel Ferrara; produced by Rochelle Weisberg. 1999. USA: Navaron Productions.

The Elephant Man. DVD. Directed by David Lynch; produced by Stuart Cornfeld. 1980. USA: Brooksfilms.

The Evil Dead. DVD. Directed by Sam Raimi; produced by Bruce Campbell. 1981. USA: Renaissance Pictures.

The Exorcism of Emily Rose. DVD. Directed by Scott Derrickson; produced by Paul Harris Boardman. 2005. USA: Lakeshore Entertainment; Screen Gems; Firm Films.

The Exorcist. DVD. Directed by William Friedkin; produced by William Peter Blatty. 1974. USA: Warner Bros. Pictures; Hoya Productions.

The Exorcist III. DVD. Directed by William Peter Blatty; produced by Carter de Haven. 1990. USA: Morgan Creek Productions.

The Fly. DVD. Directed and produced by Kurt Neumann. 1958. USA: Twentieth Century Fox Film Corporation.

The Fly. DVD. Directed by David Cronenberg; produced by Stuart Cornfeld. 1986. USA/UK/Canada: Brooksfilms.

The Fog. DVD. Directed by John Carpenter; produced by Charles B. Bloch. 1980. USA: EDI; AVCO Embassy Pictures; Debra Hill Productions.

Forbidden Planet. DVD. Directed by Fred M. Wilcox; produced by Nicholas Nayfack. 1956. USA: Metro-Goldwyn-Mayer.

The Ghost goes West. Rene Clair Alexanda Korda. 1935 UK London Film Productions.

The Grudge. DVD. Directed by Takashi Shimizu; produced by Doug Davison. 2004. USA/Japan: Senator International; Columbia Pictures; Vertigo Entertainment.

The Haunting. DVD. Directed by Robert Wise; produced by Denis Johnson. 1963. USA/UK: Argyle Enterprises.

The Hills Have Eyes. DVD. Directed by Alexandre Aja; produced by Wes Craven. 2006. USA/France: Craven-Maddalena Films; Major Studio Partners; Dune Entertainment.

The Hills Run Red. DVD. Directed by Dave Parker; produced by Stephen Bender. 2009. USA: Dark Castle Entertainment; Ludovico Technique; Fever Dreams.

The Hole. DVD. Directed by Nick Hamm; produced by Jeremy Bolt. 2001. UK: Impact Pictures; Canal+; Granada Film Produtions.

The Hole. DVD. Directed by Joe Dante; produced by Chris Bender. 2009. USA: BenderSpink; Bold Films; The Hole.

The Horror of Frankenstein. DVD. Directed and produced by Jimmy Sangster. 1970. UK: Hammer Film Productions; EMI Films.

The House on Haunted Hill. DVD. Directed and produced by William Castle. 1959. USA: William Castle Productions.

The House on the Edge of the Park [Le casa sperduta nel parco]. DVD. Directed by Ruggero Deodato; produced by Franco Di Nunzio. 1980. Italy: F. D. Cinematografica.

The Human Centipede (First Sequence). DVD. Directed by Tom Six; produced by Ilona Six. 2009. Netherlands: Six Entertainment.

The Hypnotist / London After Midnight. DVD. Directed and produced by Tod Browning. 1927. USA: Metro-Goldwyn-Mayer.

The Innocents. DVD. Directed and produced by Jack Clayton. 1961. USA/UK: Twentieth
    Century Fox Film Corporation; Achilles.
The Invasion. DVD. Directed by Oliver Hirschbiegal; produced by Jessica Alan. 2007.
    USA/Australia: Silver Pictures; Warner Bros. Pictures; Vertigo Entertainment.
The Invisible Man. DVD. Directed by James Whale; produced by Carl Laemmle Jr.
    1933. USA: Universal Pictures.
The Invisible Woman. DVD. Directed by A. Edward Sutherland; produced by Burt Kelly.
    1940. USA: Universal Pictures.
The Island of Dr. Moreau. DVD. Directed by Don Taylor; produced by Samuel Z. Arkoff.
    1977. USA: American International Pictures; Major Productions; Cinema 77.
The Last Exorcism. DVD. Directed by Daniel Stamm; produced by Marc Abraham.
    2010. USA/France: Strike Entertainment; Louisiana Media Productions; StudioCanal.
The Last House on the Left. DVD. Directed by Dennis Iliadas; produced by Jonathan
    Craven. 2009. USA: Film Afrika Worldwide; Rogue Pictures; Scion Films.
The Living Dead at the Manchester Morgue [*Non si deve profanare il sonno dei morti*].
    DVD. Directed by Jorge Grau; produced by Edmondo Amati. 1974. Spain/Italy:
    Flamina Produzioni Cinematografiche; Star Films S.A.
The Mist. DVD. Directed and produced by Frank Darabont. 2007. USA: Dimension
    Films; Darkwoods Productions; The Weinstein Company.
The Mummy. DVD. Directed by Karl Freund; produced by Carl Laemmle Jr. 1932. USA:
    Universal Pictures.
The Mummy. DVD. Directed by Stephen Sommers; produced by Patricia Carr. 1999.
    USA: Universal Pictures; Alphaville Films.
The Ninth Gate. DVD. Directed by Roman Polanski; produced by Mark Allan. 1999.
    Spain/France/USA: Via Digital; Kino Vision; Artisan Entertainment.
The Old Dark House. DVD. Directed by James Whale; produced by Carl Laemmle Jr.
    1932. USA: Universal Pictures.
The Omen. DVD. Directed by Richard Donner; produced by Harvey Bernhard. 1976.
    UK/USA: Twentieth Century Fox Film Corporation.
The Omen. DVD. Directed by John Moore; produced by David Harfield. 2006. USA:
    Twentieth Century Fox Film Corporation; 11:11 Mediaworks.
The Orphanage [*El orfanato*]. DVD. Directed by Juan Antonio Bayona; produced by
    Belén Atienza. 2007. Spain/Mexico: Televisio de Catalunya; Telecinco; Rodar y
    Rodar Cine y Television.
The Others. DVD. Directed by Alejandro Amenábar; produced by Fernando Bovaira.
    2001. USA/Spain/Italy/France: Lucky Red; Cruise/Wagner Productions; Dimension
    Films.
The Possession of Joel Delaney. DVD. Directed by Waris Hussein; produced by Martin
    Poll. 1972. USA: Paramount Pictures; Haworth Productions; Incorporated Television
    Company.
The Rite. DVD. Directed by Mikael Håfström; produced by Christopher Almerico. 2011.
    USA/Hungary/Italy: Mouse Films; New Line Cinema; Contrafilm.
The Rocky Horror Picture Show. DVD. Directed by Jim Sharman; produced by Lou
    Adler. 1975. UK/USA: Twentieth Century Fox Film Corporation.
The Ruins. DVD. Directed by Carter Smith; produced by Gary Barber. 2008.
    DreamWorks SKG; Spyglass Entertainment; Red Hour Films.
The Sect / The Devil's Daughter [*La setta*]. DVD. Directed by Michele Soavi; produced
    by Dario Argento. 1991. Italy: ADC Films; Penta Film.

The Seventh Seal [*Det sjunde inseglet*]. DVD. Directed by Ingmar Bergman; produced by Allan Ekelund. 1957. Sweden: Svensk Film.

The Seventh Victim. DVD. Directed by Mark Robson; produced by Val Lewton. 1943. USA: RKO Radio Pictures.

The Shining. DVD. Directed by Stanley Kubrick; produced by Jan Harlan. 1980. UK/ USA: Warner Bros. Pictures; Hawk Films; Peregrine.

The Sick House. DVD. Directed by Curtis Radclyffe; produced by Ashish Bhatnagar. 2008. UK: Hopscotch Films; iDream Productions.

The Sixth Sense. DVD. Directed by M. Night Shyamalan; produced by Kathleen Kennedy. 1999. USA: Barry Mendel Productions; Hollywood Pictures; The Kennedy/ Marshall Company.

The Skeleton Key. DVD. Directed by Iain Softley; produced by Daniel Bobker. 2005. USA/ Germany: Universal Pictures; ShadowCatcher Entertainment; Double Feature Films.

The Skin I Live In [*Le piel que habito*]. DVD. Directed by Pedro Almodóvar; produced by Agustin Almodóvar. 2011. Spain: Blue Haze Entertainment; Canal+ España; El Deseo D.A. S.L.U.

The Stepford Wives. DVD. Directed by Bryan Forbes; produced by Gustave M. Berne. 1975. USA: Palomar Pictures; Fadsin Cinema Associates.

The Strangers. DVD. Directed by Bryan Bertino; produced by Thomas J. Busch. 2008. USA: Rogue Pictures; Intrepid Pictures; Vertigo Entertainment.

The Student of Prague [*Der Student von Prag*]. DVD. Directed by Stellan Rye and Paul Wegener; produced by Paul Wegener. 1913. Germany: Deutsche Bioscop GmbH.

The Texas Chain Saw Massacre. DVD. Directed by Tobe Hooper; produced by Kim Henkel. 1974. USA: Vortex.

The Texas Chainsaw Massacre. DVD. Directed by Marcus Nispel; produced by Jeffrey Allard. 2003. USA: New Line Cinema; Focus Features; Radar Pictures.

The Thing. DVD. Directed by John Carpenter; produced by Stuart Cohen. 1982. USA: Universal Pictures; Turman-Foster Company.

The Thing. DVD. Directed by Matthijs van Heijningen Jr.; produced by Marc Abraham. 2011. USA/Canada: Morgan Creek Productions; Universal Pictures; Strike Entertainment.

The Thing From Another World. DVD. Directed by Christian Nyby; produced by Howard Hawks. 1951. USA: Winchester Pictures Corporation.

The Tortured. DVD. Directed by Robert Lieberman; produced by Troy Begnaud. 2010. USA/Canada: Twisted Pictures; LightTower Entertainment; MP Productions.

The Toxic Avenger. DVD. Directed by Michael Herz and Lloyd Kaufman; produced by Michael Herz. 1984. USA: Troma Entertainment;.

The Uninvited. DVD. Directed by Lewis Allen; produced by Charles Brackett. 1944. USA: Paramount Pictures.

The Uninvited. DVD. Directed by Charles Guard and Thomas Guard; produced by Doug Davison. 2009. USA/Canada/Germany: DreamWorks SKG; Cold Spring Pictures; MacDonald/Parkes Productions.

The Vanishing [*Spoorloos*]. DVD. Directed by George Sluizer; produced by Anne Lordon. 1988. Netherlands/France: Argos Films; Golden Egg; Ingrid Productions.

The Wages of Fear [*Le salaire de la peur*]. DVD. Directed and produced by Henri-Georges Clouzot. 1953. France/Italy: Fono Roma; CICC; Filmsonor.

The Ward. DVD. Directed by John Carpenter; produced by Adam Betteridge. 2010. USA: FilmNation Entertainment; Premiere Picture; Echo Lake Productions.

The Wave [*Die Welle*]. DVD. Directed by Dennis Gansel; produced by Christian Becker. 2008. Germany: Rat Pack Filmproduktion GmbH; Constantin Film Produktion; B.A. Produktion.

The Wicker Man. DVD. Directed by Robin Hardy; produced by Peter Snell. 1973. UK: British Lion Film Corporation.

The Wicker Man. DVD. Directed by Neil LaBute; produced by Nicholas Cage. 2006. USA/Germany/Canada: Warner Bros. Pictures; Alcon Entertainment; Millenium Films.

The Witches of Eastwick. DVD. Directed by George Miller; produced by Neil Canton. 1987. USA: Warner Bros. Pictures; The Guber-Peters Company; Kennedy Miller Productions.

The Wolf Man. DVD. Directed and produced by George Waggner. 1941. USA: Universal Pictures.

The Woman. DVD. Directed by Lucky McKee; produced by Josh Garrell. 2011. USA: Modernciné.

The Woman in Black. DVD. Directed by James Watkins; produced by Tobin Armbrust. 2012. UK/Canada/Sweden: Cross Creek Pictures; Hammer Film Productions; Alliance Films.

Theatre of Blood. DVD. Directed by Douglas Hickox; produced by Gustave M. Berne. 1973. UK: Cineman Productions.

Timber Falls. DVD. Directed by Tony Giglio; produced by Doug Croxall. 2007. USA: Rifkin-Eberts; Ascendent Pictures; A-Mark Entertainment.

Tokyo Gore Police [*Tôkyô zankoku keisatsu*]. DVD. Directed by Yoshihiro Nishimura; produced by Yoshinori Chiba. 2008. Japan/USA: Fever Dreams; Nikkatsu.

Toolbox Murders. DVD. Directed by Dennis Donnelly; produced by Tony DiDio. 1978. USA: Cal-Am Productions; Tony DiDio Productions.

Toolbox Murders. DVD. Directed by Tobe Hooper; produced by Ryan Carroll. 2004. USA: Alpine Pictures; Scary Movies LLC; Toolbox Murders Inc.

Trailer Park of Terror. DVD. Directed by Steven Goldmann; produced by Jonathan Bogner. 2008. USA: Trailer Park Partners; Bogner Entertainment; Lightning Entertainment.

Tremors. DVD. Directed by Ron Underwood; produced by Ellen Collett. 1990. USA: Universal Pictures; No Frills Film Production.

Triangle. DVD. Directed by Christopher Smith; produced by Julie Baines. 2009. UK/Australia: Icon Entertainment International; Pictures in Paradise; UK Film Council.

Trick 'r Treat. DVD. Directed by Michael Dougherty; produced by Ashok Amritraj. 2007. USA: Warner Bros. Pictures; Legendary Pictures; Bad Hat Harry Productions.

Troll Hunter [*Trolljegeren*]. DVD. Directed by André Øvredal; produced by Marcus Brodersen. 2010. Norway: Filmkameratene A/S; Film Fund FUZZ; SF Norge A/S.

Tromeo and Juliet. DVD. Directed by Lloyd Kaufman and James Gunn; produced by Franny Baldwin. 1996. USA: Troma Entertainment.

Twelve Monkeys. DVD. Directed by Terry Gilliam; produced by Robert Cavallo. 1995. USA: Universal Pictures; Atlas Entertainment; Classico.

Twilight Zone: The Movie. DVD. Directed by Joe Dante, John Landis, George Miller and Steven Spielberg; produced by John Landis. 1983. USA: Warner Bros. Pictures.

Urban Legend. DVD. Directed by Jamie Blanks; produced by Brad Luff. 1998. USA/France: Canal+ Droits Audiovisuels; Original Film; Phoenix Pictures.

Videodrome. DVD. Directed by David Cronenberg; produced by Pierre David. 1983. Canada: Victor Solnicki Productions; Famous Players; Filmplan International.

Village of the Damned. DVD. Directed by Wolf Rilla; produced by Ronald Kinnoch. 1960. UK: Metro-Goldwyn-Mayer British Studios.

Village of the Damned. DVD. Directed by John Carpenter; produced by Andre Blay. 1995. USA: Universal Pictures; Alphaville Films.

Villmark [Dark Woods]. DVD. Directed by Pål Øie; produced by Jan Aksel Angeltvedt. 2003. Norway: Norsk Filmfond; Spleis A/S.

Voodoo Man. DVD. Directed by William Beaudine; produced by Jack Dietz. 1944. USA: Banner Productions; Monogram Pictures.

w Delta z (Waz) / The Killing Gene. DVD. Directed by Tom Shankland; produced by Michael Casey. 2007. UK: Vertigo Films; UK Film Council; Ingenious Film Partners.

War of the Worlds. DVD. Directed by Byron Haskin; produced by Frank Freeman Jr. 1953. USA: Paramount Pictures.

Wasting Away. DVD. Directed by Matthew Kohren; produced by Sheldon Brigman. 2007. USA: Shadowpark Pictures; Wasted Pictures.

Werewolf of London. DVD. Directed by Stuart Walker; produced by Stanley Bergerman. 1935. USA: Universal Pictures.

What Lies Beneath. DVD. Directed by Robert Zemeckis; produced by Steven Boyd. 2000. USA: DreamWorks SKG; Twentieth Century Fox Film Corporation; ImageMovers.

White Zombie. DVD. Directed by Victor Halperin; produced by Edward Halperin. 1932. USA: Edward Halperin Productions; Victor Halperin Productions.

Witchboard. DVD. Directed by Kevin Tennet; produced by Roland Carroll. 1986. UK/USA: Paragon Arts International.

Witchfinder General. DVD. Directed by Michael Reeves; produced by Louis M. Heyward. 1968. UK: Tigon British Film Productions; American International Productions.

Wolf. DVD. Directed by Mike Nichols; produced by Robert Greenhut. 1994. USA: Columbia Pictures Corporation.

Wolf Creek. DVD. Directed by Greg Mclean; produced by George Adams. 2005. Australia: Australian Film Finance Corporation; South Australian Film Corporation; 403 Productions.

Wrong Turn. DVD. Directed by Rob Schmidt; produced by Hagen Behring. 2003. USA/Germany: Summit Entertainment; Constantin Film Produktion; Media Cooperation One.

Wrong Turn 5. DVD. Directed by Declan O'Brien; produced by Jeffery Beach. 2012. USA: Summit Entertainment; 20th Century Fox Home Entertainment; Constatin Film Produktion.

Young Frankenstein. DVD. Directed by Mel Brooks; produced by Michael Gruskoff. 1974. USA: Crossbow Productions; Gruskoff/Venture Films; Jouer Limited.

Zombie Strippers! DVD. Directed by Jay Lee; produced by Andrew Golov. 2008. USA: Stage 6 Films; Larande Productions; Production Headquarters.

Zombieland. DVD. Directed by Ruben Fleischer; produced by Ryan Kavanaugh. 2009. USA: Columbia Pictures; Relativity Media; Pariah.

Zombies of the Stratosphere. DVD. Directed by Fred C. Brannon; produced by Franklin Adreon. 1952. USA: Republic Pictures.

Bibliography

Asma, Stephen T. *On Monsters: An Unnatural History of Our Worst Fears*. Oxford: Oxford University Press, 2009.

Carolyn, Axelle. *It Lives Again! Horror Movies in the New Millenium*. Prestatyn, Wales: Telos Publishing, 2009.

Carrol, Noëll. *The Philosophy of Horror: Or, Paradoxes of the Heart*. London: Routledge, 1990.

Clover, Carol J. *Men, Women and Chain Saws: Gender in Modern Horror Film*. London: BFI, 1992.

Field, Syd. *Screenplay: The Foundations of Screenwriting, A Step-By-Step Guide from Concept to Finished Script*. New York: Delta, 2005.

Janocovitch, Mark. *Horror, the Film Reader*. Abingdon: Routledge, 2002.

Jones, Alan. *The Rough Guide to Horror Movies*. New York: Rough Guides, 2005.

King, Stephen. *Danse Macabre*. New York: Everest House, 1981.

—*On Writing*. London: New England Library, 2001.

King, Vikki. *How to Write a Movie in 21 Days*. London: HarperCollins, 1988.

Kristeva, Julia. *Powers of Horror: An Essay on Abjection*. New York: Columbia University Press, 1982.

Marriott, James. *Horror Films*. London: Virgin Books, 2004.

McKee, Robert. *Story: Substance, Structure, Style and the Principles of Screenwriting*. London: Methuen Publishing Ltd., 1999.

Medway, Gareth J. *Lure of the Sinister: The Unnatural History of Satanism*. New York: New York University Press, 2001.

Newman, Kim. *Nightmare Movies: Horror on Screen since the 1960s*. Bloomsbury 2011.

Pirie, David. *A New Heritage of Horror: The English Gothic Cinema*. London: I. B. Tauris, 2008.

Russell, Jamie. *Book of the Dead: The Complete History of Zombie Cinema*. Godalming, UK: FAB, 2005.

Watson, Devin. *Horror Screenwriting: The Nature of Fear*. Studio City, CA: Michael Wiese Productions, 2009

Zinoman, Jason. *Shock Value (How a Few Eccentric Outsiders Gave Us Nightmares, Conquered Hollywood, and Invented Modern Horror)*. London: Duckworth Overlook, 2012.

Index